Bill
From one buff
Civil War buff
to another, thanks for all
Adm.

America's
Buried History

Landmines in the Civil War

Kenneth R. Rutherford

SB

Savas Beatie
California

Library of Congress Cataloging-in-Publication Data

Names: Rutherford, Ken, 1962- author.
Title: America's Buried History: Landmines in the Civil War / by Kenneth R. Rutherford.
Other titles: Landmines in the Civil War
Description: El Dorado Hills, California: Savas Beatie, [2020] |
    Includes bibliographical references.
Identifiers: LCCN 2020005531| ISBN 9781611214536 (hardcover: alk. paper) |
ISBN 9781611214543 (ebk)
Subjects: LCSH: United States—History—Civil War, 1861-1865—Equipment and supplies. |
    Land mines—United States—History—19th century. | Submarine mines—
    United States—History—19th century. | Confederate States of America. Army Torpedo
Bureau. | United States—History—Civil War, 1861-1865--Campaigns.
Classification: LCC E468.9 .R88 2020 | DDC 973.7/8--dc23
LC record available at https://locexternal.service-now.com/pub/?id=cip_data_block_
viewer&lccn=2020005531

First Edition, First Printing

SB

Savas Beatie
989 Governor Drive, Suite 102
El Dorado Hills, CA 95762
Phone: 916-941-6896
(web) www.savasbeatie.com
(E-mail) sales@savasbeatie.com

Savas Beatie titles are available at special discounts for bulk purchases in the United States by corporations, institutions, and other organizations. For more details, please contact Savas Beatie at sales@savasbeatie.com, or visit our website at www.savasbeatie.com for additional information.

Proudly published, printed, and warehoused in the United States of America.

For one of the most beautiful people I know—
Kim Rutherford

Confederate torpedoes, shot, and shell in the
Charleston, South Carolina Arsenal yard in April 1865. *Library of Congress*

Table of Contents

Preface

Soldiers in the 30th Ohio Volunteer Infantry knew the dangers they faced on December 13, 1864, but they followed orders and charged toward Confederate-held Fort McAllister nonetheless.

Sgt. Lyman Hardman was moving ahead with his comrades during the afternoon attack when he was thrown violently to the ground by an explosion. The sudden change of circumstances left him momentarily dazed. When he recovered his senses and realized what had happened, he searched his body for wounds and discovered shattered bones in his left foot, a burned leg, hand, and face, and a badly swollen eye, among other injuries. Hardman was not the only man from the 30th Ohio to fall in that manner. Private James S. Horner of Company D saw a comrade's foot blown off at the ankle joint.[1]

"At least five boys in blue [were] torn into fragments" during the battle, and scores hurled to the ground" in a crater, recalled another Ohio soldier. The next morning, a man fighting in the 70th Ohio visited a comrade who had lost both legs in the short but deadly fight. "There was no hope or possibility of his

---

1 Roger S. Durham, *Guardian of Savannah: Fort McAllister, Georgia, in the Civil War and Beyond* (Columbia, SC, 2008). 155; Joseph A. Saunier, ed., *A History of the Forty-Seventh Regiment, Ohio Veteran Volunteer Second Brigade, Second Division, Fifteenth Army Corps, Army of Tennessee* (Hillsboro, OH, 1903), 365.

living," he wrote with sadness. "He was torn to pieces from his stomach [down], all his bowels was mashed."[2]

Each of these men were victims of what the Federals called "infernal machines"—Confederate landmines, or "torpedoes." The Rebels had planted them liberally near the fort. "[They] exploded as they were trodden upon," a 30th Ohio lieutenant colonel remembered, "and many a gallant soldier was mutilated and fairly torn to pieces."[3]

I can relate.

On December 16, 1993, almost 129 years to the day of the Fort McAllister attack, I was traveling with my Somalian colleagues in a Toyota Land Cruiser in the Upper Juba Region of southern Somalia near the border with Ethiopia. At the time, I was in the war-torn country as a humanitarian relief worker. My aim on that brutally hot day was to review a potential project site.

As I sat in the middle front seat, I angled my legs to the right because of the stick shift, focusing on my papers and to-do lists while the Somalis in the vehicle talked amongst themselves. Our driver suddenly slowed the vehicle as we approached a donkey cart. It was then I went blind. The papers on my lap had disappeared. As the heavy dust slowly cleared, I could make out a foot on the floorboard. "*Whose foot is that?*" I wondered.

It was mine. We had struck a landmine.

I tried to step out of the vehicle, but my legs wouldn't move. I grabbed the steering wheel and finally pushed myself out and slumped to the ground outside the Land Cruiser. As I looked at my legs, there was that severed foot again—and *a lot* of blood. With a determination and calmness that remain a mystery to me, I tried to put my foot back on, but it kept falling off.

Then I noticed that my handheld radio, the one I almost always kept in my briefcase for security reasons, lay next to me. For this trip I had clipped to my belt. If the radio had been in the briefcase near my feet in the Land Cruiser when we hit the landmine, it would have been destroyed. It would have been impossible for me to call for help.

"*Kilo Romeo. Kilo Romeo,*" I said calmly into the radio, announcing my call sign. "We are bleeding. I am O-positive. Send for an airplane."

---

2 Charles Bateman, Service and Pension Records, National Archives, Washington, DC, as quoted in Durham, *Guardian of Savannah*, 174.

3 William E. Strong, "The Capture of Fort McAllister, December 13, 1864," in *Georgia Historical Quarterly* (2004), vol. 88, no. 3. Fall 2004, 413.

As I lay grievously wounded, I thanked the Lord for a wonderful life. I had an awesome family, the best of friends, had attended excellent schools, and lived in a terrific community. I stared at a beautiful cobalt blue sky.

Would this be my last view on Earth? The thought crossed my mind and drifted away. I was comfortable, calm, and ready for my next life.

Then I thought of my fiancé, Kim, and it struck me that I had never loved someone as much as I loved her. We had to have a life together. "God," I prayed, "I just changed my mind. I want to marry Kim, have children with her, and become a professor. And whatever comes after that is icing on the cake. I commit to you that if these things happen, I will be the most grateful servant, never asking for anything more."

Thankfully I was rescued by colleagues, including members of a local Islamic militia. I nearly bled to death during a medical emergency flight to Kenya. My shattered right leg was amputated in a Nairobi hospital. Later, I had surgeries in four other hospitals in two countries. My remaining leg was amputated, too. To this day, I can still smell and taste my own blood. I wasn't the only landmine casualty that day. A Somali passenger riding with us lost part of his right foot, and a donkey cart owner near the blast lost one of his arms. Our driver was found wandering in the desert later that day.

The experience forever altered my life, crystallizing my vision for what I was put on Earth to do. My passion became alleviating negative effects of landmines, including aiding victims of those awful weapons. Unfortunately, landmines have been used in more than 80 countries, killing and maiming more people than biological, chemical, and nuclear weapons combined.

In August 1997, weeks before her tragic death, landmine survivor Jerry White and I escorted Princess Diana on her last humanitarian mission. It was the first overseas trip for the Landmine Survivors Network, an organization Jerry and I co-founded in 1996. In Bosnia-Herzegovina, we campaigned to draw international attention to the impact of landmines. In doing so, we met with Bosnian Muslims, Croatian Catholics, and Serbian Orthodox Christians who had suffered life-changing injuries due to landmines. Princess Diana, Jerry, and I even gave a cake to a landmine survivor and sang "Happy Birthday" to him.

On September 6, 1997, the afternoon before Princess Diana's funeral, I shared with her sons, Princes William and Harry, how their mother had transformed landmines from a security issue into a humanitarian issue. At the 20th anniversary of his mother's trip to Bosnia in 2017, Prince Harry told me in London that his mother had been shocked and appalled by the awful effects of landmines.

Fort Johnson marker, Richmond National Battlefield Park. Henrico, Virginia. *Author*

Since Princess Diana's death on August 31, 1997, I have written scores of articles and published a few books about landmines, including *Disarming States: The Global Movement to Ban Landmines*, and a co-edited book entitled *Landmines and Human Security*. All of this brings us back to the subject of *America's Buried History*.

Until I read a marker in 2011 at Fort Johnson in Henrico County, Virginia, I had no idea landmines were used during the American Civil War. Motivated, I began conducting Civil War mine research almost immediately, diving into articles and books before turning to official records, personal memories, and letters from the soldiers themselves. In addition to visiting museums and examining private mine collections, I toured battlefields and most other locations where landmines factored into combat operations. Because naval mines were also used during the war, I explored that topic in depth as well.

Because of my own experience, I had mixed feelings as I imagined how Union soldiers must have felt crossing mined areas at Forts Wagner, Blakeley, McAllister, and Fisher, at Port Hudson and elsewhere. Slowly, the largely untold story of the use of mines during the Civil War came into focus for me. Armed with this new information, I'm excited to educate others about the world's first conflict in which this dreadful weapon was widely used.

Acknowledgments

This book could not have been written without the support of many people, including global landmine and explosive ordnance experts, librarians, and the James Madison University community.

I thank Keven M. Walker, chief executive officer of the Shenandoah Valley Battlefields Foundation, for the opportunity to present this research in a national forum for the first time, and Terry Heder, SVBF director of interpretation, education, and history, for reading and commenting on the rough first draft.

Cameron Macauley, JMU instructor and landmine victim assistance specialist, provided unique research angles and read the manuscript. At a landmine conference dinner in Cartagena, Columbia, in 2009, he also provided inspiration for this project. Manuscript draft readers Dennis Barlow, Charles Downs, and Doug Gravitt offered excellent comments and feedback.

At JMU, I thank everyone on the Center for International Stabilization and Recovery team, especially Lindsay Aldrich, Amy Crockett, Suzanne Fiederlein, Carolyn Firkin, Heather Holsinger, Nicole Neitzey, Brenna Matlock, Paige Ober, Jennifer Riser, Letitia Turner, and Blake Williamson. CISR graduate assistants Victoria Price Matkins, Alexandra Pate, and Matthew Williams always responded quickly to assignment and research requests. I am especially indebted to student interns Caleb Gardner and Sam Friedberg for their bibliographic and photo caption work.

I also appreciate JMU Department of Political Science chair Jon Keller, who supported my travel to academic conferences. I often conducted research on landmines near the sites of those conferences. Former JMU vice provost for research and scholarship Yvonne Harris provided frequent encouragement, and Grace Barth, Head of Digital Collections at JMU Libraries was essential in obtaining high resolution photos to include in the book. Current JMU Vice-Provost for research and scholarship Keith Holland has been a strong supporter from day one.

I am especially thankful for the work of Hal Jespersen, who designed and produced the book's excellent maps. In Alabama, Nick Beeson and Seth Kinard at the History Museum of Mobile and Mike Bunn at Fort Blakeley State Park were helpful. At the Calhoun County Museum in Port Lavaca, Texas, director George Anne Cormier and assistant to the director Vicki Cox were helpful with information on the torpedo work of Edgar Singer and John R. Fretwell. Colin King and George Zahaczewky provided insight on improvised explosive devices as they relate to the American Civil War. Also, Roland Evans offered interesting opinions on post-World War I and World War II civilian landmine casualties. National Park Service ranger Robert Dunkerly shared research on landmines in the Richmond area, and Les Jensen, curator of arms and armor at the West Point Museum, allowed me to inspect torpedoes in storage at the museum.

Herbert M. Schiller pointed me in the right direction with his wonderful editing of the Gabriel Rains manuscript. He also suggested other avenues of research, including the excellent, detailed book by Mike Kochan and John Wideman about improvised explosives used during the Civil War.

I would like to thank my publisher, Savas Beatie, and its managing director Theodore P. Savas, for accepting this book and for his support in reading the manuscript, offering many helpful suggestions and additions, and performing an invaluable final edit; Sarah Keeney, marketing director, for her patience and understanding; Lee Merideth, production manager, for the final page layout and formatting; editor John Banks, for his guidance while working around my overseas work obligations, and to Joel Manuel for his final proofread.

Bill Miller-Cox invited me to tour Peninsula Campaign sites with him and to present my research at the Williamsburg Civil War Roundtable. Amy Marks, a joy to work with, provided excellent editing.

I appreciate everyone who encouraged me on this project, including Deana, Ina, and Tsyetomir of the Crystal Palace Boutique Hotel staff in Sofia, Bulgaria. While on vacation at the hotel, they allowed me to print out the manuscript so I could edit it before its final submission. I am also grateful to Brenna Hart, who was an incredibly patient host at Café One Plus while visiting her and my son Austin in Chongqing, China.

Finally, I thank my parents, Rob and Anneke Rutherford, for taking me to Gettysburg and Vicksburg when I was young. Those trips instilled a love for Civil War history that has endured to this day. Most importantly, I thank the mainstays of my life—my wife Kim and children Austin, Hayden, Campbell, Duncan, and Lucie—for their tolerance and patience as I pursued this eight-year project.

Any errors in the book are mine alone and should not be associated with anyone else.

Introduction

During the Civil War particularly, and in the 19th century more broadly, the term "torpedo" was used to define a type of explosive device that was deployed covertly, either on or just under the soil, or fixed to a river bank or bottom hidden by the water from unsuspecting ships. In today's terms, these torpedoes are now referred to as landmines, sea mines, improvised explosive devices (IEDs), or booby traps. In this book, I use the terms "torpedoes" and "landmines" interchangeably when referring to an explosive device designed to be placed under, on, or near the ground and to be exploded by the presence, proximity, or contact of a person and that will incapacitate, injure, or kill one or more persons.[4]

Landmines and their antecedents, especially those with origins in the Civil War, have been used widely through both world wars and in many modern conflicts. Those used in the 20th and 21st centuries, especially in Africa, Asia, and Latin America, have caused tens of thousands of civilian casualties. The resulting international outrage transformed rapidly into a highly effective global movement to ban landmines, and made finding, clearing, and destroying mines a multimillion-dollar business.

---

4 Definition of an anti-personnel landmine as defined by the 1997 Anti-Personnel Mine Ban Treaty ("Ottawa Convention").

The seeds of modern warfare tactics and weapons were planted during the American Civil War. Under Confederate auspices, it was the first war in history to see the widespread use of victim-activated landmines. As the conflict progressed, landmine warfare advanced commensurately, and both tactics and technology evolved to include innovative types of design and deployment. During the war's later years, Confederate soldiers used both command-detonated and victim-activated landmines more frequently to defend and to protect static positions, including cities.[5]

Victim-activated landmines were a relatively new technology during the Civil War. Russian forces had used them in 1854, during the Crimean War, in defending fortifications at Sevastopol against an allied navy (French, British, Ottoman). The Russian landmines used sulfuric acid within a glass vial that, when broken by contact, created a spark or small explosion as the acid mixed with potassium chlorate and sugar; this ignited the main charge, which was typically black powder.[6]

Richard Delafield, a U.S. army officer who observed the Sevastopol fighting as a member of a military commission authorized by then-U.S. Secretary of War Jefferson Davis, described the Russians' use of victim-detonated landmines:

> [The mine was] buried in the ground, leaving the tin tube so near the surface that a man's foot, or other disturbing cause, bending it, would break the glass within, liberating the acid, which, escaping through the opening of the tin into the box, came in

---

5 "Command-detonated" and "victim-activated" landmines are modern terms not used during the Civil War.

6 A British military officer noted, "These wretched Russians have discovered a new system of annoyance . . . which consists of a series of small mines or barrels of gunpowder let into the ground between our works and theirs, and a little tin tube running along the ground a few inches above it, two or three feet long, which is filled with some composition which explodes immediately on being touched, so that any unfortunate meandering along the grass without knowing why, suddenly finds himself going up in the air like a squib with his legs and arms flying in different directions. "Letters and Papers of Colonel Hugh Robert Hibbert (1828–1895) Mainly Related to Service in the Crimean War, 1854-1855." Ref DHB/57. Letter to sister, Georgina. Before Sebastopol, June 14, 1855, as quoted in Michael P. Kochan and John C. Wideman, *Civil War Torpedoes: A History of Improvised Explosive Devices in the War Between the States*, 2nd ed. (Paoli, PA, 2011), 14, 19.

contact with the potash, or whatever may have been the priming, and by its combination instantly exploded the powder in the box.[7]

A Union cavalry officer holds the unfortunate distinction of being the first person to be killed by a landmine in the Western Hemisphere, on May 5, 1862, at Yorktown, Virginia. After the Civil War, however, most major militaries used landmines as an important component of land warfare, which resulted in hundreds of thousands of casualties.[8] By the early 1990s, it was estimated that more than 26,000 people worldwide were killed each year by landmines.[9]

*   *   *

At the outset of the Civil War in April 1861, the Union war strategy emphasized the occupation of key Southern harbors, the conquest of the Mississippi River to divide the enemy, and the establishment of a naval blockade around the Confederacy. Named after the South American boa constrictor that squeezes its prey to death, the "Anaconda Plan" intended to do much the same to the South by denying it supplies from overseas, controlling its major inland rivers, and pressing it inward until it collapsed.

Opposing such a plan required vigorously defending nearly the entire South, and the fledgling Confederacy had few resources with which to do so. From the outset the Confederate Navy, which had almost no ships, relied on a small makeshift fleet comprised of hastily recruited commercial warships to attack Union shipping, small gunboats supported by land batteries to defend its important rivers and extensive coastline, and slow-moving and unreliable ironclads to hold key harbors and other waterways. The South also relied on blockade-runners to export cotton and to import needed war materials. As the

---

7   Colonel R. Delafield, *Report on the Art of War in Europe in 1854, 1855, and 1856. . . From His Notes and Observations Made as a Member of the Military Commission to the Theater of War in Europe, Under the Orders of Hon. Jefferson Davis, Secretary of War* (Washington, DC, 1860), 109–110.

8   Landmines may have been used by the Chinese in the 3rd century in the battle of Hu-lu-ku Valley and in the 15th century wars between Pisa and Florence. Joseph Needham, *Science and Civilization in China* (Cambridge, UK, 1986), vol. 5, pt. 7, 28, 202.

9   U.S. Department of State Bureau of Political-Military Affairs, *Hidden Killers: The Global Landmine Crisis* (Washington, DC, 1994). This was the first report to estimate the magnitude of the landmine threat in terms of numbers of mines laid and numbers of mine-related deaths and injuries.

war dragged on, the enemy used various inlets and other stations to support a growing number of warships. The Union blockade became increasingly effective with each passing month.[10]

For the most part, the Union's Anaconda strategy worked. Within a few years the North had established a fairly tight blockade along the coast, and it was no longer possible for the Confederacy to export cotton in large quantities. The South's "white gold" failed to produce the income needed to help prevent the depreciation of its currency and fund the war effort. By war's end, more than 150 blockade-runners had been captured and the blockading fleets were comprised of more than 400 ships.[11]

The South's economy was based on agriculture, and there were few industries capable of producing the war materials the Confederacy needed to fight the war ahead; thus, it had no choice but to import many of its weapons. The Southern president, Jefferson Davis, appointed Josiah Gorgas as the Chief of Ordnance with the rank of major. His responsibilities included the Bureau of Foreign Supplies. Gorgas, who would prove to be one of Davis' best appointments of the entire war, recognized immediately the Confederacy's manufacturing weakness and dispatched agents to Europe to procure arms even as he took steps to increase the domestic production of war materials. "It soon became obvious that in the Ordnance Department we must rely greatly on the introduction of articles of prime necessity through the blockade of ports," he wrote in his postwar memoir.[12]

The efforts of Gorgas and others around him were surprisingly successful. At the war's outset only 25,000 small arms were available to the South. Another 185,000 firearms were imported between January 1, 1862 and July 1, 1863, while nearly 40,000 more were manufactured, and 150,000 were captured. Overall, about 50 percent of Confederate firearms were imported during this period. Just as or more important was the selection of George W. Rains to develop the domestic production of gunpowder. Rains established and operated

10 Don Farrant, "When Yankee Ships Patrolled the Georgia Coast," in *North South Trader's Civil War* (1990), vol. 17, no. 3, 24.

11 Farrant, "Yankee Ships," 24.

12 General Josiah Gorgas, Confederate States of America, *Army Ordnance Magazine* (January–February 1936), as quoted in Henry L. Gaidis, "Confederate Ordnance Dream: Gen. Josiah Gorgas, CSA, and the Bureau of Foreign Supplies," in *North South Trader's Civil War* (November–December 1982), vol. 10, 7.

the Augusta Powder Works in Augusta, Georgia, which began producing in quantity in early 1862, and would continue producing and shipping gunpowder and other important munitions until late April 1865.[13]

Other shortages of all kinds plagued the South, including a population inadequate to the needs of a large-scale war, inland rivers west of the Appalachian Mountains that ran basically north and south like giant arrows deep in the Confederate heartland, and a meandering coastline riddled with harbors and inlets that practically begged to be invaded. In short, defending the Confederacy against a determined enemy was going to be exceedingly difficult.

As the war moved into its second year, the Davis administration sought more creative ways to fight it, including leveraging low-cost weapons with minimal material input due to a lack of financial and material resources. One of the solutions to holding key pieces of Southern territory was the development of new tactics for destroying enemy ships.

Initially, a significant amount of energy was directed toward challenging the superior Federal Navy by using floating or static naval mines. This defensive weapon was ideally suited to protecting inland waterways and the extensive coastline, and Confederate troops assisted in their deployment.

Landmine development, including technology and tactics, benefited from the military's initial focus on the use of naval mines. The Confederacy continued to develop landmines from a variety of artillery shells with increased technological ingenuity adapted to local circumstances, including the type of combat engaged in, and the geographical conditions present. Confederate soldiers eventually configured spur-of-the-moment landmines in a relatively ad hoc manner. Details were rarely written down, and most of what was recorded was destroyed near the end of the war to avoid the possibility of some leading advocates being charged as war criminals. The simplicity and cost-effectiveness of landmines made their continued use attractive. Today we call these buried or hidden artillery rounds Improvised Explosive Devices, or IEDs.

Despite the expanding development and use of landmines, many American military officers, both Confederate and Union, looked upon them with intense disfavor. Landmines were disparaged as the "tools of cowards or offenses against democracy and civilized warfare."[14] In addition, some American

13 Ibid., 8.

14 Jack Kelly, *Gunpowder: Alchemy, Bombards and Pyrotechnics: The History of the Explosive that Changed the World* (New York, NY, 2004), 202.

officers on both sides believed landmines concealed their "lethality" and were "un-sportsman-like."[15] "If any one had to contend with the abuse and sneers, and ridicule whilst in the performance of torpedo [landmine] duty day and night, that fell upon me during the war," complained Hunter Davidson, a commander in the small Confederate Navy, "he would realize that as late as the summer of 1863, some of the ablest men of the day did not regard torpedo [landmine] warfare as worthy of consideration."[16]

In 1863, the Confederate high command and Congress allocated $100,000 to establish the Torpedo Bureau, which became the world's first institution devoted to landmine warfare. By the end of the war, the Confederacy considered landmines and naval mines to be accepted tools of warfare, though most Union officers had not yet arrived at that conclusion.

*   *   *

America's Buried History details how landmine development and the tactics of employing them began and evolved during the Civil War, and how the war's progression mirrored mine development on land and sea. As strange as it sounds today, it was an alliance of a few professionally trained soldiers, ill-equipped home guard units, businessmen, and Masonic members who developed and improved the use of landmines across the Confederacy—a harbinger of future warfare in countries around the world.

More than 50 years later, after the outbreak of World War I, landmines would saturate battlefields once again. Their prolific use continues to kill and maim thousands of innocent victims every year.

Few realize the world's first widespread deployment of landmines took place during the Civil War. It took some digging and patching together the story to uncover that part of America's buried history.

15 "Foreword," William Schneck, Colonel (USAR), U.S. Army Corps of Engineers, in Kochan and Wideman, *Civil War Torpedoes*.

16 Hunter Davidson, Commander, CSN, "Electrical Torpedoes as a System of Defense," in *Southern Historical Society Papers*, 52 vols. (Richmond, VA, 1876), vol. 2, 1-6.

Chapter 1

1861: Matthew Fontaine Maury—
A Man with a Plan

On April 21, 1861, Governor John Letcher convened an urgent meeting in the governor's mansion in Richmond. A vastly superior Federal navy was blockading Virginia's rivers and ports, strangling commerce with Europe and creating great angst within the Old Dominion and across the South. How was he to defend his state? Letcher, a newspaper editor-turned-politician, looked to a man with a plan: Matthew Fontaine Maury, a veteran of the U.S. Navy. Although no one realized it at the time, 55-year-old Maury would become the leading figure in the Confederacy's efforts to develop naval mines and the first to deploy "torpedoes" in combat.

Born in 1806 near Fredericksburg, Virginia, Maury moved with his family to Franklin, Tennessee, when he was four years old. In 1825 he was appointed a midshipman in the U.S. Navy, following in the footsteps of his older brother John, who had died a year earlier of yellow fever while at sea. As a 19-year-old, Matthew made his first voyage across the Atlantic on the *Brandywine*. The trip was notable for terrible weather and the presence aboard of Gilbert du Motier, Marquis de Lafayette, the French aristocrat and ex-military officer who had aided the American military during the Revolutionary War.

In 1836, Maury published *A New Theoretical and Practical Treatise on Navigation*, which was soon adopted as a textbook by the U.S. Navy. "From the time of entering the service," a newspaper account noted, "Maury exhibited

Matthew Fontaine Maury, in his pre-Civil War U.S. Navy uniform. *Library of Congress*

those characteristic traits and qualities which finally rendered him famous throughout the world." After his marriage to Anne Herndon, he reestablished his residency in his native state of Virginia. In 1839, when he was 33, Maury broke his right leg in a stagecoach accident in Ohio. To his dismay and the benefit of the future Confederacy, the injury ended his days at sea.[1]

Maury was a brilliant man with interests in astronomy, history, the world's oceans, meteorology, education, and cartography. His *Physical Geography of the Sea*—the first comprehensive book on oceanography—"excited more attention in Europe," a Southern newspaper bragged, "than any recent work of popular science." It was soon translated into several languages.[2]

When the Civil War began in April of 1861, Maury was superintendent of the National Observatory in Washington, a position he had held since 1842. "This institution . . . has already attained a reputation scarcely inferior to that of the oldest and most celebrated institution of its kind," boasted a Washington newspaper in 1857 in praise of Maury's leadership there.[3]

The day before his meeting with Governor Letcher on April 21, 1861, Maury resigned his commission as commander in the U.S. Navy. Like fellow Virginian Robert E. Lee's decision to side with his native state, his choice to be true to the Old Dominion proved a boon for the Confederacy. "Lincoln offered $3,000 for Matthew Maury's head," a Fredericksburg newspaper wrote facetiously weeks later. "We are not surprised. Maury's head is worth all the heads in the Northern United States. They need brains as well as behavior."[4]

Without delay, Maury began participating in war planning meetings at the governor's mansion as part of Letcher's advisory council, a de facto war ministry that built up Virginia's forces and laid the groundwork for the defense of the state. For Maury—dubbed the "most scientific man in the South"—the task was as monumental as it was difficult.

The meager Confederate Navy was no match for the mighty Federal sea arm on Virginia's waterways and along her coast. As a result, Maury became a powerful advocate for a relatively new defensive tactic: mines triggered by electricity, or "galvanic current" as it was called at the time. He eagerly went about selling the Confederate high command on the idea of an innovative

1 "In Memoriam, Matthew Fontaine Maury," *Times-Picayune*, March 30, 1873.

2 "Southern Writers," *Fayetteville Semi-Weekly Observer*, January 9, 1860, 2.

3 "The National Observatory," *Washington Union*, August 27, 1857.

4 *Richmond Enquirer*, May 21, 1861.

coastal defensive system of electrical (battery-operated electrical circuit) minefields supported by small and maneuverable armored boats.[5]

Electrically detonated mines first came to Maury's attention on April 13, 1844, when Samuel Colt successfully tested his waterborne explosives in the Anacostia River near Washington. Naval mine technology had progressed significantly since the early 1840s when Colt launched his groundbreaking experiments.

By the eve of the Civil War, naval mines, while not yet tested under battle conditions, could be detonated in two ways. The first way was by contact activation when a ship or other vessel came into contact with the explosive and triggered the device. The second type of naval mine functioned by a command-control system that required an operator in a concealed location to manually trigger a distant explosive device connected by an electrical wire or pull cord. Under Maury's leadership, defensive naval mines that included electrically detonated anchored or moored contact mines were produced. Eager to combat the Union's menacing warships, the Jefferson Davis administration was intrigued with Maury's innovative strategic thinking. Mines required few materials to produce, an important consideration for the resource-starved Confederacy.

In June 1861, Maury tested his naval mines for the first time at Rockett's Landing on the north side of the James River in Richmond. Confederate officials watched from shore. One of them was the former U.S. Secretary of War and a Louisiana congressman named Charles Magill Conrad. Two keg mines were floated to the middle of the James. Bobbing gently, they drifted toward a buoy upon which they were to become entangled and explode. To the dismay of Maury and the onlookers, the weapons failed to detonate. Maury ordered his son to row a boat to the buoy, take up the rope connected to the mine's trigger, and yank it.[6]

BOOM!

A huge geyser of river water soared into the sky and dead and stunned fish floated to the surface of the James. The Maurys, described in one account as having been "drenched in the baptismal water of modern mine warfare in North

---

5 Dean Snyder, "Torpedoes for the Confederacy," *Civil War Times*, March 1985, 41; John Grady, *Matthew Fontaine Maury, Father of Oceanography: A Biography, 1806-1873* (Jefferson, NC, 2015), 194.

6 Grady, *Matthew Fontaine Maury*, 206-207.

America," were jubilant. Still, the explosives test could hardly be described as an unqualified success.[7]

The next month on July 7, again under Maury's direction, naval mines were deployed in combat for the first time at Aquia Landing on the Potomac River 15 miles from Maury's hometown of Fredericksburg. The Rebels were keen to defend the vital shipping port against Union gunboats. That afternoon, two oak barrels were filled with 200 pounds of explosive powder. Using two boats, 10 men guided the clunky weapons into the Potomac and released Maury's mines into the tide. Each cask was connected to a span of rope roughly 600 feet long. Corks kept the rope afloat while the explosive casks submerged.[8]

As the barrels slowly approached enemy vessels, the men hiding ashore pulled the ropes. In theory, the yank was supposed to light a fuse that would trigger an explosion below the waterline of the enemy ships. Instead of a mighty *kaboom!*, however, there was . . . nothing. As it turned out, water had ruined the fuses, which failed to light. Maury believed the failure was because the fuses would not burn under water pressure and set about trying to fix it.[9]

Embarrassingly for Maury, the mines drifted past their targets and floated into nearby Aquia Creek. The captain of the Union warship *Pawnee* spotted two objects there of "exceedingly suspicious look" nearing the Federal squadron and sent out a party to examine the "queer-looking things." As a small Union boat closed in on the objects, its crew "grew increasingly suspicious of them, discovering they floated with steady purpose toward the Federal vessels, and in their own language looked 'diabolical.'"[10]

Eventually, Maury's mines were hoisted aboard the *Pawnee* and examined by the curious crew. Later, the "infernal machines" were transferred to another ship and taken to the Washington Navy Yard for "scientific investigation" and to be photographed. The weapon "attracted hundreds of cautious but curious visitors," a newspaper reported, "who peeped at it from all possible points of view, though at a respectful distance."[11]

---

7 John Grady, "Damn the Torpedoes," *New York Times*, February 6, 2012.

8 "Civil War—Aquia Landing," Stafford County Museum, undated.

9 Grady, *Matthew Fontaine Maury*, 206.

10 "An Infernal Machine Discovered Floating in the Potomac," *Richmond Dispatch*, July 18, 1861.

11 Ibid.

It did not take long for the Northern press to point the finger of blame at Maury. The Confederate officer's invention of command-controlled naval mines, sneered the *New York Times*, was nothing more than a "wretched failure." The embarrassment of the failed experiment, coupled with media criticism and wavering support from superiors, depressed Maury, who eventually renewed his research at a cousin's townhouse in Richmond intent on perfecting his defensive weapon.[12]

Convinced he was on the right path and that he could deliver an electrical charge from a battery to a naval mine, Maury began experimenting with fuses and gunpowder. He needed essential materials, but obtaining batteries, copper, and the like was difficult in an increasingly resource-deprived city. Maury even asked women to contribute "items made of rubber, [but] received enough to make only a few hundred feet of waterproof cable." Maury's luck changed in February 1862 when a strong storm tossed up miles of insulated telegraph cable that had been laid along Willoughby Spit in Hampton Roads between Virginia's Fort Monroe and the Eastern Shore onto Confederate-controlled shores. Maury used the serendipitous find to help produce his electrical mines.[13]

That August, Maury was named head of the Submarine Battery Service, which officially oversaw the development of electrically detonated naval mines as part of a comprehensive program of harbor defense improvement. In practice, Maury was the Confederacy's naval mine expert. Secretary of the Navy Stephen Mallory believed ironclad vessels were the essential counter-tactic to Federal blockades, but he also supported Maury and his ideas about how to use naval mines to augment the static Confederate coastal defenses. Mallory allocated Maury $50,000 and "a few men to work out of an office at Ninth and Bank streets to perfect the Confederacy's secret weapon."[14]

With increased financial and political support, Maury renewed his focus on improving the effectiveness of contact-activated explosive devices while developing electrically detonated mines. At first the only battery Maury could find for the electric torpedoes was a Wollaston comprised of 36 gallons of sulfuric acid. The University of Virginia loaned him a Cruikshank, the first

---

12 Grady, *Matthew Fontaine Maury*, 206.

13 Robert Collins Suhr, "Torpedoes, the Confederacy's Dreaded 'Infernal Machines,' Made Many a Union Sea Captain Uneasy," *America's Civil War* (November 1991), 59.

14 Matthew Fontaine Maury to B. Franklin Minor, July 19, 1861, Grady, *Matthew Fontaine Maury*, 206.

electric battery designed for mass production, and eventually established a small research center for mine development. A laboratory, under the direction of Virginia professors Socrates Maupin and James Lawrence Cabell, was created to research mine warfare. The university also sought the aid of Charlottesville factories and foundries to make percussion caps and other war materiel for mines.[15]

President Abraham Lincoln, meanwhile, was increasing pressure on Maj. Gen. George B. McClellan, the Union general in chief, to capture Richmond, which was already potentially vulnerable to Union gunboats steaming up the James River. Aside from the political advantage of taking Richmond, the city was an attractive target because of its large cache of Confederate ordnance and munitions, as well as its manufacturing capabilities. The capital was home to the Tredegar Iron Works, the largest munitions and iron production foundry in the Confederacy. Tredegar and an adjacent armory complex, a gunpowder laboratory on Brown's Island, and nearby woolen and flour mills, made the city the industrial heart of the Confederacy.[16]

Although several small forts on the James River were supposed to protect the Confederate capital, President Davis was worried about whether his military could prevent Union gunboats from steaming upriver to shell Richmond. The forts "may be successful against wooden fleets," he argued, "[but] iron-clad vessels of which we have not had sufficient experience to form a correct judgment, can pass these works, as the channel is too wide and deep for obstructions."[17]

Appointed by Mallory to supervise construction of coastal defenses, Maury built new earthworks and reinforced others in order to protect the vulnerable city from enemy access via waterways. The Confederacy's strongest and best known defensive position on the James was at Drewry's Bluff, seven miles downriver from the capital. The artillery position was tucked into the elbow of

---

15 R. Thomas Campbell, *Hunters of the Night: Confederate Torpedo Boats in the War Between the States* (Shippensburg, PA, 2000); Minutes, May 27, 1861, *Proceedings of the Advisory Council of Virginia, 1861*; Matthew Fontaine Maury to James L. Cabell, May 31, 1861, in Grady, *Matthew Fontaine Maury*, 195.

16 For more on the amazing facility, see, generally, Charles B. Dew, *Ironmaker to the Confederacy Joseph R. Anderson and the Tredegar Iron Works* (Yale University Press, 1966).

17 Robert Jones, "Exploded Fort Huger Cannon," *North South Trader's Civil War* (2012), vol. 36, no. 1.

the river where the waterway turned back north, offering a clear field of fire eastward along a stretch of the James that would have to be traversed by enemy warships. The bluff provided an excellent field of plunging fire against any approaching enemy vessels.[18]

Maury reinforced the position by placing a strong line of electric naval mines across the James below the bluffs. The mines would be manually activated by a spark passing through electrical cable running from telegraph batteries on the riverbank to each mine. The weapons would only be detonated when Federal boats passed by, thus avoiding the risk inadvertent damage to passing Confederate ships. Unlike the indiscriminate contact mines, which were unable to distinguish between friend or foe, the command mines were under human control and could be deployed to target specific enemy shipping. Along with man-made obstructions like the guns atop Drewry's Bluff, the naval mines made the river almost impenetrable by Yankee warships.

News of these defensive tactics soon reached Federal ears, and any attacks that were planned at that time were called off. Although the Union threat had been neutralized in the short term, Richmond's James River defenses would be tested during the spring and summer during the Peninsula Campaign.

Columbus, Kentucky: Boom . . . or Bust?

The first bishop to enter military service in North America urgently needed the aid of the Confederacy's leading naval mine expert. "I feel constrained," wrote Maj. Gen. Leonidas Polk to Matthew Maury from western Kentucky on December 4, 1861, "to urge upon you the necessity of at once furnishing me an officer familiar with the subject of submarine batteries and capable of a practicable application of this species of defense to the Mississippi River."[19]

In September 1861, Polk had sent troops from Tennessee to Columbus, Kentucky, a strategically important position along the Mississippi River directly across from Belmont, Missouri. Kentucky, however, had declared its

---

18 Grady, *Matthew Fontaine Maury*, 207.

19 Maj. Gen., Leonidas Polk, Commanding, Headquarters, Western Division, to Hon. S. R. Mallory, Secretary of the Navy, "Report of Major-General Polk, C.S. Army, requesting the services in his department of Lieutenant Maury, C.S. Navy," *The War of Rebellion: A Compilation of the Official Records of the Union and Confederate Armies,* 128 vols. (Washington, DC, 1880–1901), Series 1, vol. 22, 793. All references are to Series 1 unless otherwise noted.

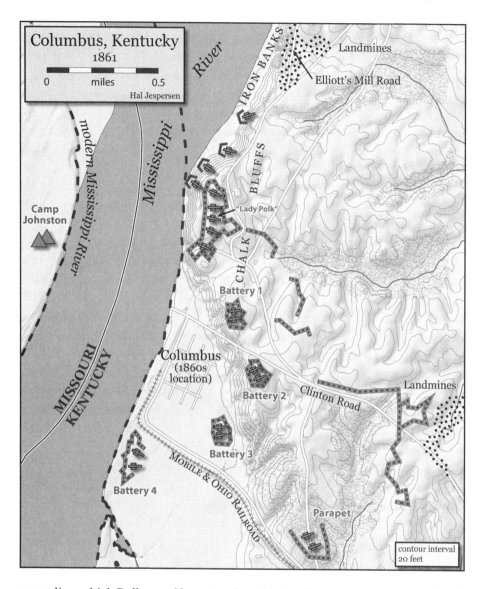

neutrality, which Polk—and by extension, the Confederacy—had now violated. The move was a major strategic blunder. After the town's occupation, the neutral border state's legislature requested Federal aid and went almost full tilt in support of the Union. By whatever means necessary, the 55-year-old bishop general aimed to hold the town in a region he believed vital to the Confederacy.

The fort in Columbus—called by some the "Gibraltar of the West"— was quickly improved. Extensive breastworks were built, and the river side eventually bristled with 140 guns. Randolph Bluff loomed over the town, making the fort nearly impregnable by a river assault. The Confederates even deployed command-detonated landmines on two roads leading into town, the first time the weapons were used in the Western Hemisphere. The key question remained to be determined: Could mines really affect the outcome of a battle for the critical town, which comprised the all-important western anchor of Gen. Albert S. Johnston's long Confederate defensive line?

With his hands full in the Eastern Theater, Maury sent naval lieutenant Isaac N. Brown to help strengthen Polk's defenses at Columbus. A 20-year veteran of the U.S. Navy, Brown had worked hard to further develop Maury's naval mining ideas after consulting with him during the summer, and would eventually command the ironclad CSS *Arkansas* on the Yazoo and Mississippi rivers during the summer of 1862. Brown quickly put his stamp on the defenses, deploying hundreds of contact and electrically detonated naval mines in the Mississippi River. Word of what the Confederates were up to reached a startled Union high command. "From information received through a gentleman up from Memphis," one Federal report stated, "there are about 600 torpedoes [naval mines] in the river from Columbus to the city." Was the Mississippi now blocked to all shipping?[20]

To support Brown's mine deployment, naval officer Lt. Beverley Kennon sent 150 electrically fired "submarine batteries" to Polk from New Orleans. These naval mines were intended to be used by Confederate troops stationed along the Mississippi, Tennessee, and Ohio rivers and any others under Brown's command. Some of these naval mines were made of cast iron at Memphis and Nashville, and held 100-200 pounds of powder. The Memphis Ordnance Office ordered the manufacture of at least 50 of A. L. Saunders's mechanically fired naval mines. "The cases are to be charged with powder . . . when ready for submerging," Saunders wrote to Polk. "The levers are only to be screwed in after the anchor and weight are properly deposited in the bed of the river with the cordage attached to the cases."[21]

To further protect the town, wooden gunboats were positioned on the Mississippi and an immense iron chain—perhaps a little more than a mile

20 Brigadier-General U. S. Grant, Headquarters District of Cairo, to Captain J. C. Kelton, Asst. Adjt. Gen., Dept. of the Missouri, Saint Louis, Missouri, January 6, 1862, *OR* vol. 7, 534.

21 *Wisconsin Daily Patriot*, March 12, 1862; "Discovery of an Elaborate Infernal Machine," Special Correspondence of the *Chicago Times*, Columbus, Kentucky, March 9, 1862.

long—was strung across the river to prevent Union vessels from slipping past. It was secured to the Columbus side with a huge anchor believed to have weighed four to six tons. Each link of the massive chain was 11 inches long and six inches across, and many were interspersed with contact naval mines designed to explode when bumped by a ship. The chain came to the attention of Union Brig. Gen. Ulysses S. Grant, the commander of the District of Southeast Missouri. Grant, who was more ambitious and talented than anyone realized at the time, had his sights set on taking control of the Mississippi River valley. "The rebels have a chain across the river about 1 mile above Columbus," wrote Grant from his base in Cairo, Illinois, to Captain J. C. Kelton, a staff officer with the Department of the West. "It is sustained by flats at intervals, the chain passing through staples placed about the water's edge, the chain passing under the boats. Between each pair of the boats a torpedo is attached to the chain, which is expected to explode by concussion."[22]

In addition to the naval mines in the river, Lt. Brown ordered the planting of command-controlled landmines on the roads leading into the city from the north and east. The weapons were placed "tactically to channelize advancing Union forces into roads where they could be brought under focused artillery and small arms fire." Each mine contained a four-pound artillery shell filled with canister as well as an electrical sparking device to detonate it by wire from a battery connected to a triggering location.[23]

A letter written in Columbus appeared in an 1862 issue of *Scientific American* describing the landmines as being "made of cast iron" and "constructed under Right Rev. Major-General Bishop Polk." The landmine itself, it continued,

is shaped like an old-fashioned tea kettle in some respects and has a sort of cap on the top similar to the lid of an iron tea kettle, which is fastened to it by a set of iron of screws. About two inches from the bottom are two orifices from which run copper wires, insulated with gutta percha and tarred cord, which are laid in trenches and

---

22 Brigadier-General U. S. Grant to Captain J. C. Kelton, January 6, 1862, *OR* vol. 7, 534.

23 Charles Lee Lewis, *Matthew Fontaine Maury, Pathfinder of the Sea* (Kessinger, 2010), 10-12; Kochan and Wideman, *Civil War Torpedoes*, 187. From primary sources, landmines were categorized with different terms as well as different spellings. For example, the term "subterra" was also spelled "sub-terra."

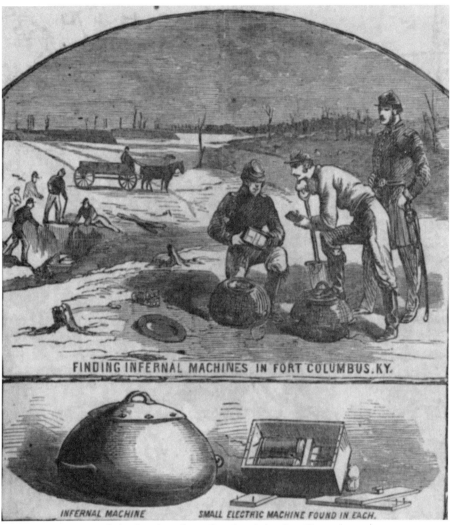

FINDING INFERNAL MACHINES IN FORT COLUMBUS, KY.

INFERNAL MACHINE   SMALL ELECTRIC MACHINE FOUND IN EACH.

Rebel infernal machines found at Columbus, Kentucky.

Sketch by Mr. Alexander Simplot. Harper's Weekly, March 1862

communicate with a galvanic battery inside of the fortification on the bluff. This infernal machine is a specimen of many that lie buried in and about Columbus.[24]

24 "Infernal Machines in the Mississippi," *Scientific American* (April 1862), vol. 6, no. 14, 210-211.

In October 1861, Columbus became one of the first targets of an offensive Grant would lead along the Mississippi, Tennessee, and Cumberland rivers. He ordered his troops to attack Belmont, Missouri, located across the Mississippi River from Columbus, and then cross the river and storm the heights of the Kentucky town. Grant's forces, however, were surprised to find Confederates in strong fortifications in Belmont and were turned back after sharp fighting.

After Belmont, Grant decided that instead of assaulting the impressive fortifications of Columbus directly, it would surely fall if nearby supporting Confederate forts to the east and southeast were captured. As part of that operation, Grant ordered his troops and the Western Gunboat Flotilla, comprised of the ironclads *St. Louis*, *Carondelet*, *Louisville*, and *Pittsburg*, together with the wooden gunboats *Conestoga*, *Tyler*, and *Lexington*, to steam up the Tennessee and Cumberland rivers to capture Forts Henry and Donelson in northwestern Tennessee. Each fort had significantly weaker garrisons than the Columbus stronghold. Record spring flooding that February of 1862 contributed to the vulnerability of both forts, and Grant's fleet safely passed over metallic contact naval mines anchored in the rivers to defend them.

Fort Donelson on the Cumberland was much stronger and better constructed than the flooded and undermanned Fort Henry, which fell quickly on February 6. Grant marched his army overland the short distance to Donelson and besieged it. He knew Donelson would be a much more difficult operation than the Henry affair. Donelson's guns were distributed on three levels, from the shoreline up to the 100-foot bluff overlooking the Cumberland. The fort was also protected by a three- mile ring of infantry entrenchments, much of which were reinforced by abatis (sharpened felled trees), and an army that numbered some 17,000 men under Brig. Gen. John B. Floyd. With reinforcements arriving daily, Grant was able to extend his nearly 25,000 men in a large semi-circle and trap the Southerners, whom he hoped could be starved into submission.

In an effort to break out, the Confederates launched an attack against the Union right on February 15. An escape route was cleared, but the Southern command proved utterly inept and the men "were ordered to return to their entrenchments—a result of confusion and indecision among the commanders." The next day Floyd, a former U. S. Secretary of War, turned over command to Brig. Gen. Gideon Pillow because he was worried about what might happen to him if captured. Floyd eventually escaped on a river steamer with two regiments—abandoning the balance of his men to their fate. Pillow, who also feared retribution if captured, turned over command to Brig. Gen. Simon Buckner and made a disgraceful exit across the Cumberland in a small boat.

Buckner demonstrated the courage needed for the occasion and surrendered the Confederate garrison unconditionally on February 16.[25]

Grant's victory proved catastrophic for the South. The capture of Forts Henry and Donelson left the Southern forces at Columbus unprotected and vulnerable to being cut off from Gen. Johnston's Confederate force at Bowling Green, Kentucky. The entire perimeter defense set up in the Western Theater collapsed almost overnight. Although Polk was willing to make a fighting stand, he was ordered to save his command and evacuate Columbus. Before doing so, he moved supplies, ammunition, heavy cannon, and gun crews down the Mississippi River to an enlarged sandbar called Island Number 10, just south of the confluence with the Ohio River below the Kentucky border.

On March 2, Polk ordered a complete withdrawal from Columbus after destroying buildings and supplies. Federal forces entered the town the next day. Coupled with the occupation of Columbus, Union victories at Henry and Donelson opened two major river arteries—the Tennessee and Cumberland—that led directly into the South's heartland.

Unfortunately for the Confederate cause, the mines at Columbus and elsewhere had fizzled. Water had ruined the gunpowder in the electrically detonated river mines, which was why none of the weapons exploded. After the Confederate evacuation, Union forces found more than 400 naval mines in the river. According to a Northern reporter, the weapons were

> round, about three feet long and a foot and a half in diameter, with one end tapering off to a point. The river is very high, and the number cannot be made out. It took three steamers five days to sink what are in the bottom of the river. The very high stage of water has prevented any damage to either gun-boat or transport.[26]

Before taking over Confederate fortifications, Union forces heard stories about the "infernal devices" buried on the bluff, so the soldiers took all necessary precautions. The weapons were never activated because the Rebels abandoned the area without a fight, leaving the mines in place.

The rumors of landmines in the fortifications were confirmed two days later in the northern and northeastern areas of Columbus. After noticing "ridges of

25 "Fort Donelson," National Battlefield Tennessee and Kentucky, National Park Service, 2018.

26 "Infernal Machines in the Mississippi," *Scientific American*, 216; *Harper's Weekly*, March 29, 1862, 203.

new earth, similar to ridges formed by covering up gas or water pipes in a city and tracing them to a cavern," explained a Union captain named W. A. Schmitt of the 27th Illinois, he and his comrades in his company "found a strong, rude wooden frame, covered by earth to attract no attention. Inside this," he continued with details rarely recorded with such clarity,

with the assistance of a light, he found implements similar to those used in a telegraph office, with wires running in a dozen different directions. Following the raised rows of earth he soon came to a spot where something had evidently been buried. Digging down some five feet, he came to a large iron cask, about three feet high, and a foot and half through, in shape as near as can be described to a well-formed pear, with an iron cap fastened by eight screws. Taking off the cap we found grape, canister, and four eight-pound shells surrounded by about two bushels of coarse powder. On the bottom of the cask there was a wooden box containing several batteries, with hollow wires attached to two larger wires, covered with a substance impervious to water, connecting with the cavern before spoken of. A dozen of these iron pots or casks were thus united with this cavern. Half a dozen of these caverns have been found, and probably 75 or 100 of these infernal machines are thus buried in the earth, some distance from the enemy's work; and the time to be exploded would be when our infantry had driven them inside their works—a sentinel would give the operator inside the cavern a signal, and he would send the electric spark through all the wires.[27]

Captain Schmitt had no way of knowing he had just described one of the world's first deployed electrically activated landmines, or anti-personnel devices. They were command-detonated mines—in other words, the device would be exploded by someone else at a given moment designed to inflict maximum casualties. A deadlier alternative was soon to come when victim-activated landmines became popular with Confederate forces throughout the South.

27 Ibid., 202-203.

Chapter 2

1862: Legitimate or "Cowardly"?

In March 1862, the Union army launched its Peninsula Campaign with more men and materiel than any other campaign in Virginia during the Civil War. Major General George B. McClellan conceived a strategic plan to strike the Confederate capital at Richmond, by way of the peninsula between the York and James rivers. It was a sound concept that enabled the Union to use its naval superiority to protect McClellan's flanks and its vast fleet to carry his troops. McClellan landed a force of nearly 120,000 men at Fort Monroe on the peninsula's extremity, about 80 miles southeast of Richmond. The Federals began fighting their way toward the Confederate capital on April 4.

The Emergence of Victim-activated Mines

A Confederate army under Gen. Joseph E. Johnston, about 65,000 strong, was responsible for defending Richmond. McClellan's Army of the Potomac on the Virginia Peninsula, however, outnumbered Johnston's army nearly two to one, and was one of the best-equipped armies in history.

Before McClellan began moving his troops northwest from the area around Fort Monroe up the Peninsula and before Johnston shuttled his men south to the capital and then out on the Peninsula, the Confederacy's first steam- powered ironclad made her appearance. Based out of Norfolk, the CSS *Virginia* steamed into Hampton Roads off Fort Monroe on March 8 and devastated much of the

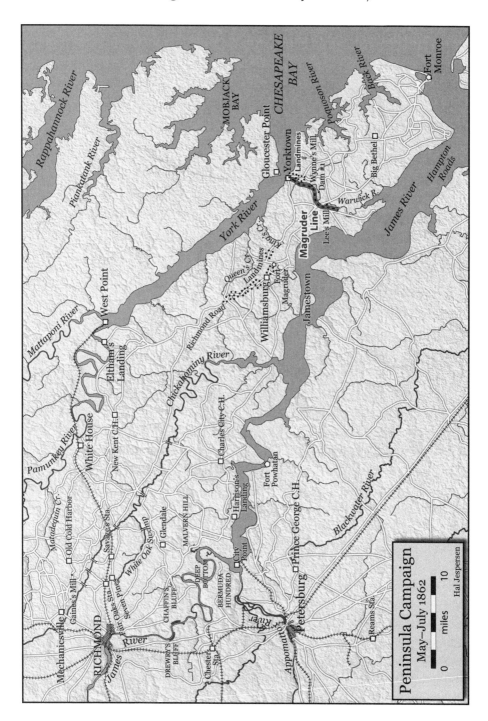

Peninsula Campaign
May–July 1862

Hal Jespersen

miles
0   10

Gen. Joseph E. Johnston, who would feud often with Gabriel Rains about using landmines against unsuspecting enemy soldiers. *Library of Congress*

wooden Union fleet. Only the fortuitous arrival of the USS *Monitor* prevented additional losses when, on March 9, the ironclads dueled to a stalemate. The mouth of the James River, however, was directly across Hampton Roads, and the *Virginia's* presence threatened all Union naval activity on it. The *Virginia* disrupted McClellan's plan of amphibiously enveloping Yorktown, his army's first objective. His overland path up the Peninsula to Richmond was also blocked by Maj. Gen. John B. Magruder's forces anchored in massive fortifications at Yorktown.

The Peninsula Campaign that followed witnessed the first use of innovative weapons and tactics including the ironclads just discussed, and even hot air balloons for observation. What most people, including most students of the Civil War, do not realize, is that at the siege of Yorktown in early April, victim-activated landmines (also known as "sub-terra shells" or "infernal machines") were deployed for the first time in the Western Hemisphere. In the fighting to come at Williamsburg and outside Richmond, these victim-activated mines would delay, and in many cases, maim or kill, pursuing Federals.

The Exploits of Gabriel James Rains

Under Magruder's command, the defenders of Yorktown reinforced the remains of the British earthworks from the American Revolution and constructed additional defenses in anticipation of McClellan's advance up the Peninsula. By April 1862, Yorktown was again surrounded by a formidable wall of works and faced a besieging force. Another major line of earthworks were constructed several hundred yards west of Yorktown. Known as the Warwick-Yorktown line, this defensive front ran south from the town for

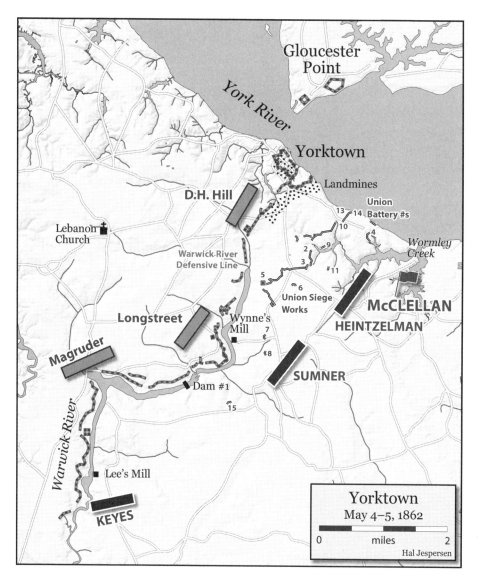

almost 12 miles to the James River, incorporating many natural features to increase its strength.

McClellan's army ran up against Magruder's defensive line once it marched away from Fort Monroe. To increase the appearance of strength, several Confederate embrasures were filled with "Quaker guns," which were simply painted logs shaped to resemble cannons and placed into position to deceive the enemy. Despite his overwhelming superiority, McClellan was fooled by Magruder's pretense of power and was disinclined to launch a direct assault.

Without naval support for his flanks and confronting strong defensive fortifications in their front, McClellan's forces were held up for nearly a month attempting to overcome the unexpected resistance. In the woods east and south of Yorktown, the Union army constructed heavy siege batteries with 103 guns—among the most advanced and powerful weapons in the world— designed to destroy the Confederate defenses in preparation for an assault.

On April 16, Union reconnaissance forces probed a perceived weakness in the Confederate line at Lee's Mill (also known as the "Battle of Dam No. 1"), but initial success there failed when the Federals were repulsed by a heavy counterattack. It appeared that the fortifications at Lee's Mill were too strong to take without suffering significant losses.

Over the next few weeks Johnston and the bulk of his army arrived at Yorktown as McClellan worked to get his batteries into place. He planned to open his massive bombardment at dawn on May 4, followed by a major infantry assault. Every battery (except two) was prepared to participate. Johnston, however, knew the time had arrived and ordered a withdrawal of the Confederates on the night of May 3. The defenders evacuated under a heavy rain that would continue without a break for the next 30 hours. The Confederates unleashed a tremendous preemptive night bombardment of their own to cover their retreat northwest toward Williamsburg.[1]

To McClellan's surprise, at dawn the advancing Union troops found only abandoned mud-filled Rebel trenches. No bloody assault would be needed. Yorktown was in Union hands. The news spread like wildfire. "Loud cheers resounded along the line, from the York River to Warwick Creek, when the result was officially announced," recalled Capt. Henry Blake of the 18th Massachusetts, "and the bands, which had been dumb so long, again enlivened the soldiers; and the notes of a thousand drums, fifes, and bugles filled the woods with a discord of melody." Federals raced to win everlasting glory by being the first to place their units' colors atop the Confederate earthworks.[2]

---

1 Earl C. Hastings, Jr., and David Hastings, *A Pitiless Rain: The Battle of Williamsburg, 1862* (Shippensburg, PA, 1997), 28.

2 Henry Blake, *Three Years in the Army of the Potomac: "From Year to Year, the Battles, Sieges, Fortunes, That I Have Passed"* (Boston, MA, 1865), 66.

Explosion of a torpedo.

Landmine exploding among Union troops at Yorktown. *A. R. Waud, Harper's Weekly, May 24, 1862*

The initial jubilation proved short-lived when the advance on the enemy's works encountered a new weapon. The Confederates had planted victim-activated landmines—powder-filled artillery shells topped with friction primers set to explode when stepped on or moved—just a few inches under the soil. Union soldiers found the mines throughout the area—"in the vicinity of the springs, hospitals, and other places which they supposed the soldiers would visit," recalled one eyewitness. Nearly 30 Union soldiers were killed or maimed by what were soon referred to as "infernal machines."[3]

Some Federals encountered the "torpedoes" well in front of the town's defenses. Union Brig. Gen. William F. Barry, chief of artillery for the Army of the Potomac, reported the horrifying experiences with landmines when his men approached and entered Yorktown. "Before reaching the glacis of the main work, and at the distance of more than 100 yards from it," he recalled, "several of our men were injured by the explosion of what was ascertained to be loaded shells buried in the ground." The shells, buried just below the surface, were eight- or 10-inch mortar or Columbiad shells filled with gunpowder. The mines exploded, Barry recalled, when stepped on or simply jostled.[4]

Jesse A. Gove, colonel of the 22nd Massachusetts, wrote of the effects of "inhuman missiles of war" placed in or near houses or "in the roads and thoroughfares in town." Six men in Gove's Company G were wounded when one of them stepped on a mine buried in the road. Another mine exploded in a column of cavalry near the abandoned works. The colonel was unsure how many men were injured in the blast. Another victim was a telegraph operator working as part of the Union balloon battlefield reconnaissance hot crew. The unlucky man "stepped on one of them a [landmine], which exploded with deadly effect," recalled Colonel Gove. "It was a 10-inch shell, concealed by the sand, and in the middle of the road."[5]

Robert Knox Sneden had enlisted in the 40th New York Infantry (the "Mozart" Regiment) and was serving on the Peninsula as a staff officer and topographical engineer for Maj. Gen. Samuel Heintzelmen's III Corps. Sneden, who would survive captivity at Andersonville and become an accomplished

---

3 Ibid., 167; General E. P. Alexander, "Sketch of Longstreet's Division: Yorktown and Williamsburg," *Southern Historical Society Papers*, vol. 10, 38.

4 William F. Barry, Brigadier-General and Inspector of Artillery, U.S. Army, to Brigadier-General G. W. Cullum, Chief of Staff, Headquarters of the Army, August 25, 1862, *OR* vol. 11, pt. 1, 349.

5 Report of Col. Jesse A. Gore, Twenty-Second Massachusetts Infantry, of Occupation of Yorktown, May 4th, *OR* vol. 11, pt. 1, 399-400. It is believed that the telegraph operator killed in Yorktown by a landmine near the telegraph pole on May 5, 1862, was the first and only casualty suffered by anyone in the Union balloon crews during the entire war.

illustrator after the war, witnessed a landmine casualty involving another telegraph operator who had entered a house to take down a Confederate telegraph location. While removing a ground wire, he stepped on a hidden shell and triggered a huge explosion. The force of the blast was so powerful that it blew off the man's legs and collapsed the side of the house. The victim, Sneden recalled, died in "great agony."[6]

In a twist of fate, Confederate forces suffered casualties from their own landmines as they worked their way to Williamsburg along muddy roads. At roughly 3:00 a.m. on May 4, Confederate cavalry stragglers from the rear guard entered Yorktown and inadvertently triggered torpedoes. The evacuation, recalled Reverend Nicholas A. Davis of the 4th Texas, the last infantry unit to leave Yorktown,

> might have been accomplished with some degree of secrecy had not the whiskey drinking propensities of some our cavalry led them into a trap which had been arranged for the reception of the Yankees. Secret mines had been placed in several houses, to explode on entrance. Ignorant of that fact, our enterprising troopers burst open a door, and though unsuccessful in their search for liquor, came out of the house considerably "elevated" themselves.[7]

Some Federals narrowly avoided severe injuries or death after triggering a landmines. Marching toward abandoned Confederate works outside Yorktown, for example, soldiers in the 77th New York heard a pistol-like report within their ranks and scattered. Someone found a piece of old cloth where the sharp sound emanated. When a colonel lifted it with the point of his sword, he discovered a mine carefully buried in the ground. Only the fuse had exploded.[8]

Never in American history had soldiers encountered such weapons. "On the morning of May 4th, 1862," recalled Union Brevet Brig. Gen. Fred T. Locke some years later,

---

6 Robert Knox Sneden, *Eye of the Storm: A Civil War Odyssey*, Chares F. Bryan Jr. and Nelson D. Lankford, eds. (New York, NY, 2000), 60.

7 Alexander, "Sketch of Longstreet's Division," 38; Norman Youngblood, *The Development of Mine Warfare: A Most Murderous and Barbarous Conduct* (Westport, CT, 2006), 41.

8 Richard Wheeler, *Sword Over Richmond: An Eyewitness History of McClellan's Peninsula Campaign* (New York, NY, 1986), 144.

our pickets sent in a prisoner who said he was a Union man, had been impressed into the rebel service, and was one of a party detailed to bury some shells in the road and fields near the works. . . . A cavalry detachment passing along the road leading to Yorktown had some of its men and horses killed and wounded by these shells. . . . In the casemates and covered ways about the fortifications I saw a number of large shells, placed so that they could easily be fired by persons unaware of their presence.[9]

Union assistant surgeon W. E. Waters was equally horrified by the use and effects of the landmines. "One of the most barbarous practices of civilized warfare was adopted by the enemy, in placing on all the approaches to the abandoned fortifications numerous torpedoes, which, when trod upon, exploded," he complained, "killing and wounding men and horses." One Union soldier was killed and six more wounded by a mine explosion in a deserted trench at Lee's Mill.[10]

The Yorktown victim-activated landmines were placed under the supervision of Brig. Gen. Gabriel Rains, the 58-year-old commander of a mixed Alabama and Georgia brigade in Maj. Gen. Daniel Harvey Hill's division. Rains, who was a virtual unknown at the time, would earn significant, if infamous, notoriety as the most significant figure in Confederate landmine warfare.[11]

Gabriel was born in 1803 in New Bern, North Carolina, one of eight children of his cabinet-making father named Gabriel and his wife Hester. He graduated from the U. S. Military Academy at West Point in 1827, 13th in a class that also included future Confederate bishop general Leonidas Polk.

9 Fred T. Locke, Assistant Adjutant-General to Fitz John Porter, Director of the Siege, and Colonel Edward C. James, of the Engineer Corps, letter to editors and published in "Confederate Use of Subterranean Shells on the Peninsula," in Robert Underwood Johnson and Clarence Clough Buell, eds., *Battles and Leaders of the Civil War*, 4 vols. (1884), vol. 2, 201.

10 W. E. Waters, Assistant Surgeon, U.S. Army, "Extract From a Narrative of His Services on the Medical Staff," in *The Medical and Surgical History of the War of the Rebellion*, 6 vols. (Washington, D.C., 1870-1888), Vol. 1, Appendix, "Containing Reports of Medical Directors, and Other Documents," edited under the direction of Surgeon General Joseph K. Barnes, U.S. Army, 80; Report of Brigadier General Erasmus D. Keyes, U.S. Army, commanding, Fourth Corps, Headquarters Fourth Army Corps, New Kent Court-House, Virginia, to Brigadier General S. Williams, Adjunct General, Army of the Potomac, May 14, 1862, *OR* vol. 11, pt. 1, 511.

11 On June 5, 1860, Gabriel Rains was promoted to lieutenant colonel in the U.S. Army. He resigned his commission on July 31, 1861, to join the Confederate States Army.

Rains's younger brother George, who would follow in his older brother's footsteps and graduate from West Point in 1842, would gain extensive business and scientific experience before the Civil War before establishing and running the Confederate Powder Works in Augusta, Georgia.

The Rains brothers had a fondness for science, in general, and the use of chemicals in particular. "George is certainly one of the best," his mother said, "but I can't keep the boy decent. He burns up with his 'chemicals,' as he calls them, the best clothing I can have made for him. I never feel sure that he has a single suit not in holes."[12]

By 1839 Rains was a captain in the Regular Army and was assigned to Fort Micanopy in Florida's northern interior, about 25 miles from Fort King. In April 1840, the area near Fort King became a hotbed of Seminole activity. According to Rains, the Seminoles realized that King was not as strong as Fort Micanopy and moved quickly to exploit the situation. "It became dangerous to walk even around the post," Rains recalled, "and finally two . . . men were waylaid and murdered [by the Seminoles] in full view thereof."[13]

It was Rains who came up with the idea of using victim-activated explosives "with variable success" to deter Seminoles from attacking" his troops. Rains placed explosive shells "as booby traps about a mile from Fort King to alert the garrison of the Indians's approach and to deter Seminole ambushes." In one instance, explained Rains, the clothing of the murdered soldiers covered a torpedo, and the weapon was placed "where the Indian war parties had to get water."[14]

"A day or two" after the explosive booby trap was placed, Rains and his troops heard a blast and went to investigate and see firsthand the "evidence of its destructive effects." Lying in wait and concealed by thickets, however, were nearly 100 "infuriated" Seminoles "ready for action," continued Rains. The mine was defective and had not exploded correctly. The Indians attacked the small group, killing seven soldiers and wounding several others, including Rains, who was carried to the fort by his men with what they believed was a mortal chest wound. Despite the casualties, the victim-activated weapon "was

---

12 "Recollections of New Bern Fifty Years Ago," *The Newbernian* (New Bern, NC), September 8, 1877.

13 Gabriel J. Rains, "Torpedoes," *Southern Historical Society Papers*, vol. 3, 258.

14 Alexander, "Sketch of Longstreet's Division," 39; Rains, "Torpedoes," 258.

successful in startling the enemy and protecting the fort," claimed one account. Rains was promoted for gallant and meritorious conduct under fire.[15]

When the Civil War began, Gabriel was a lieutenant colonel in the Regular Army serving as a mustering officer for Vermont soldiers. In July 1861, he resigned his commission, a decision criticized by at least one Northern newspaper. "This is only another instance showing how the service was permeated by treason," accused the *Boston Traveler*, "and the difficulties under which the administration has labored in separating the chaff from the wheat."[16]

Rains expected a long and difficult war. "The Southerners think that there is no *fight* in the Yankees [emphasis in original]; but these men," he explained, pointing to his Vermont soldiers before the fighting started, "are going to fight. The Southern people are fighters. And how the blood will flow!" Initially commissioned a colonel in the Confederate Army, Rains was appointed a brigadier general in late 1861. At 58, he was one of the older officers in the Southern army.[17]

On the Virginia Peninsula in the spring of 1862, Rains, apparently without receiving permission from Maj. Gen. D. H. Hill or other higher-ranking officers, had ordered his troops to plant landmines in front of his Yorktown positions. His exploits with explosives while serving in the Regular Army in Florida were no secret to at least some officers in the Union army. General Barry was highly critical of Rains for reintroducing the tactic at Yorktown. Planting mines was a "dastardly business," he exclaimed before adding that "a similar mode of warfare [was] inaugurated by Rains while disgracing the uniform of the American Army during the Seminole war in Florida."[18]

Rains' Confederate troops at Yorktown deployed the booby traps using tactics similar to what the general had employed against the Seminoles. Explosives were hidden in inconspicuous places throughout town around telegraph poles, under pieces of discarded clothing, inside food barrels, and elsewhere. Innocent-looking objects such as common work tools were used as triggering devices. As noted earlier, unsuspecting Federal soldiers were killed

---

15 Rains, "Torpedoes," 258-259; W. Davis Waters, "Deception is the Art of War: Gabriel J. Rains, Torpedo Specialist of the Confederacy," *North Carolina Historical Review* (1989), vol. 66, no. 1, 32.

16 "Turned Traitor," *St. Johnsbury* (VT) *Caledonian*, January 17, 1862.

17 "Death of Gen. G. J. Rains," *Burlington Free Press and Times*, September 1, 1881, 2.

18 William F. Barry to G. W. Cullum, August 25, 1863, *OR* vol. 11, pt. 1, 350.

or wounded by these mines, which unnerved their comrades who witnessed or heard of these horrific events. The weapons made it difficult for soldiers to carry out tasks because they were afraid of triggering the explosives.

In his Yorktown after-action report, Union Brig. Gen. Fitz John Porter explained that his troops "experienced some losses from shells planted in the ground, which exploded when trod upon. Many of these shells were concealed in the streets and houses of the town," he continued, "and arranged to explode by treading on the caps or pulling a wire attached to the doors."[19]

A *New York Times* reporter confirmed similar observations: "Inside the fort [Yorktown], especially near the grounds, and in the streets, and places our men would walk, newly turned earth and other indications gave evidence of buried torpedoes." According to one Union soldier, "[s]ome were also found near wells and springs of water, a few in some flour barrels and sacks in the telegraph office, and one or more near a magazine."[20]

"In some cases, articles of common use, and which would be most likely to be picked up, such as engineers' wheelbarrows, or pickaxes, or shovels, were laid upon the spot with apparent carelessness," reported General Barry. "Concealed springs or wires leading from the friction primer of the shell to the superincumbent articles," he continued,

> were so arranged that the slightest disturbance would occasion the explosion. These shells were not thus placed on the glacis at the bottom of the ditch, &c., which in view of the anticipated assault, might possibly be considered a legitimate use of them, but they were basely planted by an enemy who was secretly abandoning his post on common roads, at springs of water, in the shade of trees, at the foot of telegraph poles, and, lastly, quite within the defenses of the place—in the very streets of the town.[21]

As the previous reports made clear, explosive devices connected by trip wires were placed inside houses in all sorts of nefarious ways. Those weapons were particularly frightening to Federal soldiers. Several explosives were

---

19 Report of Brig. Gen. Fitz John Porter, U.S. Army, as Director of the Siege of Yorktown, from April 7-May 5, *OR* vol. 11, pt. 1, 313-314.

20 "The Advance Through Yorktown: Letters from our Special Correspondents, Yorktown, Sunday, May 4, 1862," *New York Times*, May 7, 1862, 8; Oliver Otis Howard, *Autobiography of Oliver Otis Howard, Major General, United States Army*, 2 vols. (New York, NY, 1907), vol. 1, 218.

21 William F. Barry to G. W. Cullum, August 25, 1863, *OR* vol. 11, pt. 1, 349.

planted in one dwelling. Under a table in a corner, a coffee pot was attached by a string to a weight that, when moved, was designed to fall on a torpedo and trigger the explosion. Several shells were placed at the foot of cellar stairs, and another room had a large shell on the table. No one could see how it was to be detonated, so everyone avoided entering the room.[22]

Union forces reported other incidents involving the "devilish ingenuity" of explosive booby traps in Yorktown. A New York soldier picked up a pocket knife he spotted lying on the ground. While attempting to do so, "he found a cork tied to it. Without any suspicion he gave it a pull to see what the cord was fastened to, and the next instant was blown into fragments, the cord having been fastened to the machinery of a concealed torpedo and the slightest pull had exploded." The man, a Union chaplain recalled, was torn "into a hundred fragments."[23]

Searching for torpedoes ahead of his column, Col. Edwin C. Mason of the 7th Maine accidentally crushed a percussion cap with his foot. Fortunately, the shell failed to explode. When Mason moved the dirt away, he saw the "red wax at the top of the buried shell" and counted himself an extremely lucky man. Mason called for volunteers who scoured the road on their hands and knees and found more than a dozen similar mines. Mason saved his men, but "several horses and men among the first passing troops were killed or wounded by [landmines]," admitted a Union general.[24]

The torpedo explosions were ignited by direct contact with the primer of a buried shell or a concealed trip wire attached between an article and the primer. Many landmines had a foot or two of telegraph wire sticking out of the ground, apparently designed as a trip wire to catch a foot or a horse's hoof and trigger the shell. A "number of our men were killed by them before the disgraceful trick was discovered and information of the fact could be given to the troops," Barry wrote. "Careful examinations were at once made, and sentinels were posted wherever the existence of these infernal machines was ascertained or suspected."[25]

---

22 Ibid., 349-350.

23 Gilbert Adams Hays, *Under the Red Patch: Story of the Sixty-Third Regiment, Pennsylvania Volunteers, 1861-1864* (Pittsburgh, PA, 1908), 83-84.

24 Howard, *Autobiography*, vol. 1, 218-219.

25 Waters, "Deception is the Art of War," 34; Barry to Cullum, *OR* vol. 11, pt. 1, 349.

Casualties decreased as awareness of landmines spread. More were soon located and marked with flags or stakes. Soldiers began to carefully examine roads looking for "fatal iron fuses, whose touch is death." Engineer teams were sent to clear the explosive booby traps and landmines, dangerous work that consumed hours. According to one Union report, "[o]ur sapper engineers after two hours' work had safely unearthed many of these cowardly missiles."[26]

Union officers posted sentinels at suspected and uncovered mined positions, typically where "newly made earth revealed the location of these concealed infernal machines," Captain Blake explained. The red flags were brought out, and the Federal officers detailed men to stay behind and warn upcoming columns when clusters of shells were found. African-Americans sometimes "came out of their hiding places" to give "all information that they were capable of" regarding mines.[27]

A *New York Times* correspondent traveling through town as part of a military escort noted that guards were posted to warn soldiers of the presence of landmines. "[W]e passed on," he wrote, "feeling our way cautiously along the road thus prepare[d] for us by those, who too weak to trust to honorable warfare, thus indulge their devilish instincts of hate."[28]

"Horrible Mangling"

The Federal pursuit of withdrawing Southern forces northwest to Williamsburg was hampered by heavy rain. Army of the Potomac veterans involved in the movement described it as one of the most memorable aspects of their service. III Corps staff officer Robert Sneden wrote in his postwar memoir about traveling on the Yorktown-to-Williamsburg turnpike chasing retreating Confederate soldiers. "The roads were sandy but full of sloughs of mud and water," he began,

with here and there broken corduroy stuff sticking out of the red mud, and these mud holes were numerous. The wagon trains crawled along slowly, until an opening in the woods allowed one train to pass the other. After going two miles the wagons stuck in

26 Luther S. Dickey, *History of the Eighty-Fifth Regiment, Pennsylvania Volunteer Infantry, 1861-1865* (New York, NY, 1915), 37; Sneden, *Eye of the Storm*, 60.

27 Sneden, *Eye of the Storm*, 60.

28 "The Advance Through Yorktown," *New York Times*, May 7, 1862, 8.

the mud every few minutes, while the mules were belabored unmercifully by the teamsters, while the air was blue with their swearing.[29]

The Union soldiers marching from Yorktown in the early morning darkness were especially wary of landmines, many of which had been marked with small flags planted in the ground. Some soldiers slipped through narrow passages among the landmines while others "became hoarse calling to the soldiers not to move to the right or left" to avoid stepping on the deadly devices.[30]

To delay pursuers, Rains ordered the planting of more victim-activated landmines in the rain-soaked soil on May 5. He and his men found an abandoned ammunition wagon on the road north of Williamsburg. They took four of the five loaded shells, attached a "sensitive fuse primer," and planted them near some trees that had fallen across the road.[31]

Union soldiers also came across several heaps of dirt on the road to Williamsburg and wasted an hour carefully digging through them in search of mines. Nothing was found. Other Federals chasing the retreating Confederates discovered Rains's landmines buried ingeniously in the road. The shells were exploded "with terrific effect" by the first Federal cavalry to arrive on the scene. General Barry witnessed the "horrible mangling" of a Yankee cavalryman and his horse on the Williamsburg Road who had the misfortune of triggering one of the "infernal devices."[32]

Later that same day, a Federal division under Gen. Joseph Hooker collided with Confederates manning Fort Magruder, an earthen fortification along the Williamsburg Road. Union forces were driven back in the fighting at Williamsburg, the first large-scale pitched battle of the Peninsula Campaign. More than 40,000 troops from McClellan's Army of the Potomac engaged nearly 32,000 Confederates commanded by Maj. Gen. James Longstreet. The battle ended without a clear-cut winner, though the Confederates were able to resume their withdrawal up the Peninsula toward Richmond during the night.

Rains continued seeding the ground with more landmines behind the army, especially along the Richmond Road passing through Williamsburg. The fear of

---

29 Hastings and Hastings, *A Pitiless Rain*, 89; Sneden, *Eye of the Storm*, 63.

30 Howard, *Autobiography*, vol. 1, 222-223.

31 Jefferson Davis, *The Rise and Fall of the Confederate Government*, 2 vols. (New York, NY, 1881), vol. 2, 97.

32 Sneden, *Eye of the Storm*, 64; Barry to Cullum, *OR* vol. 11, pt. 1, 350.

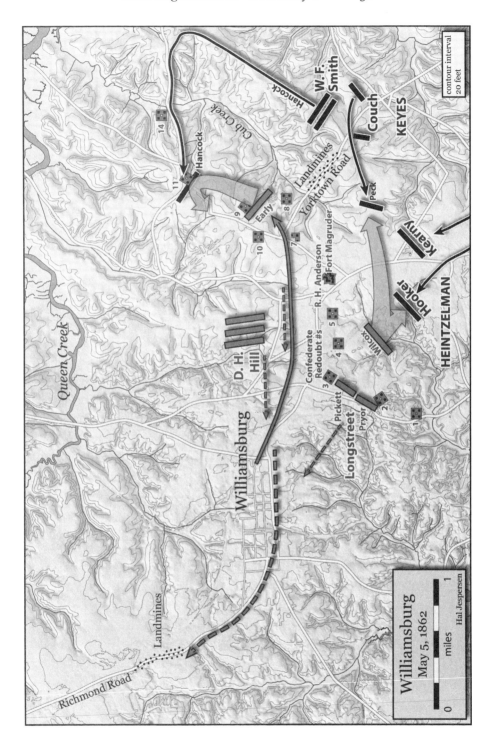

Williamsburg
May 5, 1862

miles

Hal Jespersen

a sudden explosion continued to hamper Union troops who stopped, searched, and cautiously followed in the Confederates' wake. When the Federals discovered ground that had been disturbed, they stopped moving their wagons in fear of the mines. A group of Federal cavalry ran upon the torpedoes and detonated them. The Yankees trailing the unfortunate troopers naturally hesitated to continue past the injured and dead, and in fact refused to move farther until they could examine the roadway. Eventually, the bottleneck held up part of the army for nearly three days.

"Lawful and Proper"

The enemy's use of landmines outraged General McClellan. "[T]he rebels have been guilty of the most murderous and barbarous conduct in placing torpedoes within the abandoned works near wells and springs; near flag shafts, magazines, telegraph offices, in carpet-bags, barrels of flour," he complained in a telegram to Secretary of War Edwin Stanton.[33]

As evidence of the continued deterioration in the "morality of civilized warfare," McClellan ordered Confederate prisoners to open the magazines at Yorktown, which he suspected were infested with "infernal machines." He also ordered prisoners, who had been taken captive during the siege, to unearth the concealed shells. "I shall make the prisoners remove them at their own peril," he reported to Secretary Stanton. General Barry observed that "McClellan ordered that the Confederate prisoners taken by us at Yorktown should be made to search for these buried shells and to sinter and destroy them when found."[34]

On May 11, six days after the Battle of Williamsburg, General Longstreet, the commander of Joseph E. Johnston's "Right Wing" (three divisions that included the one in which Rains commanded a brigade), forbade Rains from planting more landmines on any roads used by his command. "It is the desire of the major-general commanding that you put no shells or torpedoes behind you," Longstreet's staff officer ordered Rains, "as he does not recognize it as a proper

---

33 G. B. McClellan, Major General, Commanding, Head Quarters, Army of the Potomac, Yorktown to Hon. E. M. Stanton, Secretary of War, May 4, 1862, *OR* vol. 11, pt. 3, 135.

34 Alexander, "Sketch of Longstreet's Division," 39; McClellan to Stanton, May 4, 1862, *OR* vol. 11, pt. 3, 254, 349-350. The sintering process involved compacting and forming a solid mass of material by heat or pressure without melting it to the point of liquefaction. The physical aspects of explosives compaction significantly affect the physicomechanical (physical and mechanical) characteristics of the material of sintered specimens.

or effective method of war." Rains had run up against his first serious roadblock.[35]

Longstreet's request notwithstanding, the North Carolina scientist continued to advocate for the use of landmines during retreats and to defend fixed positions. He forwarded Longstreet's orders and his own comments to his immediate commander, Maj. Gen. D. H. Hill, who had no objections to their continued use. "In my opinion all means of destroying our brutal enemies are lawful and proper," Hill, a fellow North Carolinian, replied.[36]

Ironically, Joe Johnston learned what his own army was up to from a copy of the *New York Herald*, which had reprinted General McClellan's report on landmines at Yorktown. The surprised army commander fired off a letter on May 12 asking General Hill if it were true. Johnston had no knowledge of these devices, though one of his wing commanders had already discovered their use and had sought to stop it. Word about the mines, meanwhile, was rapidly filtering through the Confederate army.[37]

Many Confederates were horrified by the use of these weapons. When questioned, Rains insisted he knew "nothing of the locations of 'torpedoes' at the places mentioned [in Yorktown]." The deployment of mines in or around "wells or springs of water, barrels of flour, carpet-bags, and places [are] incompatible with the invention," he claimed. Rains may have been telling the truth, and was simply unaware at the time that his soldiers had placed mines in those locations. He later acknowledged that some of his men had planted torpedoes at unspecified areas that he "never saw."[38]

For his part, Johnston agreed with Longstreet that Rains should cease using landmines. In response, Rains defended their deployment as part of a rear guard action during the withdrawal to Richmond and offered his own recent experience as evidence of their effectiveness. His artillery had been held up at "a place of mud slushes" in the Richmond Road several miles out of Williamsburg,

35 G. Moxley Sorrel, Assistant Adjutant-General, Headquarters, Second Corps, Department of Northern Virginia, Christian's House, to Brigadier-General Rains, Commanding Rear Guard, May 11, 1862, *OR* vol. 11, 509.

36 Rains to D. H. Hill, Major-General, *OR* vol. 11, pt. 3, 510.

37 A. P. Mason, Assistant Adjutant-General, Headquarters, Department of Northern Virginia, to Major General D. H. Hill, May 12, 1862, *OR* vol. 11, pt. 3, 511.

38 Brigadier-General G. J. Rains, Commanding Brigade, Rear Guard to Major-General Hill, Commanding Third Division, May 14, 1862, *OR* vol. 11, pt. 3, 516.

Brigadier General Gabriel James Rains. As head of the Confederate Army Torpedo Bureau, Rains was largely responsible for developing many of the Confederacy's landmines. *Library of Congress*

he explained. The guns could neither be wheeled to fire if attacked, nor pulled out of the mud to continue retreating. When he heard Union cannon shelling the road behind his soldiers to cover the advance of their cavalry, Rains believed "[i]t was impossible for us to fight." Most of the men had had no food for "forty-eight hours, having stood all night in the rain without fire or light," and their "physical endurance had been taxed to the utmost."[39]

After attaching detonators to four small artillery shells that he had found abandoned along the road, Rains ordered his troops to bury them "to have a moral effect in checking the advance of the enemy (for they were too small to do more) to save our sick, wounded, and enfeebled, who straggled in our rear."[40]

Rains justified his use of landmines at Yorktown by explaining that their placement in the defenses there was necessary to help even the odds between Union and Confederate forces. He also pointed out that McClellan had intended to use a mine to destroy part of the defenses at Yorktown and at Fort Magruder, which Rains believed legitimized the use of his smaller mines. Finally, Rains believed Union forces had already broken the rules of civilized warfare when they began their bombardment of Yorktown "without a word of warning to innocent women and children, as at New Berne, North Carolina, my native place," and sent "death-dealing fragments among the innocent and unoffending."[41]

In mid-May, Confederate Secretary of War George W. Randolph reviewed and examined the landmine correspondence between Rains and his superiors, including Johnston and Longstreet, and an endorsement by Hill in support of

---

39 John T. Scharf, *History of the Confederate Navy From Its Organization to the Surrender of Its Last Vessel* (New York, NY, 1887), 752; Rains to Hill, May 14, 1862, *OR* vol. 11, pt. 3, 516.

40 Rains to Hill, May 14, 1862, *OR* vol. 11, pt. 3, 516.

41 Ibid.; Brigadier-General G. J. Rains, Commanding Brigade, Rear Guard, indorsement of torpedoes as read by Confederate Secretary of War, May 1862, *OR* vol. 11, pt. 3, 509, 517. On this point, Rains's claim regarding Union destruction of his hometown of New Bern is not completely accurate. On March 13, 1862, as Union Maj. Gen. Ambrose E. Burnside was preparing to capture New Bern, the retreating Confederates set fire to warehouses filled with cotton bales, military supplies, and thousands of barrels of pine tar and turpentine. During the next 24 hours straggling soldiers, sailors, and a few residents looted and vandalized New Bern until Burnside's troops restored order. After the Union occupation, New Bern was transformed into a fortified city and remained under Union control for the duration of the war. The town had various spellings throughout its history, including *New Berne*, *Newbern*, and *New Bern*. In 1897, the name was designated as New Bern.

Rains. Randolph's judgment was that if no strategic advantage could be earned from the use of landmines, their use simply for the purpose of causing fatalities was wrong. "[The goal is] to take life with no other object than the destruction of life," explained the war secretary. "Hence it is inadmissible to shoot sentinels and pickets, because nothing is attained but the destruction of life." He continued:

> It would be admissible, however, to shoot a general, because you not only take life but deprive an army of its head. It is admissible to plant shells in a parapet to repeal an assault or in a road to check pursuit because the object is to save work in one case and the army in the other. It is not admissible to plant shells merely to destroy life and without other design than that of depriving your enemy of a few men, without materially injuring him.[42]

Randolph—a lawyer by profession—placed great emphasis on the intended "purpose" of a landmine's use. His review resulted in an official statement from the War Department on the subject of "sub-terra shells" that recognized their application under certain conditions, and, by doing so, indirectly validated Rains's claims.[43]

Soon after Randolph's decision, Johnston launched a major counter-offensive on May 31 at Seven Pines, just a handful of miles east of Richmond. Johnston was seriously wounded late in the day and President Davis, who was on the field with his military advisor, Gen. Robert E. Lee, appointed Lee to replace Johnston. By June of 1862 the Confederacy was already in dire straits. Federal forces were positioned on the outskirts of Richmond, the important port of New Orleans was in Union hands, as was a large swath of the Mississippi River, and U. S. Grant had scored another major victory along the Tennessee River at Shiloh that also killed Gen. Albert S. Johnston, one of the South's most promising field generals.

While Lee assumed the reins of command and schemed about how to defeat McClellan, Maj. Gen. D. H. Hill was gathering evidence to write his report on the role of his command at Seven Pines. Hill reprimanded Rains for what he deemed a poor performance in failing to deliver a second flank attack with his

---

42 Gabriel Rains, to Maj. Gen. D. H. Hill, on the Confederate Secretary of War's indorsement of torpedo use under certain conditions, *OR* 11, pt. 3, 516.

43 Ibid.

infantry brigade after an assault against a Federal redoubt. Secretary of War Randolph tried to tactfully deal with the issue of what to do with Rains by suggesting a voluntary transfer to the James River defenses, where there was no question that mines were needed. This seemed like a viable solution. Lee, who was trying to weed out officers who were not up to the task of leading men in the field, relieved Rains of his brigade command on June 16. Two days later, Rains was assigned to protect the James and Appomattox rivers, and work extensively with naval mines to do so.[44]

Robert E. Lee, who was more talented and much more aggressive than most people in or out of the military believed, ordered that a series of entrenchments be constructed to help hold the capital, reorganized and reinforced his new army, and ordered Maj. Gen. Thomas J. "Stonewall" Jackson to transfer his command from the Shenandoah to Richmond. Lee then launched a major offensive to sever the Union supply lines east of Richmond and turn McClellan's flank. He would either force the Army of the Potomac away from the capital or crush it. The Seven Days' Battles that followed (June 25 - July 1, 1862) indeed turned McClellan's flank and forced the Federals back to the James River, 35 miles south and east of Richmond. The seat of the Confederate government was free from the immediate prospect of a siege or worse.

The Defense of the James River

Rains would not be the first torpedo expert to operate on the James River. Lee had previously ordered Matthew Maury to use his electric naval mines to help defend the James, together with obstructions that would prevent the easy approach of the Union Navy close enough to shell Richmond. Maury deployed four large naval mines and 15 smaller ones near the north bank of the river at Chaffin's Bluff, just downstream from Drewry's Bluff. The mines were connected by fine-conducting platinum wire and heated by means of a galvanic current from a battery on shore, where the detonators were manned. Fixed tightly "in a small bag of rifle powder to serve as a bursting charge . . . the two terminals were then connected with the platinum wire making a span between

---

44 Ibid.; A. P. Mason, Assistant Adjutant-General, Special Orders No. 135, "By Command of Gen. R. E. Lee," Hdqrs. Dept. of Northern Virginia, to James Longstreet, Major-General, Commanding, June 16, 1862, *OR* vol. 11, pt. 3, 605. Longstreet forwarded Lee's orders to D. H. Hill "detaching General Rains" on June 17, 1862. See *OR* vol. 11, pt. 3, 605.

the terminals of say one-half inch." Electricity, passed through a hot platinum wire, ignited the primer that surrounded it, exploding the charge. Combined, the naval mines contained 12,000 pounds of gunpowder.[45]

The key to defending the river was Drewry's Bluff, a high bank overlooking an elbow in the James reinforced by heavy artillery. Back on May 15, a small Union fleet that included the USS *Monitor* steamed up to attempt a passage but was turned back by the river obstructions—including the water torpedoes—and heavy plunging fire from atop the bluff. This relatively "easy" victory, which was followed by a final inspection of the naval mine defensive systems on the James by President Davis, General Lee, and Secretary of the Navy Mallory, convinced the Confederate high command to "withdraw large numbers of troops from that quarter for offensive operations elsewhere." The troops had been used to reinforce Johnston's army, which in turn became Lee's.[46]

The electric naval mines became a mainstay of the defenses of the James River and other Southern rivers and harbors across the Confederacy. By June, Maury and Lt. Hunter Davidson had 15 casks in the river arranged in rows and spaced about 30 feet apart. The men, however, requested more gunpowder and materials to build an effective defense everywhere one was needed. With the assistance of Davidson and Lt. Robert Minor, Maury devised a method of reliably detonating the explosives as deep as 15 feet below the surface. However, the technology could not be exploited initially or widely because there was not enough wire for a comprehensive galvanic torpedo system. They would have deployed more mines, Maury later reported, if these materials had been available to do so.[47]

Several months later on October 12, Maury left Charleston for England aboard the Confederate blockade runner *Herald*. There, he was to procure materials and "study explosives and set up laboratories for the manufacture of new torpedoes" for the Confederate war effort. One concern with Maury's electric mines was the high probability of malfunction in combat conditions.

45 Acting Master, U.S. Navy, Henry Rogers, telegraphic engineer, for Acting Rear Admin. Lee, U.S. Navy, regarding magneto-electric machines for use in the James River, September 16, 1862, *Official Records of the Union and Confederate Navies*, 30 vols. (Washington, D. C., 1884-1922), vol. 8, 72; Matthew Fontaine Maury Lectures to Dutch, Swedish, and Norwegian Officers in MP, in Grady, *Matthew Fontaine Maury*, 218.

46 Dean Snyder, "Torpedoes for the Confederacy," *Civil War Times*, March 1985, 43-44.

47 Commander, Mathew Fontaine Maury to Confederate Secretary of the Navy Stephen R. Mallory, June 19, 1862, *ORN* vol. 1, 544-546.

Before Maury's departure for England, leadership for Confederate naval torpedo operations was assigned to Davidson, the former commander of the gunboat CSS *Teaser*. He would hold that position for the remainder of the war.[48]

Rains, meanwhile, had set about his new task in earnest along the James River. To earn political support and commensurate financial resources for his landmine research, Rains had written a report on the effectiveness of mine warfare that won President Davis's backing. Only one copy of Rains's report was made, partly due to Davis's fear that "no printed paper could be kept secret" and the design of mines "would be deprived of a greater part of its value if its peculiarities were known to the enemy."[49]

Rains's advocacy for torpedo use was vindicated on October 25, 1862, when the Confederate government created the Army Torpedo Bureau. The measure passed "both houses with acclamation." Because of the clandestine nature of the Torpedo Bureau, Rains ran the department mostly in secret. His official role was "as general superintendent of the conscription service for the Professional Army of the Confederate States." As his biographer dryly observed, "The man who had ushered in a new weapon now summoned soldiers for the Confederacy."[50]

The creation of the Army Torpedo Bureau solidified Rains's status as a key architect of landmine weapons and mine warfare. The bureau was responsible for the making, handling, and laying of landmines to support infantry operations. In addition to being responsible for landmine production and deployment, Rains supervised a staff of civilian and military engineers and their assistants. The law creating the bureau added momentum to Rains's landmine research and development. As a capable engineer with experience with contact-activated explosives in Florida and with landmines during the Peninsula Campaign, he was exceedingly well prepared for the job.

---

48 George M. Brooke, *John M. Brooke: Naval Scientist and Educator* (Charlottesville, VA, 1980), 282-283.

49 Confederate President Jefferson Davis to Brig. Gen. G. J. Rains, June 3, 1863, *OR* vol. 52, pt. 2, 487.

50 Rains, "Torpedoes," 256. The same legislation also created the Confederate States Submarine Battery Service and the Secret Service Corps. See Special Orders No. 294, "By command of the secretary of war," JNO Withers, Assistant Adjutant-General, December 16, 1862, *OR* Series 4, vol. 2, 241. W. Davis Waters, *Gabriel Rains and the Confederate Torpedo Bureau* (Savas Beatie, 2017), 43.

The Confederate Congress later supported Rains's landmine production and deployment efforts by appropriating $100,000 for his use. As a result, the bureau became the world's first institution devoted to landmine warfare, eventually setting up production and distribution facilities in several states to produce and field the mines. Although the largest facility was in Richmond, the bureau also established sizeable operations in Charleston, South Carolina, Mobile, Alabama, Savannah, Georgia, and Wilmington, North Carolina.

With the creation of the Army Torpedo Bureau, the Confederate high command's vows to stand up to the Union with "civilized" warfare caved in to the harsh realization that mines helped defenders hold crucial territory and slow aggressive pursuits. The weapons were easy to deploy and involved low-cost technology. The dramatic change in its landmine policy was due primarily to the immediate necessity of defense overriding the longer-term moral concerns regarding conventions of war.

Debate about the civility of landmine use would never arise again among Confederate leaders, at least in public. President Davis later formally acknowledged to the Confederate House of Representatives that torpedoes and submarine batteries were part of the overall defensive effort to protect major Southern cities and coastal areas from Union naval attacks. For the rest of the war, he encouraged and supported widespread landmine use.[51]

With the South facing chronic shortages in the raw materials necessary to carry on war, it was imperative that Rains's landmines be both low cost and effective as force multipliers. The deprivation of provisions led him and other explosive ordnance personnel to develop alternative explosive devices that used available resources.

Rains's experience with non-electrical, command-detonated explosives helped propel his development of contact- and victim-activated mines. He improved and improvised Maury's design by using a less expensive, more dependable, and more available fuse system to ignite the explosive. Rather than use electricity to detonate mines, for example, Rains designed a system to detonate more reliably on contact. In other words, the landmines and naval mines were triggered by the act of the victim himself.[52]

---

51 Confederate President Jefferson Davis to the House of Representatives of the Confederate States, March 25, 1862, *OR* Series 4, vol. 1, 1,021.

52 Electrical wire was hard to obtain and very expensive when it was available, which, in turn, made electric torpedoes very expensive.

On August 29, 1862, Rains received orders to report to the port city of Wilmington, North Carolina. Before he did so, he turned over his "submarine defense" duties in Virginia to Lieutenant Davidson. The mining of the James River became a solely naval responsibility.[53]

Besides the high-level political support from the Confederate Congress and Davis administration, three synchronous factors advanced and supported Rains's work. First, he conducted most of his landmine research in secret in Richmond, which was not only the center for political and financial support from the Confederate government, but the home of the Tredegar Iron Works, a key manufacturer of landmine materials.[54]

Second, the abrupt resignation of Confederate Secretary of War George Randolph led to the appointment of James A. Seddon, who was personally selected by President Davis to fill the post. Seddon was more supportive of Rains than Randolph had been, and Davis and Rains were relatively close acquaintances, having first met in 1834 while serving as Army officers at Fort Gibson in Indian Territory. There, then-Lt. Davis was arrested for "missing a morning bugle call and answering an officer in a disrespectful manner." Two days later he went before a court-martial proceeding that lasted six days. Rains was called as a witness and his testimony helped clear Davis of the charges. The Mississippian had a long memory and had not forgotten Rains's assistance. Through his personal appeal to Davis, Rains won the new secretary of war's approval for his landmine research. He had once again secured the backing and the blessings of the War Department.[55]

Third, Rains's enormously talented younger brother George W. Rains became an important supporter of, and supplier to, the production of landmines. As noted, the younger Rains established the Augusta Powder Works in Georgia,

---

53 Gideon Welles to Charles Wilkes, August 29, 1862, *ORN* vol. 7, 687; *OR* vol. 11, pt. 1, 4; Special Order No. 206, September 3, 1862, *OR* vol. 51, pt. 2, 615; JNO Withers, Assistant Adjutant-General, Special Orders No. 659. *OR* vol. 29, pt. 2, Special Orders No. 198, August 20, 1862, 577.

54 The Army Torpedo Bureau was purposefully not made public because it was intended to be a secret organization, and it operated under the name of the Conscription Bureau.

55 Grant Foreman, *Advancing the Frontier, 1830-1860* (Norman, OK, 1993), 46-47; Rembert W. Patrick, *Jefferson Davis and His Cabinet* (Baton Rouge, LA, 1976), 133.

which by war's end would provide more than three million pounds of gunpowder for the Confederacy.[56]

During the early months of the bureau's existence, Gabriel Rains worked on developing a sensitive primer fuse. At Yorktown, the landmine consisted merely of an artillery shell capped with a friction primer buried in the ground. Although the basics of this design—a pressure-sensitive fuse connected to a powder-filled shell—remained the same throughout the war, Rains made substantial modifications to the individual components, specifically a more sensitive primer that he developed during the winter of 1862–1863. Although the friction primer was designed to explode the artillery shell on impact with the ground, it could not be assured that the pressure of a walking human or horse would generate such force. To counter this problem, Rains replaced the old artillery-style friction primers with a sulfuric acid fuse similar to those used by the Russians during the Crimean War.[57]

The new Rains fuse was designed to explode with the slightest of pressure. The combination was enclosed in a metal container and topped with a thin copper or lead cap. The pressure would crush the cap and trigger the primer to ignite, which would light a short fuse, exploding the gunpowder and detonating the prime charge. The primer was soon known as the "Rains fuse."

The Rains fuse consisted of a paper tube filled with black powder that was inserted through a hole in the center of a wooden disc and extended down to the powder in the mine (usually an artillery shell). When someone stepped on the soft copper cone, the primer activated and immediately ignited the percussion

---

56 Theodore Savas, "The Best Powder Mill in the World: Rains and His Mission," in C.L. Bragg, Gordon A. Blaker, Charles D. Ross, Stephanie A. T. Jacobe and Theodore P. Savas, *Never for Want of Powder: The Confederate Powder Works in Augusta, Georgia* (Columbia, SC. 2007), 29.

57 Youngblood, *The Development of Mine Warfare*, 46. The fuse was composed of a soft lead cap that covered a small glass tube containing sulfuric acid. The tube rested in a 50/50 mixture of chlorate of potash and white sugar. When the cap was dented, the glass tube broke and the acid combined with the potash mixture, igniting the main fuse. For more information, see J. S. Barnes, *Submarine Warfare, Offensive, and Defensive* (New York, NY, 1869), 68. It is not known whether Rains was familiar with Nobel's work. Given the similarities between Rains' early fuses and Nobel's, it seems logical to infer that Rains had at least some knowledge of mine warfare in the Crimea, either from Delafield's writings or from the discussion of Jacobi's (Nobel's) mines in H. L. Scott, *Military Dictionary* (New York, NY, 1861), 318.

A Rains Fuse, Richmond National Battlefield Park Headquarters. *Author*

mixture, which then fired the black powder in the tube, sending a jet of flame down into the black powder charge in the shell, which would then explode.

When applied to wartime conditions, the fuse was activated by crushing the lead cover or metal foil. The weight of a person, horse, or wagon was more than enough to cause the explosion. Although the formula for the device was kept secret during the war, Confederate engineer Viktor Von Scheliha, an Austrian officer, later revealed that the Rains mixture was composed of a metal cone of tinned copper filled with a percussion mixture of 50 percent potassium chlorate, 30 percent antimony trisulfide, and 20 percent pulverized glass placed on top of a circular wooden disc.[58]

Unlike similar devices, the Rains fuse was intended solely for static defense. When set and armed, the weapon was just as dangerous to friend as it was to foe. For the rest of the war Confederate forces would use the Rains fuse throughout the South. Rains affixed the primer to shells to create landmines and

58 Youngblood, *The Development of Mine Warfare*, 46.

"submarine batteries," and to barrels of powder to create naval torpedoes.[59] Confederates would use the Rains primer or variations thereof in landmines, naval mines (floating and moored), frame torpedoes (bottom sea mines), spar torpedoes (explosives attached to the end of a long pole that was then rammed into Union vessels), and dart-shaped hand grenades.

By the end of 1862, mines were used again in the Western Theater, especially in the Mississippi Valley. On December 12, 1862, a Maury-designed torpedo in the Yazoo River sank the gunboat USS *Cairo*. Although the *Cairo* was the first ship sunk in combat by a torpedo, water torpedo warfare was difficult to implement in the inland waterways because currents carried trees and other debris that often uprooted or detonated the torpedoes. As a result, these were used much less in the Mississippi River and its tributaries than in the eastern and southern coastal areas.

About 150 miles south of where the USS *Cairo* went down was Port Hudson, Louisiana, a bastion along the Mississippi River where the longest military siege in U.S. History was about to play out. It was also the campaign in which command- and victim-activated landmines were used for the first time.

---

59 P. G. T. Beauregard to H. W. Mercer, n.d., *OR* vol. 16, 757; W. H. C. Whiting to James A. Seddon, January 28, 1863, *ORN* vol. 8, 858.

Chapter 3

1863: The Landmine Comes of Age

Once his first full year as Army Torpedo Bureau director was over and his ideas more settled and accepted, Brig. Gen. Gabriel Rains entered what would be the most intense and productive period of his entire military career. During this time he concocted more creative combinations of chemicals to produce even deadlier landmines. His efforts were boosted with the allocation of additional officers to the bureau, including an assistant adjutant general. From December of 1862 through May of 1863, while he was "officially" overseeing conscription, Rains directed ordnance experimentation and invented "a new primer that would explode from the slightest pressure." The "Rains primer," as it would soon be known, enhanced his reputation among Confederate political leadership and military commanders.[1]

Ironically, the first landmine casualty of the new year was Rains himself. On January 24, while working with his primers in his Richmond laboratory, one accidentally exploded in his right hand, injuring his thumb and forefinger. According to a government clerk working with him, the injury was so severe

---

1 Special Order No. 1, January 2,1863, JNO Withers, Assistant Adjutant-General, Adjt. and Insp. General's Office, Richmond, Virginia, *OR* series 4, vol. 2, 279; John B. Jones, *A Rebel War Clerk's Diary at the Confederate States Capital*, 2 vols. (Philadelphia, PA, 1866), vol. 1, 246.

that Rains "could barely sign his name to official documents." He told the clerk that he "would not use such a weapon in ordinary warfare," but would resort to it as a "means of defense against an army of Abolitionists, invading our country for the purpose of avowed . . . extermination."[2]

As the South reeled from battlefield defeats and dwindling resources, the Davis administration increased its support to Rains for the production and deployment of his torpedoes. Anxious to get away from the fiction of running conscription, which ate away at his time, Rain prepared a book of drawings exclusively for President Davis of various landmines and torpedoes, and of his ideas for improving their use. The ploy worked, and the president was fascinated by the possibilities. That May, Davis relieved Rains from his Richmond-based duties at the Bureau of Conscription so he could spend his time in the field advancing landmine warfare. To Rains's dismay, the president ordered him west to Mississippi for immediate service under Joseph E. Johnston.[3]

Port Hudson: Innovation Born from Necessity

By early the spring of 1863, Port Hudson, Louisiana, was firmly in the cross hairs of the Lincoln administration and was the target of a major offensive by Maj. Gen. Nathaniel Banks's Army of the Gulf. Together, Port Hudson and Vicksburg, Mississippi, about 100 miles to the north, helped the Confederacy hold open a vital section of the Mississippi River. If one fell, the other would suffer the same fate, allowing Federals to control the river and effectively divide the Southern Confederacy in two, which also was part of Winfield Scott's original "Anaconda Plan."

---

2 Jones, *A Rebel War Clerk's Diary*, vol. 1, 245-246. Coincidently, a few months earlier another explosives developer, former Rhode Island senator Charles Tillinghast James, a Union supporter and superintendent of the Slater cotton mills in Providence, was also a casualty from an accident during an explosives experiment. He was killed on October 17, 1862, at Sag Harbor, New York, when a workman tried to remove a cap from one of the shells with pliers and the projectile exploded, killing both men. James is credited with numerous inventions, including a rifled cannon and several patterns of artillery projectiles. Jack W. Melton, "The Projectiles of Charles Tillinghast James," *North South Trader's Civil War* (July-August 1997), vol. 24, no. 4, 36.

3 Waters, *Gabriel Rains and the Confederate Torpedo Bureau*, 55.

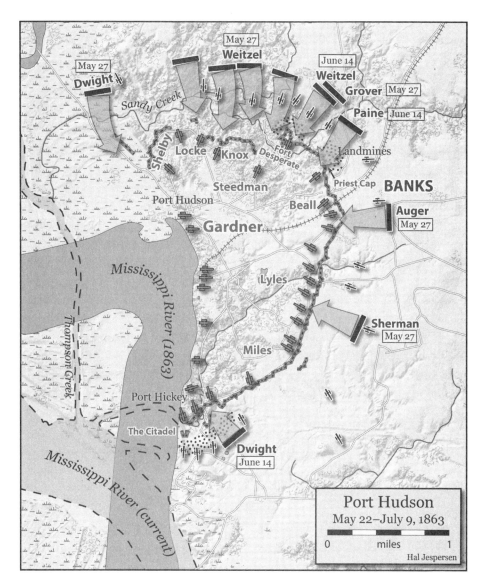

Port Hudson was manned by about 7,000 soldiers under Maj. Gen. Franklin Gardner. The 39-year-old native of New York had arrived at Port Hudson on December 27, 1862, a few months before Union troops appeared in his front. He immediately set about reinforcing the fortifications with earthen parapets and supporting roads, and by realigning gun batteries—totaling 30 siege guns—for more accurate fields of fire. Improvised naval mines were placed in the Mississippi River, explosive devices stuffed into cotton bales, latched to logs, and floated downriver to collide with Union vessels. These attacks were unsuccessful because of incessant Union patrols and "intelligence provided by a local African-American."[4]

Although relatively isolated and rather small, the garrison held a strong defensive position. The 80-foot bluff overlooking the Mississippi River gave the artillerists a clear line of fire against any Union vessels that steamed within range from either direction. Port Hudson would not fall from that direction. The landward side, however, even with its swamps, thick woods, and gullies that made any approach difficult, was also its weakness. Augmenting the natural features were extensive field works including earthen parapets, breastworks, and rifle pits—all of which encircled the small town for four and a half miles. Confederate Lt. Howard C. Wright, a member of the 30th Louisiana and a newspaperman in New Orleans before the war, estimated that the extensive line would require at least "15,000 men to hold, with a reserve of three to five thousand." General Gardner did not have anywhere close to that number of soldiers to man the lines. How could he hold them against any determined assault?[5]

The Confederates were in dire straits. They had been under siege since late May, when Banks's nearly 30,000-man army arrived and surrounded them. Food and supplies of every kind began to run short almost immediately. "[A]mmunition appeared to be as plentiful with them as air," Wright wrote about the Federals, "while with us it had to be husbanded with the greatest distinction. They fired from morning to night, and from night to morning, only giving time for their pieces to cool, and any object, however trivial, was aimed at."[6]

Necessity being the mother of invention, the Confederates found creative ways to hold the extensive Port Hudson works. Engineers dug galleries and tunnels from the interior of the fort to the external earthworks so that "men

---

4 Lawrence Lee Hewitt, *Port Hudson, Confederate Bastion on the Mississippi* (Baton Rouge, LA, 1987), 1. Gardner had connections on both sides of the Mason Dixon line. He was born in New York, and appointed to West Point from the state of Iowa. He went South when the war came, however, because his mother was from a wealthy plantation-owning family in Louisiana, and he had married Marie Celeste Mouton, the daughter of Louisiana's governor Alexandre Mouton. Ezra Warner, *Generals in Gray: Lives of the Confederate Commanders* (Baton Rouge, 1983), 97.

5 Lt. Howard C. Wright, "Port Hudson: Its History From an Interior Point of View as Sketched From the Diary of an Officer," *St. Francisville* [LA] *Democrat*, 7.

6 Ibid., 28.

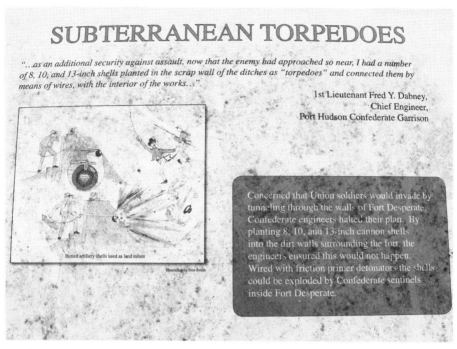

SUBTERRANEAN TORPEDOES

"...as an additional security against assault, now that the enemy had approached so near, I had a number of 8, 10, and 13-inch shells planted in the scrap wall of the ditches as "torpedoes" and connected them by means of wires, with the interior of the works..."

1st Lieutenant Fred Y. Dabney,
Chief Engineer,
Port Hudson Confederate Garrison

Concerned that Union soldiers would invade by tunneling through the walls of Fort Desperate, Confederate engineers halted their plan. By planting 8, 10, and 13-inch cannon shells into the dirt walls surrounding the fort, the engineers ensured this would not happen. Wired with friction primer detonators the shells could be exploded by Confederate sentinels inside Fort Desperate.

Buried artillery shells used as land mines

Illustration by Don Smith

Command-detonated landmines, Fort Desperate, Port Hudson State Historic Site. *Author*

could crawl into the other ditch and sharp shoot from that." The defenders also built upper works for commanding positions for their marksmen, which enabled "them to shoot down into the enemy's ditches so soon as they should approach near enough." Ravines were stuffed with sharpened tree branches to impede attackers trying to use them for cover or as a means to approach the Confederate works. In a last-ditch effort to hold the vital position, command-detonated and victim-activated mines were used on the same battlefield for the first time.[7]

The command-detonated landmines were deployed at Fort Desperate, so named for the dire and hopeless situation in which its defenders found themselves. At Priest Cap, a redan south of Fort Desperate, victim-activated landmines triggered by trip wires were set in place. Victim-activated mines were also deployed at The Citadel, a well-fortified bluff at the extreme southern end of the Port Hudson defensive line.

---

7 Association of Defenders of Port Hudson, "Fortification and Siege of Port Hudson," *Southern Historical Society Papers* (January-December 1886), vol. 14, 334.

Once Banks arrived and the siege got underway, Confederate officers instructed their soldiers to be "very economical" in their use of ammunition, which was nearly exhausted. To boost their supply, defenders refocused efforts on gathering large amounts of unexploded Federal ordnance and other ammunition inside their stronghold and within their defensive perimeter. Unexploded Union artillery shells were found in abundance because the malfunction rate on fixed ammunition sometimes reached as high as 90 percent.

"The shells fired at us were principally percussion, intended to burst on striking any hard substance," explained Lieutenant Wright,

> but not one-tenth of them exploded. Percussion shells may be very effective when fired against wooden vessels, but in the field or at such a place as Port Hudson they are not worth much, as they hardly ever explode and do not obtain the momentum of a solid shot. The whole place became strewn with iron missiles, so that a person could not travel the road, go through the woods, or even pick his way through the thick blackberry bushes without stumbling over them at almost every step. . . . Large numbers of them were picked up and collected in the hope of their being serviceable on our side during the siege, but the sabots, or soft metal base which fits the grove of the gun, were generally destroyed.[8]

The Federal artillery shells were used in the Confederate cannons, if possible. Union bullets were melted and remolded for use in Enfield rifles. Unexploded eight-, 10-, and 13-inch Union mortar shells were converted into landmines.

With the enemy closing in on Fort Desperate, the 15th Arkansas and Battery B, 1st Mississippi Artillery, worked to strengthen its defenses. Captain Louis Girard anticipated that Union engineers would dig a tunnel under his position and plant explosives. Counteracting that threat was problematic, but there was at least one way to help keep infantry away. At vulnerable points, Girard supervised the deployment of several rows of command-detonated landmines to counteract any threat from that quarter. Engineer officers could detonate the mines, which were connected by wires running back to Fort Desperate, by merely pulling on the wires.[9]

---

8 Wright, "Port Hudson," 28, 23.

9 Ibid., 50; Association of Defenders of Port Hudson, "Fortification and Siege of Port Hudson," 334.

The first major assault against Port Hudson occurred on May 27, when some 6,000 Federals advanced through the tree-choked gullies toward Fort Desperate on the Confederate left flank. Roughly 1,200 defenders, augmented with command- detonated landmines, waited for them to step into killing range. For the first time in the Civil War, landmines would be ignited during actual combat.[10]

The Federals charged through ravines, but heavy fire from within the fortifications, coupled with pulls on the landmine wires, inflicted significant casualties. Attacks against other points in the line were also launched, and the fighting lasted throughout the day, to little effect. General Banks, meanwhile, turned up the pressure against Fort Desperate by ordering his troops to continue tunneling and sapping operations (the latter entailed digging trenches) to get closer to Confederate lines, while sharpshooters picked off anyone who lifted his head too high.

On June 13, Banks ordered an hour-long artillery barrage of Fort Desperate. The guns opened at 11:15 a.m., and shells rained on the Confederates "at the rate of more than one a second." The defenders hugged the earth and refused to surrender.[11]

At 3:30 the following morning, another Union assault struck a heavily fortified compound of front-line earthworks known as Priest Cap, a pair of strong battery positions southeast of Fort Desperate. Smaller attacks were made against the The Citadel at the southernmost bastion of Port Hudson defenses, and again at Fort Desperate. Over the course of four hours, the Federals launched "[s]even distinct and separate charges." The assaults were turned back with heavy losses and Banks resumed siege warfare.[12]

Confederates ingeniously laced the terrain in front of Priest Cap, a vulnerable part of the line, with trip-wire victim-activated landmines and mortar shells. Hundreds of sharp wooden stakes, the points thrusting outward, covered the outer edge of the parapet. Scores of artillery shells were attached to crude *chevaux-de-frise*, portable obstacles of wooden spikes. The desperate

---

10 The fighting of May 27 was also noteworthy for another reason. For the first time, African-American troops, composed mostly of former slaves, participated as the 1st and 3rd Louisiana Native Guard in the fighting. After the Union occupation, Port Hudson became a recruiting center for U.S. Colored Troops.

11 Hewitt, *Port Hudson*, 171.

12 Wright "Port Hudson," 40-41.

Confederates even stretched piano wire about 18 inches above the ground to trip charging soldiers.[13]

As Federal saps inched closer to Priest Cap, defenders deployed more landmines on the battlefield. "Torpedoes were . . . placed at proper positions," confirmed one Confederate. "These precautions were only taken to delay and retard an assaulting party should they attempt to charge in the night time from their ditches and carry our work by surprise." On June 29, the Federals nearly captured The Citadel, and the following day, another Union assault failed after some initial successes. When unsuspecting soldiers from the 6th Michigan and 165th New York were pushed back into the bottom of a ditch outside the position, they stepped on the landmines and, recalled one eyewitness, "were blown to pieces."[14]

On July 4, one week after the assaults at The Citadel, Confederate forces under Lt. Gen. John C. Pemberton surrendered to General Grant at Vicksburg. When word reached Port Hudson, General Gardner realized his situation there was hopeless. He surrendered his command on July 9, ending the 48-day siege of continuous fighting. The loss of Vicksburg and Port Hudson effectively split the Confederacy in two. From that day forward, getting large quantities of supplies and manpower across the river in either direction would be exceedingly difficult.

A close look at what unfolded at Port Hudson makes it clear that the Confederates managed to hold out as long as they did by increasing their firepower with innovative improvised weapons. Landmines played a crucial role for the defenders during the longest siege in American military history. The weapon used so effectively at Port Hudson, however, was not deployed at Vicksburg for reasons that have never fully been explained. Ultimately, a delaying tactic by Gabriel Rains may have been at least partly to blame.

Mississippi: "A Terror to All Invading"

Jefferson Davis was deeply concerned with the dire military situation in his home state of Mississippi. By the last week of May 1863, John Pemberton's Confederate army, which had been beaten in the field at Champion Hill and

---

13 Edward Bacon, *Among the Cotton Thieves* (Detroit, MI, 1867), 287.

14 Association of Defenders of Port Hudson, "Fortification and Siege of Port Hudson,"
335; Bacon, *Among the Cotton Thieves*, 263.

again at the Big Black River Bridge the next day, was trapped inside Vicksburg's entrenchments. The defenders were outnumbered by Maj. Gen. Ulysses Grant's army, and were enduring the early stages of what would be a prolonged siege. To Davis's dismay, landmines had not been deployed to aid in the defense of the beleaguered bastion. Taken in by the power of these new cost-effective weapons, and having only recently consumed a book on the subject prepared just for him, the Southern president ordered Gabriel Rains to abandon his secret work in Richmond (and any covering efforts related to the Conscription Bureau) and travel to Mississippi. His task was to find out what could be done to help Vicksburg and to use his mines to advantage. To Rains's dismay, he was to report to Gen. Joseph E. Johnston, the department commander who was busy organizing a relief army near Jackson to try and help save Pemberton's army.

Rains protested the assignment. He and Johnston had tangled during the Peninsula Campaign in 1862, when the general condemned his use of landmines. By 1863, the so-called "infernal machines" were recognized by the Confederacy as legitimate weapons of warfare. Had Johnston changed his mind on the subject? How could Rains work effectively under him if he had not? To set Rains's mind at ease, President Davis directed Secretary of War Seddon to inform Johnston of what he expected in sending Rains west. "GENERAL: Brig. Gen. G. J. Rains, having been detailed for duty in connection with torpedoes and sub-terra shells, has been ordered to report to you," began the important telegram on May 27, 1863. "The president," it continued,

> has confidence in his inventions, and is desirous that they should be employed both on land and river, if opportunity offers, at Vicksburg and its vicinity. Should communications allow, you are desired to send him there; but if otherwise, to employ him and his devices against the enemy, where most assailable in that way, elsewhere. All reasonable facilities in the supply of men or material for the fair trial of his torpedoes and shells are requested on your part.[15]

Rains remained skeptical of the assignment and whether he could supply enough torpedoes to alter the outcome of the campaign against Vicksburg. By early June the Confederacy's landmine expert had yet to leave Richmond. Davis had expected Rains would made haste for Mississippi, and was shocked that he

---

15   J. A. Seddon, Secretary of War, to General Joseph E. Johnston, Commanding, May 27, 1863, *OR* 18, pt. 1, 1,082-1,083.

had not. "I learn that you have not started," wrote the frustrated president to his stationary general, who threatened to replace him. This was enough to light the necessary fire and Rains departed the capital a few days later.[16]

On his way to meet with Johnston in Mississippi, Gabriel stopped in Augusta, Georgia, where he visited with his brother, Lt. Col. George W. Rains. The skillful director of the Confederate government's gigantic powder mill supplied his brother with materials to supplement his landmine equipment. Gabriel stowed the supplies in a wooden chest, which held sensitive primers, chemicals, and other tools necessary to produce mines. It was late June by the time Rains reached Jackson, Mississippi. When he did, he unpacked his instruments, built a laboratory in his hotel room, and began making landmines.

He was too late.

On July 4, before even a single mine could be smuggled into Vicksburg, Pemberton surrendered his army, and Union forces under Maj. Gen. William T. Sherman were marching on Jackson. Long after the war, the failure to use mines around Vicksburg and Rains's part in the fiasco continued to plague Davis. After writing in his memoir about what he had ordered, Davis added, "There could scarcely have been presented a better opportunity for this [landmine] use than that offered by the heavy column marching against Jackson, and the enemy would have been taken at great disadvantage if our troops had met them half way between Jackson and Clinton."[17]

Johnston, meanwhile, contemplated holding out in Jackson but at the last moment decided it best to abandon the Mississippi capital. On the eve of the evacuation, the general ordered Rains to deploy landmines to provide more time for a Confederate withdrawal. "[Johnston] asked if I could not check the advance of the enemy (under Genl Sherman) by the shells" along the banks of the Pearl River and two roads leading into the city, explained Rains, who instructed soldiers to bury landmines where civilians would not be exposed to them. Later, he informed Johnston that he could, when so directed,

plant the shells on the city side of Pearl River though I assured him on the coming of the enemy, the women and children would naturally fly that way, it being in rear of the town, and would be destroyed by the shells. I left the Genl's quarters and sent for Col. Parker whom I informed of the Genl's wishes, but I directed him to have the shells, the

---

16 Ibid., vol. 52, pt. 2, 487.

17 Davis, *Rise and Fall of the Confederate Government*, vol. 2, 424-425.

largest we could get, planted on the opposite bank of the river to the city, and in the two roads leading there from.

As it turned out, Rains's landmines were deadly and effective against the Federals on the roads leading to Jackson. A correspondent for the *Memphis Bulletin* reported that a landmine explosion severely wounded two men from the 6th Iowa near the Pearl River. One had "both legs cut and all mashed to pieces," explained the reporter. The other soldier suffered a severe head wound and "the surgeon in charge of them tells me [they] will die."[18]

While riding near the river, two reporters noticed landmines in the road "half imbedded in the dust [with] little cords and pieces of fine wire, 25 and 30 feet in length." The landmines could be triggered, one of them noted, "by a horse striking his foot against the cords or wires, or a footman even stumbling against them."[19]

Civilian diarist John B. Jones, an observant and opinionated clerk in the war department in Richmond, told his journal, "[I]t appears that hundreds of the enemy and their horses were killed and wounded by the shells planted by him beneath the surface of the earth, and which ignited under the pressure of their weight." Although he exaggerated the effects of the landmines, Jones observe with some accuracy that Union soldiers "knew not where to avoid them."[20]

In Jackson itself, Rains saw to it that the roads were lined with mines. "[Many] were the poor victims, both of citizens and soldiery, who that day fell by them, mangled and maimed for life," exclaimed a New Orleans newspaper. In addition, it continued, the "[t]orpedoes were strewn along the roads and in the wagon ruts near Pearl River," exposing the civilians there to grave danger.[21]

General Sherman reported that the retreating Confederates had "placed loaded shells with torpedoes in the roads leading out from the river," one of which exploded and injured "a citizen severely, and another killed" a man and wounded two Union soldiers. One of the first civilian casualties was William Heinasy, a baggage master on the Southern Railroad who was seriously injured by a device that killed his horses. Two civilians riding in a cart were tossed from

---

18 Gabriel J. Rains, *Confederate Torpedoes: Two Illustrated 19th Century Works* (McFarland, 2014), 68; *Memphis Bulletin*, August 1863, 9.

19 Ibid.

20 Jones, *A Rebel War Clerk's Diary*, vol. 2, 8.

21 *New Orleans Picayune*, August 1863, 9.

the conveyance when it struck a mine buried in a rut. The cart was "torn to pieces" and the horse killed. The man and woman were unhurt.[22]

Federal troops pressured the citizens of Jackson to identify landmine locations. Unable to secure their cooperation, the acting Jackson provost marshal used Confederate prisoners for that dangerous task.[23]

In part because Rains's landmines delayed pursuing Federals, Johnston's forces retreated from Jackson without incident. The weapons were highly regarded for their effectiveness. Clerk John Jones, who read dispatches and kept a close ear on the pulse of the war department in Richmond, explained how they "discomfited the cavalry and checked the advance of the columns of the enemy which were halted with a space of 9 miles between the opposing armies." The lesson learned, he added, was that landmines "became a terror to all invading."[24]

The triggering of landmines at Jackson had a reverse domino effect. Once they inflicted casualties in the Union cavalry riding in the vanguard of Sherman's army, the spooked troopers retreated, taking the infantry marching behind them with them because "they supposed it [the explosion] masked a battery sure enough." One account wildly exaggerated the effect and claimed the Union army "retreated 40 miles," but the misstatement emphasized the point that Rains's mines were successful—and he was quite pleased. "[T]hus the 2nd time the shells saved our general," he wrote, unable to resist taking a jab at Joe Johnston.[25]

On August 3, about two weeks after the evacuation of Jackson, Johnston ordered Rains to pack up once more and head to Mobile, Alabama, to support the defensive efforts there. Although he had been unable to help in Vicksburg, the landmine expert's work elsewhere in Mississippi was considered somewhat successful. After only a short time in Mobile, however, during which Rains clashed with local Confederate authorities, President Davis directed him to travel to Charleston, South Carolina. Landmines were already being deployed

---

22 Report of W. T. Sherman, Major-General, Commanding, Headquarters Fifteenth Army Corps, Camp on Big Black, July 28, 1863, *OR* 24, pt. 2, 536; *New Orleans Picayune*, 9.

23 Ibid.

24 Rains to W. T. Walthal, for Jefferson Davis to use in writing his memoirs (*Rise and Fall of the Confederate Government*), Aiken, South Carolina, June 21, 1879, as explained quoted in Waters, *Gabriel Rains and the Confederate Torpedo Bureau*, 130; Jones, *A Rebel War Clerk's Diary*, vol. 2, 8.

25 Kochan and Wideman, *Civil War Torpedoes*, 27.

there in large numbers to defend Battery Wagner, located on a narrow beach outside the city on Morris Island. Mobile was in less danger than Charleston, where his expertise was sorely needed.[26]

South Carolina: A "Great Torpedo Man"

With important railroad lines, armament and munitions factories, and a vitally important harbor, Charleston was a high-value target for Union forces. The South Carolina city also had major symbolic value. The shooting war began in the harbor with the firing on Fort Sumter, the crumbling hulk of which was now manned by Confederate forces. Sumter, together with Battery Wagner on Morris Island and Fort Moultrie, helped defend the city against attacks from the sea. As Federal Rear Admiral Christopher Rodgers observed with obvious distaste, "No city in the South was so obnoxious to Union men as Charleston."[27]

Gen. Pierre G. T. Beauregard had his hands full. In the early spring of 1863, while General Grant was planning his final offensive against Vicksburg and Banks was organizing to move against Port Hudson, the commander of Department of South Carolina, Georgia, and Florida was trying to figure out how he was going to keep Union forces out of Charleston. He was vastly outmanned, under-supplied, and outgunned. Maneuver wasn't an option because he was pinned to the city of Charleston and its immediate environs. Beauregard faced the prospect of a major Federal amphibious offensive against Charleston on any given day, and he had no naval force worthy of the name to send out to meet enemy ships. The situation in his department was so bad that even though Beauregard wanted to reinforce Confederates under direct threat in Florida in late March, he was unable to do so because he didn't have a regiment to spare.[28]

Within Confederate circles, General Beauregard had been one of the first high-ranking proponents to enthusiastically urge the use of mine warfare. He

26 Special Orders No. 145, Benjamin S. Ewell, A. A. G. Morton N. Mississippi, "By command of General Jackson." August 3, 1863, *OR* vol. 26, pt. 2, 136; Waters, "Deception is the Art of War," 46.

27 Roger Pinkney, "Iron Angel of Death," *Civil War Times*, October 1999, 27.

28 G. T. Beauregard, General, Commanding, HDQS, Dept., South Carolina, Georgia, and Florida, to Brigadier-General Joseph Finegan, Commanding, Third Military District, Lake City, Florida, March 21, 1863, *OR* vol. 14, 840.

strongly encouraged research with water explosives, including floating and spar torpedoes. Beauregard even sought private aid and ordered mines from the Southern Torpedo Company, a firm formed in 1863 by Charleston businessmen to produce the explosive devices to sell to the Confederate government.[29]

In one of its more speculative efforts, the Southern Torpedo Company designed and produced a privately financed spar boat called the CSS *David*, so named for its biblical proportion to its Goliath-like opponents.[30] The 54-foot, cigar-shaped *David* was powered with steam from a discarded locomotive engine. A stationary two-and-one-half-inch iron pipe with an explosive device extended about 30 feet from its bow. The torpedo was about six feet under the surface of the water, and carried 134 pounds of rifle powder on the tip of a steel spar. The partially submerged boat was designed to deliver the explosive against a Union vessel.[31]

Under Beauregard's enthusiastic supervision, Charleston Harbor and nearby waters were seeded with mines. Pilings were driven into the channel bottom in the harbor to obstruct Federal vessels that might venture too close.

29 G. T. Beauregard, HDQS, Dept., South Carolina, Georgia, and Florida to Theodore Stoney, Secretary and Treasurer, Southern Torpedo Company, Charleston, South Carolina, November 25, 1863, *OR* vol. 28, pt. 2, 525.

30 The founders of the Southern Torpedo Company were adamant that, unless Southerners could find some means of destroying the Federal warships, the war would be lost. Another torpedo plan was proposed by inventor John S. Read, writing from Tuscaloosa to Governor Bonham of South Carolina on August 12, 1863: "Eighteen months ago [February 1862] I visited for the express purpose of exhibiting to your predecessor, Governor Pickens and his council, a plan, of my devising, for arming small, active steamers, &c., with torpedoes for attacking and destroying the enemy's ships-of-war along our coast." These plans were not acted upon, thus a "different state of affairs might have been at Charleston. The enemy is now thundering at your doors, and my present purpose is to furnish you a plan for using even pleasure yachts, and pilot-boats for destroying the enemy's ships-of-war off your port." Read argued, "little time and money are required [and] an ordinary sail-boat, with one or two torpedoes [could] destroy the largest ship-of-war." See John B. Read to South Carolina Governor M. L. Bonham, August 18, 1863, *OR* vol. 28, pt. 2, 277. The response was forwarded to General Beauregard, who passed it on to Francis D. Lee, captain of engineers. Lee replied, "I have carefully examined the plan of Mr. John B. Read, and would respectfully report that it exhibits no new plan or principle, being, in fact, but the repetition of a device now in use in this harbor." See Francis D. Lee, Captain of Engineers, to Henry Wemyss Feilden, Assistant Adjutant-General, August 24, 1863, *OR* vol. 28, pt. 2, 278.

31 One of the Southern Torpedo Company members was Dr. Ravenel, who owned Stony Landing Plantation 30 miles up the Cooper River, where Southern Torpedo Company employees could work without being observed.

Wary of torpedoes, Union ironclads avoided the area. Still, Beauregard faced shortages of almost everything critical for mine warfare, including iron for the production of the weapons, manpower to deploy them, and even trained naval engineers to man torpedo boats like the *David*."[32]

Six months earlier, on November 15, 1862, Confederate engineer Capt. Francis D. Lee had written Brig. Gen. Thomas Jordan, Beauregard's chief of staff, about the equipment he needed to produce the explosives. "My supply of iron for bolts," he began,

> although sufficient for immediate wants, is altogether inadequate for future requirements. The designs for torpedo shells, with machinery for using the same, have been perfected, and the machinist only waits a supply of iron to execute his portion of the work. The engines have not arrived from Richmond.[33]

Two days later Brig. Gen. James H. Trapier, who commanded a military district in Beauregard's department north of Charleston, also wrote to Jordan requesting more arms, more ammunition, and more trained manpower:

> The means at my command for the defense of this military district are extremely limited. The only infantry troops in the department is Colonel Cash's regiment, which, I regret to say, has arrived without arms and without ammunition. These troops are, besides, Reserves, and in service for only ninety days. It is questionable whether they can be rendered efficient in that time, even if well-armed and equipped. At present they are literally worth nothing at all.[34]

A dearth of iron needed for torpedo production in the Charleston area continued well into 1863. "The work on torpedo ram [*David*] has nearly come to a standstill for the want of iron," complained Captain Lee on March 25. "I have

---

32 The channel between Hog Island and Sullivan's Island was mined in September, and the Stono River was mined in January 1864. *OR* vol. 28, pt. 2, 293, 300, 311, 336, 539; "Controlling the Harbor," Fort Sumter National Monument, South Carolina, National Park Service, U.S. Department of the Interior, waymark, Charleston, South Carolina.

33 Report of Francis D. Lee, Captain Engineers, Prov. Army Confederate States, to Brig. Gen. Thomas Jordan, Chief of Staff, November 15, 1862, *OR* vol. 14, 680-681.

34 Report of J. H. Trapier, Brigadier-General, Commanding, to Brig. Gen. Thomas Jordan, Chief of Staff, November 17, 1862, *OR* vol. 14, 681.

exhausted every private source of supply and unless the government comes to my assistance the work must stop."[35]

A lack of trained personnel also hampered Beauregard's efforts. J. R. Tucker, a Confederate flag officer, requested more officers and men from the secretary of the navy to help build and man the torpedo rams. "We are very short of officers and men for the vessels [torpedo spar boats]," explained Tucker. "We shall require both. . . . If you could send some from Richmond it would be desirable. Very much in want of men and competent engineers."[36]

In addition to the deployment of naval mines to defend Charleston's harbor, Confederates used landmines to strengthen Fort Sumter. Its commanding officers, Col. Jeremy F. Gilmer and Lt. Col. D. B. Harris, both with the Corps of Engineers, wrote about how their troops incorporated mines into Fort Sumter's defenses:

> Prepare the bomb-proofs in the fort so as to command all points within the works by musketry fire; place mines and torpedoes in the parade; demolish all cover not needed by the garrison, or else place mines within such cover. . . . The whole safety of the place is made to depend upon quite a limited number of men, as arrangements of the fire of but few can be provided for in the bomb-proofs; upon mines and torpedoes (which are attended with many uncertainties).[37]

On the Union side, Brig. Gen. Quincy Adams Gillmore was appointed commander of the Department of the South on June 12. Trained as an engineer, he was partially responsible for the rapid advances in weapons technology that had rendered masonry forts such as Fort Pulaski—the world's first fortification targeted by rifled artillery fire—obsolete. Gillmore was also experienced at siege warfare. Beauregard was under no illusions about what Gillmore's posting meant for Charleston.[38]

---

35 Captain Francis D. Lee to Brig. Gen. Thomas Jordan, Chief of Staff, March 25, 1863, *OR* vol. 14, 681.

36 J. R. Tucker, Flag Officer, Commanding, to S. R. Mallory, July 18, 1863, *OR*, series 4, vol. 2, 664.

37 Reports of Col. Jeremy F. Gilmer and Lt. Col. D. B. Harris, C. S. Corps of Engineers., August 24 and September 22, 1863, *OR* vol. 28, pt. 1, 653.

38 Ibid., 219-224, 608-622. At Fort Pulaski (April 10-11, 1862), Gillmore began the bombardment after Col. Charles H. Olmstead refused to surrender. Within hours, Union rifled artillery, including Parrott Rifles, had breached the fort's southeast escarpment. Some of these shells began to damage the traverse shielding the magazine in the northwest

Located on the southern side of the harbor, Morris Island was central to the defense of both the harbor and the city. Before Union forces could seize the city, the island—an islet, really—had to be taken. The most important defensive fortification on Morris Island was Battery Wagner, a stronghold made of wooden logs and piled beach sand on the northern end. Roughly 1,800 Confederates manned Battery Wagner.

Soon after taking command, Gillmore targeted Battery Wagner and Fort Gregg, the latter located on the extreme northern tip of Morris Island. During the ensuing battles for the sandy island southeast of Charleston, Confederates deployed landmines in abundance. On July 10, 1863, Gillmore landed 2,000 troops commanded by Brig. Gen. George C. Strong on the southern end of Morris Island. The Federals quickly overwhelmed pickets guarding the beach and, except for the Battery Wagner area, occupied nearly the entire islet. After more fighting on July 11, Battery Wagner was reinforced with more troops—and a "large number of Rains torpedoes."[39]

Under the direction of Capt. M. M. Gray, Confederates "placed 57 shells of a Rains pattern five to 20 yards in front of Battery Wagner." The use of the Rains fuse, even in its inventor's absence, underscored its increasing acceptance and importance in defending static positions.[40]

The Battery Wagner minefield was the largest formal torpedo field in the world up to that time, and its location was ideal. A barren coastline provided clear fields of fire from Battery Wagner, and beach sand easily concealed the landmines. Because each end of the defensive position terminated at seawater, the Federals had no openings to use in order to skirt the fortification. Moreover, the landmines provided an ideal substitute for a lack of material fortifications.[41]

---

bastion. Realizing that if the magazine exploded the fort would be seriously damaged and the garrison would suffer severe casualties, Olmstead surrendered on April 11. As the event made clear, masonry forts were no match for well- handled rifled artillery.

39 P. G. T. Beauregard, General, Commanding, to General Ripley, July 10, 1863, *OR* vol. 28, pt. 2, 186.

40 Report of Confederate Captain M. M. Gray, in charge of the Torpedo Service, Charleston, South Carolina, August 12, 1863, *OR* vol. 28, pt. 1, 523.

41 Major Thomas Benton Brooks, Journal of Engineer Operations Executed Under His Direction on Morris Island, Between July 12 and September 7, 1863, as reported by Brig. Gen. Q. A. Gillmore, Commanding Department of the South, Headquarters Department of the South, Engineer's Office, Morris Island, South Carolina, September 27, 1863, *OR* vol. 28, pt. 1, 296.

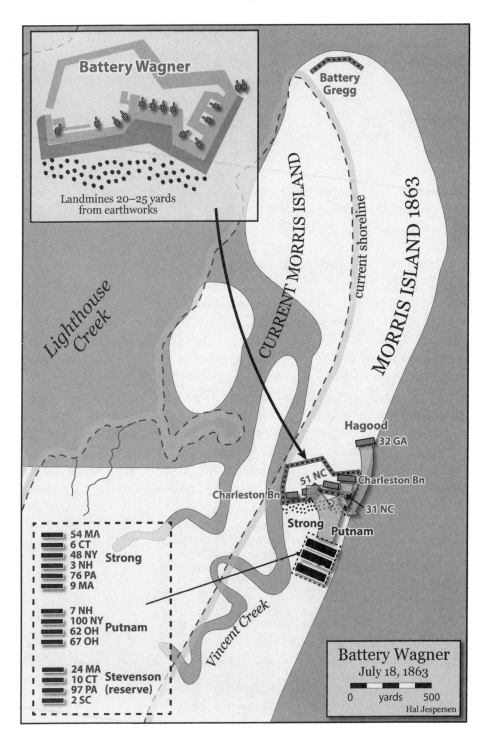

Battery Wagner

Landmines 20–25 yards
from earthworks

Battery
Gregg

CURRENT MORRIS ISLAND

current shoreline

MORRIS ISLAND 1863

*Lighthouse
Creek*

Hagood
32 GA

51 NC

Charleston Bn

Charleston Bn

31 NC

Strong   Putnam

54 MA
6 CT
48 NY   Strong
3 NH
76 PA
9 MA

7 NH
100 NY   Putnam
62 OH
67 OH

24 MA
10 CT   Stevenson
97 PA   (reserve)
2 SC

Vincent Creek

Battery Wagner
July 18, 1863

0   yards   500

Hal Jespersen

Deep-notched stakes, interconnected by tightly strung wire entanglements, were pounded into the sand, augmenting the minefield. Defenders also placed spikes in boards, with the sharpened ends protruding in the battery's ditches and in front of Wagner's stockade.

At dusk on July 18, Gillmore ordered an infantry attack on Battery Wagner. The 54th Massachusetts of the U.S. Colored Troops would lead the assault, backed by brigades of white soldiers. Before the assault was launched, an estimated 9,000 artillery rounds bombarded Wagner from land and sea. Gillmore's use of rifled artillery to shatter Fort Pulaski's brick fortifications could not be duplicated against sand and log bulwarks, which effectively absorbed and dispersed the explosives, limiting destruction. Gillmore believed the "intense shelling had incapacitated the fort's defenders," and the charge went forward. He was wrong.[42]

About 7:45 p.m., the 54th Massachusetts marched at "quick time" until it neared the glacis—the gently sloping bank near Battery Wagner and they broke into a full run.[43]

Boom . . . Boom . . . Boom!

The buried landmines delivered their intended lethal effects. Soldiers flew into the air, some suffering gruesome wounds. Combined with Confederate small arms and artillery firing canister, the black troops were mowed down in minutes. "More than half their number lay dead upon the ground," an account noted, with "their bodies ghastly mutilated & torn to pieces piled upon the glacis."[44]

The outnumbered 54th Massachusetts and other Union soldiers climbed Wagner's parapet, where intense hand-to-hand fighting erupted. The defenders beat back the attackers and held Wagner. Of the 600 black troops who charged the fort, 272 were killed, wounded, or captured. In an account that expressed the

---

42 Tim Bradshaw, "Union Veteran Made Living Selling Relics on Morris Island," in *North South Trader's Civil War* (March-April 1997), vol. 24, no. 2, 31. The rapid breaching of Fort Pulaski's walls at the distance of 1,650 yards was extremely effective due to the percussion shells that exploded on impact, shattering bricks and scattering deadly bits of masonry throughout the fort. Noah Andre Trudeau, *Like Men of War: Black Troops in the Civil War 1862-1865* (Edison, NJ, 2002), 78.

43 Quick time is the basic mobility and normal military march pace at 120 beats per minute. It is not double normal marching pace. In many other countries, including the United Kingdom, quick time is called "quick march."

44 Waters, *Gabriel Rains and the Confederate Torpedo Bureau*, 130-131.

sentiments of many on the Union side, *New York Tribune* reporter Edward L. Pierce wrote, "The Fifty-fourth did well and nobly. . . . They moved up as gallantly as any troops could, and with their enthusiasm they deserved a better fate." Robert Gould Shaw, the colonel of the 54th Massachusetts, was among the dead and was buried in a common grave with his men.[45]

After the assault, many of the Confederates assessed the minefield. According to Captain Gray, of the "57 shells of a Rains' pattern" deployed July 11, "20 of them exploded, many by the enemy's shells," and others were "damaged by the heavy rains previous to that date." All exploded mines were promptly replaced. Among them were three 15-inch shells containing 12 pounds of gunpowder, and 44 shells containing 33 to 40 pounds of powder each. These 47 mines were placed as close as 20 yards and as far out as 250 yards from Battery Wagner's sand walls, extending across the only land approach to the battery and across the islet itself. Though they used a Rains fuse, these mines differed slightly from other versions, employing a plunger suspended by a spring rather than a copper cap to break the fuse.[46]

In addition to laying new landmines, Confederates began replenishing landmine stockpiles. In doing so, they continued to construct landmines from unexploded artillery shells. Keg explosives, designed to be used in water, were also converted into landmines.

Major William Echols, the chief engineer of South Carolina, described the effort to convert artillery shells into landmines. Captain Gray, he began, "has taken 56 10-inch shells, with waterproof caps, for planting as there are no Rains' torpedoes to be had. These shells will answer the purpose, being arranged with

---

45 Garry Deal, "54th Massachusetts Ring," *North South Trader's Civil War*, vol. 27, no. 6, 60, 58. Afterwards, "[w]ord of the bravery exhibited at Battery Wagner helped spur black recruiting, and the regiment's strength, numbering 510 officers and men at the beginning of the Florida Campaign that followed. . . ." The 54th had set an example earlier in the war by refusing pay until the disparity between the wages paid to white and black soldiers was corrected. Ibid., 58.

46 In addition to the difference in breaking the fuse, "[a] stuffing nut and Indian rubber packing were used around the plunger to prevent the fuse from becoming damp. As a safeguard during transport, a spike or wire was placed in a hole in the plunger, thus preventing the accidental explosion of the mine. This variation proved readily applicable to land use." Youngblood, *The Development of Mine Warfare*, 46; Report of Captain M. M. Gray, August 12, 1863, *OR* vol. 28, pt. 1, 523.

THE SIEGE OF CHARLESTON—SOLDIERS EXPLODING TORPEDOES BY THROWING PIECES OF SHELL ON THEM FROM THE SAPS.
[From a Sketch by Mr. Theodore R. Davis.]

The Siege of Charleston: Soldiers exploding torpedoes by throwing pieces of shell on them from saps. *Harper's Weekly*

the same caps as Rains'." Gray later reported that he had 147 naval mines ready to use as landmines.[47]

Realizing further assaults against Battery Wagner were fruitless, Gillmore ordered the place taken by siege. Zigzag trenches were dug toward Wagner, enabling Union troops to avoid direct fire as they inched closer to the walls. On July 30, Beauregard sent Gillmore a message under a flag of truce. Even under a white flag the landmines continued doing their lethal work; a torpedo exploded in front of a sand wall, "killing two soldiers in a Rebel artillery company." No surrender agreement was reached, and the Union siege operation continued.[48]

On August 26, Gillmore ordered his troops to capture rifle pits 200 yards in front of Wagner's outer fortifications. The "brilliant charge" by the 24th Massachusetts, with the 3rd New Hampshire in support, overwhelmed the rifle pits by 6:30 p.m. and took 70 Confederates prisoner. Many of the captured soldiers had been afraid to try and escape by running back to the fort "because of the torpedoes scattered across the sand."[49]

After taking the rifle pits, the Federals advanced toward Battery Wagner. The area near the fort was laced with complex defensive preparations. According to Gillmore, his men found "[a]n elaborate and ingenious system of torpedo mines, to be exploded by the tread of persons walking over them." Prisoners informed their captors that the "entire area of firm ground between [Union positions] and the fort, as well as the glacis of the latter on its south and east fronts, was thickly filled with these torpedoes."[50]

---

47 W. M. H. Echols, Major and Chief Engineer, South Carolina to Lieut. Col. D. B. Harris, Chief Engineer of Department, July 20, 1863, *OR* vol. 28, pt. 2, 213.

48 Q. A. Gillmore, *Engineering and Artillery Operations Against the Defenses of Charleston Harbor in 1863* (New York, NY, 1865), 46; *OR* vol. 28, pt. 2, 21-24; A. H. Colquitt, Brigadier-General, to Capt. W. F. Nance, Assistant Adjutant-General, July 30, 1863, *OR* vol. 28, pt. 1, 446-447.

49 McIntosh, "The Confederate Artillery: Its Organization and Development," 56-70, in Miller, *Forts and Artillery*, 117. Other estimates note that the Massachusetts and New Hampshire soldiers "captured 76 of the 89 men there, who belonged to the 61st North Carolina." J. T. Champneys to W. H. Echols, September 1, 1863, *OR* vol. 28, pt. 1, 507; Beauregard to Samuel Cooper, September 18, 1864, *OR* vol. 28, pt. 1, 85; George P. Harrison to W. F. Nance, August 26, 1863, *OR* vol. 28, pt. 1, 501; *History of the Eighty-Fifth Regiment Pennsylvania Volunteer Infantry 1861-1865* (New York, NY, 1915), 277.

50 Report of Maj. Gen. Quincy A. Gillmore, U.S. Army, Commanding Department of the South, with Congratulatory Orders, *OR* vol. 28, pt. 1, 24.

The first such mine was encountered 200 yards from the battery by Federal sappers advancing beyond the rifle pits captured on August 26. The discovery slowed the Union advance, even more so after a U.S.C.T. corporal on fatigue duty was killed by a torpedo. The blast had torn his clothes from his body, and one of his arms was resting on the plunger of another landmine. The soldier's death fed rumors that he was tied to the torpedo by Confederates. A Union soldier who witnessed the explosion discounted the story, calling it "absurd." The next day, Union "[s]appers cautiously removed [the mines] and rendered them harmless by boring holes through the casings and pouring water inside; sharpshooters vainly tried to explode others at long range the next few days."[51]

Some landmine clearance efforts were especially challenging. According to Union Maj. T. B. Brooks, an assistant engineer with the Department of the South, "In endeavoring to move, by means of a rope, one which projected into the ditch, it exploded. These torpedoes give us considerable trouble and anxiety, but they are an excellent obstacle to prevent a sortie by the enemy, who are very much afraid of them."[52]

As the Federals moved closer to Battery Wagner, they discovered mines arranged to explode as soldiers in column formation advanced. The minefield covered a wide swath of land from a marsh to the beach. "The torpedoes were most numerous in the narrow front next to the beach, over which the mass of an assaulting column would have to pass," noted one account.[53]

On August 29, in preparation for yet another assault, Union sappers began clearing a landmine-infested area covering the last 100 yards to Battery Wagner. During the day, landmines could be identified by their plungers sticking out of the sand, but much of the dangerous work had to be carried out at night to avoid being seen by Confederate sharpshooters.

On August 31, as the Union soldiers pressed closer to Battery Wagner, a soldier set off another landmine while crawling "up to an advanced trench," injuring him and three other men. This last stretch was the most difficult to clear and traverse; hence the approach stalled. "The dark and gloomy days of the

---

51 Milton Perry, *Infernal Machines: The Story of Confederate Submarine and Mine Warfare* (Baton Rouge, LA, 1965), 58-59.

52 Brooks Journal of Engineer Operations, *OR* vol. 28, pt. 1, 296.

53 Ibid., 310.

siege were now upon us," Gillmore explained. "Our progress became discouragingly slow and even fearfully uncertain."[54]

At the vanguard of the Union preparation for an attack, sap rollers were used to protect the men from enemy fire as they worked. It was backbreaking and tedious work, but the Federals were slowly but surely creeping closer to their objective. When the time came, the attack would be launched at low tide because as much space as possible would be needed for the men to maneuver.[55]

The Confederates also suffered casualties in the same minefield. According to the fort's new commander, Col. Lawrence M. Keitt, on September 3, "Captain [M. M.] Gray planted a lot of torpedoes in front of this battery, during which one of his men, Thomas McNall, crawled upon a torpedo and exploded it, inflicting a very dangerous wound."[56]

Gabriel Rains Arrives in Charleston

After a short but frustrating sojourn in Mobile, Gabriel Rains reached Charleston on September 2, where he assumed "special charge of the preparation and location of torpedoes in the harbor and water approaches to the city." Captain Gray reported to Rains. No one respected, or needed, Rains' special talents more than did General Beauregard, who was one of the few early converts within the high command who understood the military value of Rains's "infernal machine." Unfortunately for the Confederates, it was much too late to save Battery Wagner.[57]

Rains, wrote one observer who met him soon after he arrived, "is [a] great torpedo man . . . a perfect monomaniac on the subject and talks of nothing else. I

---

54 Perry, *Infernal Machines*, 58-59; Brooks Journal of Engineer Operations, *OR* vol. 28, pt. 1, 296-298.

55 Ibid., 323, 301. A sap roller is a large gabion six or seven feet long filled with sticks or other impedimenta the sappers (diggers) roll in front of them as they work to protect themselves from enemy fire.

56 Lawrence M. Keitt, Colonel, Commanding, Headquarters, Battery Wagner, Morris Island, September 3, 1863, *OR* vol. 28, pt. 1, 479.

57 By command of General Beauregard, as transmitted by JNO M. Otey, Assistant Adjutant-General, Special Orders No. 172, HDQRS, Dept., South Carolina, Georgia, and Florida, September 2, 1863, *OR* vol. 28, pt. 2, 332; President Jefferson Davis to General Joseph E. Johnston, July 9, 1963, *OR* vol. 24, pt. 1, 200; Special Orders No. 145, August 3, 1863, *OR* vol. 26, pt. 2, 136.

Water Keg Naval Mine and Landmine. This type is made from a wooden keg with pointed wooden ends. Two percussion primers were set on top. This one was found at Light House inlet, near Morris Island, during the siege of Charleston in August 1863. This type was also used on land to defend Battery Wagner on Morris Island. *West Point Museum, U.S. Military Academy*

saw him get one innocent and confident young man in a corner and I am certain he torpedoed him for at least two hours." By this time the North Carolinian was widely recognized as the Confederacy's preeminent torpedo authority and specialist. Rains assumed command of mining operations at Battery Wagner and throughout the Charleston area.[58]

With Beauregard's support, Rains reinforced the city's defenses by mining rivers that emptied into Charleston's harbor and directing the deployment of landmines outside Battery Wagner. Beauregard's backing of Rains was rooted

58 Until Rains's assumption of the leadership of the Torpedo Bureau, Confederate torpedo operations were run by a variety of officers. For example, Capt. Francis D. Lee spent most of his time working on torpedo boats and spar torpedoes. In the meantime, under Rains's supervision, Captain Gray was in charge of the local Torpedo Bureau, including the torpedo production factory. This torpedo factory was located at the base of Charleston's Hazel Street on the Cooper River, produced copper spar tanks and iron castings for frame torpedoes, and constructed electric boiler mines. The Union bombardment of Charleston in 1864 forced production operations to be transferred closer to the Ashley River. Perry, *Infernal Machines*, 166-16; Tarleton to S. Lightfoot, March 2, 1864, in Tarleton Papers; S. Elliot to wife, August 20, 22, 30, and 31, 1863, in Elliot Papers, South Carolina Library, Columbia, South Carolina; A. Gonzales to T. Jordan, July 16, 1863, Department of South Carolina; *Charleston Mercury*, September 2, 1863, Stephen R. Wise, *Gate of Hell: Campaign for Charleston Harbor, 1863* (Columbia, SC, 1994), 176.

Colonel Lawrence Massillon Keitt, the commander of Battery Wagner and later of the 20th South Carolina Infantry, Kershaw's Brigade, Army of Northern Virginia. Keitt took full advantage of the opportunity to fight behind a field of mines on Morris Island. *Library of Congress*

not just in his belief in the effectiveness of the mines, but because of positive assurances he received from Secretary of War Seddon and President Davis.[59]

While Rains mapped the area and planted mines, Gillmore's engineers continued their siege operations, slowly working their way to within 100 yards of Wagner. More unexploded landmines were uncovered during their approach. Union Lt. Patrick McGuire wrote that on September 6, under his command, "one sapper of the engineers was killed and 3 infantry wounded by the explosion of a torpedo."[60]

When the Federals advanced to within 70 yards of Battery Wagner, General Gillmore reported that the "intervening space had been filled with torpedoes to destroy . . . [the] advancing column." Rear Admiral John Dahlgren suggested that before Gillmore's infantry launched their attack, his ironclads could provide a "steady fire." The warships had been bombarding the sand fort, and their shells would help provide the vulnerable foot soldiers with some cover.

59 Alfred S. Roe, *The Fifth Regiment, Massachusetts Volunteer Infantry* (Boston, MA, 1911), 22; Gabriel J. Rains to James A. Seddon, August 31, 1863, *OR* vol. 28, pt. 2, 324.

60 Brooks Journal of Engineer Operations, *OR* vol. 28, pt. 1, 301.

Preparations were set for what the Federals hoped would be the final attack and capture of the critical bastion.[61]

The Confederates had other plans. Colonel Keitt could see how close the enemy had come, and he knew what was coming next. Holding Battery Wagner was no longer possible. "The garrison must be taken away immediately after dark, or it will be destroyed or captured," the colonel messaged Beauregard's staff officer on September 6. "It is idle to deny that the heavy Parrott shells have breached the walls and are knocking away the bomb-proofs. Pray have boats immediately after dark at Cummings Point to take away the men," Keitt pleaded, adding,

> I say deliberately that this must be done, or the garrison will be sacrificed. I am sending the wounded and sick now to Cummings Point, and will continue to do so, if possible, until all are gone. I have a number of them now there. I have not in the garrison 400 effective men, including artillery. The engineers agree in opinion with me, or, rather, shape my opinion. I shall say no more.[62]

On the night of September 6, the defenders quietly abandoned the fort and relocated to Charleston. The long siege of Battery Wagner was over.[63]

When the sun rose the next morning, the Federals quickly discovered the enemy was gone. Samuel W. Gross, a Union doctor who entered the abandoned fortifications was, like all the other Federals, thankful the Confederates had left. "In front of the former work," he wrote shortly after the war, "a large number of torpedoes had been planted, and had the assault been made, the loss of life from this cause alone would have been very great."[64]

Once Battery Wagner was occupied, Gillmore's engineers had more time to study the infernal contraptions that had delayed their advance. More than 60

---

61 Rear-Admiral, A. Dahlgren, Commanding South Atlantic Blockading Squadron to Brig. Gen. Q. A. Gillmore, U.S. Army, Commanding Department of the South, September 3, 1863, *OR* vol. 28, pt 1, 78.

62 Ibid., 103. Keitt, a fire-eating former U.S. Congressman who had participated in the infamous Sumner-Brooks caning affair, was later transferred to Lee's Army of Northern Virginia as a colonel of the 20th South Carolina. He was killed in the early fighting at Cold Harbor on June 1, 1864.

63 General G. T. Beauregard, Report of operations on Morris Island, South Carolina, during the months of July, August, and September, 1863, *OR* vol. 28, pt. 1, 92.

64 S. W. Gross, "On Torpedo Wounds," *The American Journal of the Medical Sciences*, Isaac Hays, MD, ed., vol. 51 (April 1868), 369-372.

mines of three distinct types were found planted in front of the fort. All the mines were "intended to be exploded by the tread of men forming an assaulting column," observed one of the engineers. The first type was made from a reconfigured 24-pound artillery shell buried in a cylindrical tin box just beneath the sand, with the cap resting against the bottom of the box. The apparatus was buried, fuse-hole up, the explosive composition being even with the surface of the ground. Slight pressure, such as a footstep, would explode the shell.[65]

The second type of mine was made from 10-gallon kegs originally intended as floating naval mines for use against Union vessels. More than 30 of these were found. They operated by a plunger being forced down by pressure, which would ignite the explosive. In some cases, a board was placed above the plunger to expand the footprint for triggering the explosion. "A rectangular piece of board, its ends resting on the ground and plunger, to increase the chances of explosion," was how it was described. "In place of this board, a cap having three arms of iron was in a few instances substituted; stepping on one of the arms would have the same effect as on the board."[66]

The third type consisted of converted 15-inch naval shells. Although only three of these were found, they were large and could cause serious damage as they contained multiple fuses for maximizing the device's explosive power. These shells had a "metallic explosive apparatus" and were used primarily in the water until being deployed on land at Battery Wagner. Similar to the improvised gallon keg landmine ignition process, the detonation device for the naval shell was a plunger or primer covered with a board to broaden the footprint. In

---

65 Brooks Journal of Engineer Operations, *OR* vol. 28, pt. 1, 310. According to a Union observer, "[i]n its fuse hole was firmly fixed a wooden plug having a small hole through it. Extending into powder of the shell through this hole was a fuse enlarged at its upper end into a ball containing the explosive composition, which rested on the plug. Over all, enveloping the shell, was a cylindrical box of thin tin, painted black. The bottom of the box rested on the cap. *OR* vol. 28, pt. 1, 310.

66 Two types of water mines came from Rains's shop: the famous "keg" torpedo, highly efficient in its simplicity, and small wooden kegs, at first those used for beer and later some specially built for this purpose. Wooden cones were added on the ends, a coat of pitch was applied inside and outside, and a sensitive fuse was inserted into the bung. Weight attached to the bottom floated the fuse-side up. These were cheap, easy, and quick to make, and were deadly efficient. The wooden torpedoes were easily rendered harmless by pouring water into the powder through a small auger-hole bored for that purpose. More than 30 were removed in this way. *OR* vol. 28, pt. 1, 310.

addition to the three naval shell landmines that were neutralized, "[a]t least 6 torpedoes exploded accidentally, producing about twelve casualties."[67]

The Confederates had lost Battery Wagner, but the Davis administration, while disappointed, gained some encouragement from what had just transpired. Rains wrote Secretary of War Seddon that his "subterra shells" were reported by the Federals to have a "terrible" effect during their efforts to take Battery Wagner. When informed by Seddon about the positive performance of Rains's mines, President Davis responded "with gratification." Beauregard was also complimentary.[68]

General Gillmore agreed. The landmines, he reported, had fundamentally altered and impacted Federal military operations at Morris Island and Battery Wagner. "All the advantage that might have been derived from vigorous night sorties, against which the fire of the fleet could have taken no part," he explained, "was voluntarily relinquished when the system of defense by torpedo mines placed on and in advance of the glacis was resorted to."[69]

"The discovery of these torpedoes [on Morris Island]," wrote Maj. Thomas Brooks, who had led the Federal engineering operations against Battery Wagner after the siege ended, "explains what has been, to me, one of the greatest mysteries in the defense of Wagner, i.e., the fact that no material obstacle of any amount could be discovered in front of the work, not even after our two almost successful attacks. Torpedoes were the substitute."[70]

The success of the field of "subterra shells" in the defense of Battery Wagner only served to increase demands for Rains's services throughout the Confederacy. War department clerk John B. Jones in Richmond recognized the value of the landmine strategy and contradicted Union observations that grenades had been the effective Confederate defensive weapon. "The grenades reported by the enemy to have been so destructive in their repulse at Battery

---

67 Report of Major Brooks in Gillmore, *Engineering and Artillery Operations*, 163, 216-217; Brigadier-General Gabriel Rains communication with Secretary of Defense James Seddon, August 31, 1863, *OR* vol. 28, pt. 31, 310.

68 President Jefferson Davis communication with Secretary of Defense James Seddon, September 3, 1863, *OR* vol. 28, pt. 2, 343

69 Report of Maj. Gen. Quincy A. Gillmore, *OR* vol. 28, pt. 1.

70 Brooks Journal of Engineer Operations, *OR* vol. 28, pt. 1, 276.

A marker regarding the Lavaca Civil War Torpedo Works. *Author*

Wagner," noted Jones, "were his [Rains's] subterra shells, there being no hand grenades used."[71]

On September 22, about two weeks after Wagner fell, Rains proposed to Secretary of War Seddon that landmines should be deployed on the roads entering Charleston and other major Confederate cities to defend against surprise Union cavalry attacks. The proposal made sense to Seddon, who had little military manpower to spare. He thought on the subject for a few days before finally endorsing the recommendation as a labor-saving, low-cost force multiplier. Seddon sent Rains's proposal to President Davis, who quickly approved it. When Rains got word, he immediately dispatched 21 men to place landmines made from fused artillery shells in the roads leading into the city.[72]

As always, Rains was concerned about the potential for civilian casualties. Landmines deployed around Charleston were "perfectly harmless to citizens," he had assured Seddon when submitting his original proposal. The shells remain unprimed, he explained, "until the enemy approach, when the shells can be primed in a moment for their reception. I am confident that if the enemy are once or twice blown up . . . raids ever thereafter will be prevented."[73]

After the Union occupation of Charleston on February 17, 1865, Federal mine-clearing efforts received aid from unlikely sources. Several Confederates told a Federal officer they knew where mines were located in Charleston Harbor—and that they knew how to raise them. After all, they had put them there. The group's leader was none other than Capt. M. M. Gray, the former head of the Charleston Torpedo Service and now a prisoner of war. Gray, it will be recalled, had been responsible for much of the mine-laying in defense of Battery Wagner. Rear Admiral Dahlgren later accused Gray of offering his services to the Federals to "curry favor." According to Gray, Confederate

---

71 Jones, *A Rebel War Clerk's Diary*, vol. 2, 31.

72 G. J. Rains, Brigadier-General, on Special Duty, to Hon. James A. Seddon, Secretary of War, September 22, 1863, *OR* vol. 28, pt. 2, 371; J. A. Seddon, Secretary, to President J. F. Davis, September 26, 1863, *OR* vol. 28, pt. 2, 372.

73 Rains to Seddon, September 22, 1863, *OR* vol. 28, pt. 2, 371. It's unclear how or whether Rains's mines deployed on the roads near Charleston affected Federal operations in late 1863.

authorities had arrested him the previous August for deliberately sabotaging water torpedoes so they would not damage Federal ships.[74]

Despite support from Beauregard, Davis, and Seddon, Rains recognized that many Confederate authorities, especially state governors, were not yet convinced of the benefits of employing a wider mine warfare strategy. To remedy this, he suggested to Seddon that he should start communicating directly with the governors to offer his torpedo services "to assist them in the protection of their cities primarily with waterborne torpedoes and the small-scale use of subterra shells."[75]

Meanwhile, mines significantly different than those invented by Gabriel Rains were being deployed at the opposite end of the Confederate nation in Texas.

Lavaca, Texas: A New Kind of Mine

In 1862-63, Federal vessels searched for opportunities to wreak havoc along the Texas coast. Union warships sometimes shelled towns or engaged Confederate blockade runners, and on occasion, troops even went ashore to steal cattle from the state's large herds to transport to occupied New Orleans for distribution to hungry Northern soldiers and sailors.[76]

On October 31 and November 1, 1862, the Federal gunboats *Clifton* and *Westfield* entered Matagorda Bay and launched more than 250 artillery rounds into Lavaca, Texas. Captain Daniel Shea's Battalion of Texas Light Artillery, a lightly armed home guard company stationed at Lavaca, fired back at the enemy warships, which withdrew. The Union shelling destroyed or damaged homes

---

74 Reports and correspondence relating to obstructions and defenses of Charleston Harbor, Report of Rear-Admiral J. A. Dahlgren to Secretary of the Navy Gideon Welles, March 11, 1865, *ORN* vol. 16, 374-380, 411-418.

75 Gabriel J. Rains to James A. Seddon, September 22, 1863, *OR* 27, pt. 2, 37.

76 Lavaca was founded in 1842 and became a county seat four years later. After a stagecoach service was established with the relatively large inland town of Victoria, it developed into a major shipping port on Matagorda Bay. By 1850 it had 311 citizens, including 84 slaves. In 1861, railroad service started between Lavaca and Victoria, which further fueled Lavaca's growth. Kurt Johnson, Linnville, "Comanche Indians: Part of Port Lavaca's Colorful History," in *Victoria Electric Cooperative* (February 2004), 18. Lavaca was officially named Port Lavaca in 1879.

and businesses, including the Singer Iron Foundry perched atop a bluff overlooking Lavaca Bay.[77]

Eager to defend his business and the town, foundry owner Edgar Collins Singer, a 37-year-old private in the home guard unit and a gunsmith, determined to design an effective deterrent against Federal warships. Singer hailed from a family of inventors. His uncle, Isaac Singer, invented the first commercially successful sewing machine in the 1850s. Edgar began experimenting with gunpowder in a "tub behind his house," visualizing a weapon that could be detonated in the water while submerged.[78]

Singer enlisted the aid of his 47-year-old friend Dr. John Fretwell, a fellow Mason and Shea Battalion comrade. Together they invented a naval mine that would become the most widely used in the Confederacy. Its unique design even allowed it to be used as a landmine.[79]

The Fretwell-Singer mine was mechanical in nature and differed from other Confederate mines in manner of construction and detonation. Its effects were similar to Rains's mines. The Fretwell-Singer mine was an iron device with a safety lock manufactured with different weights of gunpowder charges. The black powder was placed in a tin canister with an air chamber in the top of the can to keep the device buoyant. A passing vessel caused the iron plate seated on the top of the device to fall, which pulled a safety pin that engaged a spring-loaded rod. The rod detonated two percussion caps and fired the weapon. The mine was held about three feet under the water's surface by rope attached to an anchor.

The most important part of the mine was a strong spring-action ignition system designed to explode the device. It consisted of "a buoy-like floating cone, two-thirds full of gunpowder—typically around sixty pounds," with a "saucer-like plate falling from a platform inside the cone jostled by a safety pin,

77 "A Page From Rich Calhoun History: Quiet Lavaca Bay Saw First Torpedo Test-Fired," in *Port Lavaca Wave*, January 4, 1962, Calhoun County Museum Archives, Port Lavaca, Texas.

78 Ibid.

79 J. R. Fretwell enlisted on April 20, 1861, with the Lavaca Guards, Light Infantry Company, 24th Brigade. His enlistment documents state that he was "to become Art. Co. as soon as furnished with cannon" and that he preferred "coast duty but will go anywhere in the state." J. R. Fretwell Enlistment File, Calhoun County Museum Archives, Port Lavaca, Texas.

which, in turn, released a spring-loaded plunger" that would strike "a percussion cap, which detonated the gunpowder."[80]

Lacking the money needed to mass produce their invention, Fretwell and Singer recruited their Masonic lodge members to help them secure financial support and form the operation's core labor force. Several of the Masons also served in Shea's Battalion.[81] With the exception of Kentucky-born jeweler James Jones, the torpedo project men from Lavaca were all from the North.[82] They included C. E. Frary, a Canadian-born carpenter and Singer's brother-in-law, and David Bradbury, a contractor from Maine who would soon be appointed commanding officer of Confederate torpedo operations in Texas and in other areas west of the Mississippi River.[83]

After witnessing a successful explosion of the Fretwell-Singer mine on a beached ship, Shea sent the inventors to Houston to report to Maj. Gen. John Bankhead Magruder, who knew a little something about using landmines in the field. Men under Magruder's command had deployed Rains's mines around Yorktown during the early stages of the 1862 Peninsula Campaign. Magruder was skeptical of the efficacy of Singer's mine, but he eventually gave the inventors 25 pounds of gunpowder and instructions to demonstrate their device in Buffalo Bayou in Houston. Fretwell and Singer repeated the experiment with

---

80 Henry Wolfe, Jr., "E. C. Singer and the H. L. Hunley," undated, Calhoun County Museum Archives.

81 Ibid. These same men also financed and built the *H. L. Hunley*, which was the first submarine to sink an enemy vessel in combat. She left her berth on February 17, 1864, north of Charleston, South Carolina, and rammed a mine attached to a long spar into the side of the USS *Housatonic*, a blockading warship several miles offshore. The *Hunley* never returned. She was found off Sullivan's Island by a group initially organized by local underwater archaeologist Mark Newell and generously funded by author Clive Cussler, and was raised from the ocean floor in 2000. The *Hunley* is currently housed in North Charleston, South Carolina, at the Warren Lasch Conservation Center.

82 According to Lavaca historian George Fred Rhodes (1925-2007), the men involved in the project were fellow townsmen. Rhodes oversaw the program that placed the Texas Historical Marker highlighting Singer's torpedo production facility at the intersection of Live Oak and Commerce Streets on May 31, 2003. The ceremonial program's title was "Unveiling and Dedication of Official Texas Historical Marker for Fretwell-Singer Torpedo of Port Lavaca 1862-1863."

83 Several of these men later became famous for helping to build the *Hunley*. See Mark K. Ragan, Project Historian for the Raising of the Confederate Submarine H. L. Hunley, to George F. Rhodes, Calhoun County Historical Society, March 22, 2000, Calhoun County Museum Archives, Port Lavaca.

Maj. Gen. John Bankhead Magruder, who had seeded mines in the field at Yorktown in early 1862, played a role later in the war in developing the Singer mine. *Library of Congress*

another positive result, but this test was different from the one performed earlier for Shea in Lavaca. This time, the mine was placed underwater and detonated when it struck a flat-bottomed, rectangular hulled boat.[84]

Impressed with the mine experiment at Buffalo Bayou, Magruder ordered Fretwell, Singer, and other members of the Lavaca group of torpedo men to report to Maj. Gen. Dabney H. Maury in Mobile, Alabama. Maury, commander of the District of the Gulf and the Confederate Engineering Department, was a strong supporter of mining operations, which was hardly a surprise. He was reared by his famous uncle Matthew Fontaine Maury, the former U.S. Navy commander who as the Confederacy's first chief of sea coast, river, and harbor defenses, had experimented with such explosives early in the war.[85]

In Mobile, the Lavaca men built a Fretwell-Singer torpedo mine manufacturing facility and a special torpedo launch. A small detachment stationed at nearby Fort Morgan deployed the deadly mines in Mobile Bay.[86]

84 Ragan, "Singer's Secret Service Corps," *Civil War Times* (November/December, 2007); "From Rich Calhoun History," Calhoun County Museum Archives.

85 Wolfe, "E. C. Singer and the *H. L. Hunley*"; George Fred Rhodes, Chairman, Calhoun County Historical Commission, "The *Hunley*: The Confederate Secret Weapon," paper, undated, in Calhoun County Museum Archives, Port Lavaca, Texas.

86 Did the Lavaca men hear about the success of the landmines in other parts of the Confederacy, or was their invention completely independent? No evidence has been found

Maj. Gen. Dabney H. Maury, the Confederate commander in Mobile, Alabama, and the nephew of scientist Matthew Fontaine Maury. *Library of Congress*

The Fretwell-Singer mine earned widespread support among Confederate forces because its underwater explosive device—which relied on a relatively simple system—was very effective. In early February 1863, several of the Lavaca men met with Confederate War Department officials in Richmond, where they were warmly welcomed and asked to demonstrate their invention. The next month, Secretary of War Seddon happily authorized Singer "to form a company of no more than 25 men for a special torpedo service to be attached to the Bureau of Engineers under J. F. Gilmer, subject to the immediate orders of the commander of the district in which they were operating." Singer called the torpedo service "Singer's Sub- marine Corps."[87]

Singer wisely mingled elements of capitalism with large doses of Southern patriotism by patenting his invention before signing a formal agreement with the Confederate government to produce the mines. According to the contract, the Lavaca men, also known as the Singer Torpedo men, were "to get half the

---

acknowledging or connecting landmines being developed and produced in other parts of the Confederacy to their work in Texas.

87 Ragan, "Singer's Secret Service Corps." The group was also called the "Singer Secret Service Corps" and "Singer's Torpedo Company." See, generally, Mark K. Ragan, *Confederate Saboteurs: Building the Hunley and Other Secret Weapons of the Civil War* (Texas A & M, 2015). The author is the most knowledgeable researcher on this fascinating subject.

value of any ships they sunk with their torpedoes, and, later, with submarines."[88]

After Fretwell and Singer received approval to share the mines with local forces, the weapons were deployed in Confederate waters in the spring of 1863. Separated into groups, the Lavaca men were sent to combat zones to support the various Confederate forces. They established operations in Charleston, Richmond, Savannah, and Wilmington, in addition to existing operations in Mobile. As the lead technologist, Singer went to Richmond to develop and produce more mines while Fretwell—who, as head of the Lavaca Masonic Lodge, had proven leadership skills—was "dispatched to Yazoo City, MS, to persuade Lt. Isaac N. Brown to use their torpedoes to mine the water approaches leading to the city's shipyards." Brown supported the idea, and Fretwell and his team experienced immediate success by sinking the Federal ironclad USS *Baron DeKalb* on July 13, 1863, just hours after deploying their mines in the Yazoo River off Yazoo City.[89]

That September, some of the Singer Torpedo men were ordered to report to E. Kirby Smith, a lieutenant general and commander of the Trans-Mississippi Department commander. Lieutenant Colonel Alfred L. Rives wrote to Smith that he was honored to send the men "to be employed in your department on the special service of destroying the enemy's property by torpedoes and similar inventions." Rives also described the remuneration for their work:

> Their compensation will be 50 per cent of the property destroyed by their new inventions and all the arms and munitions captured by them by the use of torpedoes or of similar devices. Beyond this they will be entitled to such other reward as Congress may hereafter provide.[90]

---

88 "A Page From Rich Calhoun History," Calhoun County Museum Archives; Rhodes, "The Hunley: The Confederate Secret Weapon."

89 Ragan, "Singer's Secret Service Corps." Lt. Isaac N. Brown was the former commander of the ironclad CSS *Arkansas*, which created havoc on the Yazoo and Mississippi rivers in July and August of 1862 before engine failure forced her destruction off Baton Rouge on August 6, 1862.

90 Alfred L. Rives, Lieutenant-Colonel and Acting Chief of Bureau, Engineer Bureau, to Lieut. Gen. E. Kirby Smith, Commanding Trans-Mississippi Department, September 15, 1863, *OR* vol. 22, 1,017.

In March of 1863, R. W. Dunn, a Kentucky-born contractor, had traveled to Richmond from Mobile for important torpedo meetings with government officials, and most likely with Singer himself. Dunn was ordered to take important Lavaca mining operations documents to Houston for delivery to Magruder. On March 16, he was pursued by Union launches from a gunboat that had fired on him during his attempt to cross the Mississippi. "I had the misfortune to loose [sic] my papers, having been closely pursued by launches from a gunboat, and fired at three times from a small swivel gun on their bows, before nearing the shore," recalled the frustrated Dunn. The top secret papers, which included the names and locations of about 50 Confederate special operatives, including Singer Corps members, were found by the enemy.[91]

Immediately after obtaining the captured Confederate documents, David D. Porter, a Union rear admiral and commander of the Mississippi Squadron, was especially incensed by the information and ordered the arrest of everyone on the list. "The persons mentioned in the following letter are rebels," he wrote, "engaged as agents for the Confederate Government, employed for the purpose of furthering the views of said Government in destroying Union vessels by torpedoes and other inventions." Every officer "belonging to the army and navy are requested to arrest them wherever found."[92]

Because the Lavaca men functioned largely on their own, they were not limited to naval operations. For example, they could engage in all kinds of combat operations, including attacks on land like sabotaging railroads. As the Federal stranglehold tightened on the Eastern seaboard and the Gulf Coast, Confederates there began adapting the Fretwell-Singer naval mine tactics and technology for use on land.[93]

---

91 Ragan, "Singer's Secret Service Corps."

92 The Confederate letter stated: "To introduce R. W. Dunn, E. C. Singer, and J. D. Braman to my friends, B. C. Adams, Grenada; Capt. Samuel Applegate, Winona; Col. H. H. Miller, commanding regiment, West Grenada and Carrollton; W. P. Mellon, Natchez; Maj. John B. Peyton, Raymond." David Porter, Rear-Admiral, Commanding Mississippi Squadron, Special Orders No. 185, U.S. Mississippi Squadron, Flag-Ship *Black Hawk*, Alexandria, Louisiana, March 21, 1864. **OR cite?**

93 Singer torpedoes were found by mounted pickets at Oyster Reef, Texas on March 29, 1864. A. C. Mathews, Major, Commanding, reported to Captain Caldwell, Federal Headquarters, on March 29, 1864, that the pickets were "two men and their horses," the names of whom were "H. J. Curtis, Company C, Ninety-ninth Illinois, and Sergt. Thomas P. Cleveland." *OR* vol. 34, pt. 2, 783.

Landmines were also deployed near the homes of the the Singer Torpedo Company members. The Confederates' 10-gun Fort Esperanza on Matagorda Island, across Matagorda Bay from Lavaca, extended 200 yards with walls 20 feet thick. In November of 1863, Fort Esperanza's commanding officer, Capt. D. Bradbury, supervised the deployment of about two dozen mines in front of the trenches.[94] Bradbury also instructed that the landmines should be deployed "with strings to set them off leading into the fort, and if they [Union soldiers] had made an assault on us they would have been very destructive." Lanyards for the command-detonated landmines extended into the fort, a unique feature. A pull on the lanyard would detonate the mine.[95]

On November 27, Federals approached Esperanza and laid siege. On December 1, four days after Union forces started their operations, the 500-man garrison learned that Kirby Smith had refused to send more reinforcements from Louisiana. Captain Bradbury made the decision to evacuate the fort. The Confederates set charges to blow up the stronghold and then withdrew along the peninsula.[96]

Once they occupied Fort Esperanza, Union forces had an unencumbered opportunity to examine its extensive landmine fields. Some of the torpedoes had been deployed near the fort in a dry moat 15 feet wide and six feet deep. Each of the landmines was built in "the style of a milk pail or a milk can with a plunger fitted in the top," wrote one Federal, in a way that "[i]f a soldier stepped on the plunger of one of these torpedoes it would have meant certain death to him."[97]

A Union captain and engineering officer named J. T. Baker was in charge of the captured Fort Esperanza. The landmine threat, he explained, was very real. "Enough tin Singer torpedoes were assembled at Port Lavaca, Texas," he

---

94 According to Calhoun County tax assessor-collector Katie Guidry, "the underwater ruins of Fort Esperanza can be seen today when the tide is low." "Indianola and the Civil War," in *The Texas Public Employee* (April 1968), 15, Calhoun County Museum Archives, Port Lavaca, Texas.

95 Captain Bradbury, Communication Related to His Torpedoes to Colonel James Duff, Commanding, Victoria, Texas, January 9, 1864, *OR* vol. 34, pt. 2, 854.

96 H. B. Atkinson, diary, "Civil War in Calhoun County" (New Canton, IL), undated, in Calhoun County Museum Archives, Port Lavaca, Texas.

97 William H. Chenery, *The Fourteenth Regiment Rhode Island Heavy Artillery (Colored) in the War to Preserve the Union 1861-1865* (Providence, RI, 1898), 22.

reported, "to present a serious obstacle for the Federals who attacked the southern Texas coast in the fall of 1863."[98]

Confederate commanders also ordered their troops to deploy a "double line" of landmines to protect Fort Griffin, a fortification near Sabine Pass on the Texas-Louisiana border. The weapons were similar in design and in potential explosive effects to those placed at Fort Esperanza. The mines were command-detonated, with the explosives connected by "explosion-lines or lanyards [that] reached entirely inside the Fort, so that in case of an assault, they could be pulled at the proper time (when the dead angles were crowded) with perfect safety to the garrison."[99]

By the end of 1863, word of the success of the Fretwell-Singer mines had spread throughout the Confederacy. More Lavaca men were transferred to Mobile, where their torpedoes aided in the defense of the city. Singer's men and their mines were in demand elsewhere in the dwindling Confederacy as well—especially in war-ravaged Virginia.[100]

98 J. T. Baker, Ex-Capt. U.S. Vol's Engineer to Bvt. Maj. C. J. Allen, Corps U.S. Eng'rs, October 2, 1865, quoted in Perry, *Infernal Machines*, 46.

99 V. Sulakkowski, Chief of Engineers, to Major J. Kellersberg, Chief Engineer, Eastern District Texas, Sabine Pass, October 5, 1863, *OR* vol. 26, pt. 2, 298; W. R. King, *Torpedoes: Their Invention and Use, From the First Application to the Art of War to the Present Time* (Washington, DC, 1866), 506.

100 A Fretwell-Singer landmine deployed outside of Richmond was found in 1865 and is now in the West Point Military Museum.

Chapter 4

1864: Contagion

After a hard day of mounted fighting at Yellow Tavern, just six miles from Richmond, Maj. Gen. Philip Sheridan's weary Union cavalrymen advanced through heavy rain on the Brook Pike on the night of May 11-12, 1864. Flush with victory and news that Confederate cavalry commander Maj. Gen. James Ewell Brown ("Jeb") Stuart had been mortally wounded, Sheridan's troopers rode on in a generally good mood, unaware that they were completely vulnerable to a new form of war they had yet to encounter.

Boom!

A buried torpedo was tripped by accident and exploded along a road leading to the Confederate capital. The blast killed several horses and injured some of Sheridan's unsuspecting troopers.

Boom! . . . Boom! . . . Boom!

"The enemy, anticipating that I would march by this route, had planted torpedoes along it," reported a frustrated Sheridan, who went on to describe the devices in some detail. "[T]he torpedoes were loaded shells planted on each side of the road, and so connected by wires attached to friction-tubes in the shells, that when a horse's hoof struck a wire the shell was exploded by the jerk on the improvised lanyard." Alonzo Foster, a Union cavalryman from New York riding with Sheridan, recalled the harrowing scene after the war. "It was thundering and lightening in the great style overhead," he wrote, remembering the scene, "and the torpedoes [were] blowing up under foot. Altogether, I certainly don't expect to see the like again, and don't especially want to."[1]

For six long and bloody weeks beginning in early May and running through the middle of June 1864, Gen. Robert E. Lee's Army of Northern Virginia and Maj. Gen. George G. Meade's Army of the Potomac fought their way south and east from the Rapidan River all the way to the banks of the James River. The new general in chief of the Union armies, Ulysses S. Grant, accompanied the Army of the Potomac into the field rather than remain tied to a desk in Washington. The Overland Campaign began in the Wilderness (May 5–7) before the Union army slid by its left flank southeast to Spotsylvania Court House (May 8–21), where Lee's army blunted the enemy advance, fought it to a standstill, and the armies dug in across miles of Virginia landscape. When massive assaults failed to drive the Army of Northern Virginia from the field there, Meade's army slipped by its left once more and met Lee's command dug in behind the North Anna River (May 23–26), where the opposing forces clashed once more before Meade withdrew and flanked Lee again, this time moving southeast to Cold Harbor, where the armies faced off on ground that had been fought over during the Seven Days' Battles two years earlier.

The opposing armies were less than 10 miles outside Richmond and 25 miles from the James River. The mounted fight at Yellow Tavern (May 11) between Sheridan and Stuart was only a small part of the ongoing operations, but an important one in the context of this study. While Confederate mines did not play a large role in the Overland Campaign—and were not even deployed at Cold Harbor that June—they became a real concern for the Union army. The torpedoes maimed unsuspecting Federals and the Union high command was generally incensed by the deployment of Rains's "infernal machines."

After encountering the deadly mines immediately after Yellow Tavern, an angry Sheridan ordered 25 Confederate prisoners to clear the devices. Crawling on a muddy road in front of sullen Union troops, the unfortunate captives searched in the darkness for the deadly weapons planted by their comrades. "This kind of work required a delicate touch, and was unpleasantly exciting,"

---

1 Major-General Sheridan, U.S. Army, Commanding Cavalry Corps, Report of the operations of the Cavalry Corps, Army of the Potomac (April 6, 1864–August 4, 1864), to Maj. Gen. A. A. Humphreys, Chief of Staff, Army of the Potomac, May 13, 1864, *OR* vol. 36, pt. 1, 791; P. H. Sheridan, *Personal Memoirs*, 2 vols. (New York, NY, 1888), vol. 1, 380; Gordon C. Rhea, *To the North Anna River: Grant and Lee: May 13–25, 1864* (Baton Rouge, LA, 2000), 41.

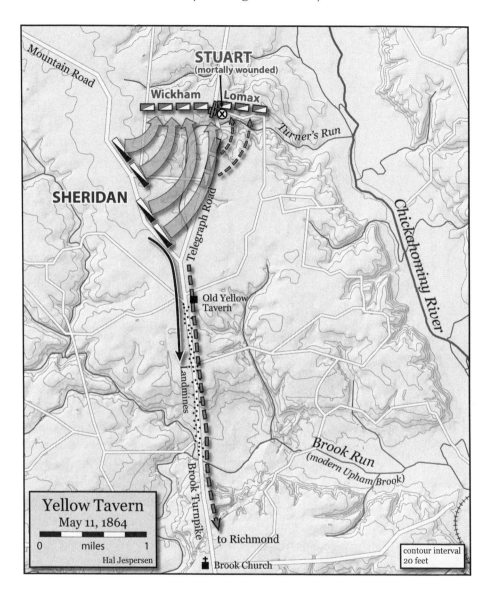

wrote one of the Rebels years after the war. A Union trooper from Ohio discovered a thin line and followed it into the woods, where he captured the Rebel tasked with yanking it. He cut the line into segments and handed them out as souvenirs.[2]

2 S. H. Nowlin, "Capture and Escape," in *Southern Bivouac* (1883), vol. 2, 70; Rhea, *To the North Anna River*, 41.

The Confederate mining efforts led to Sheridan laying some of his own—perhaps a first during the war. After his troopers triggered the mines in the dark and Sheridan used POWs to clear the way, one of the captives reported that the owner of a nearby house was a "principal person who had engaged in planting these shells." Sheridan ordered the unexploded mines uncovered by the prisoners placed in the man's cellar and arranged in a manner sure to detonate if the enemy disturbed them. The Confederate sympathizer and his family were taken prisoner and held until after daylight.[3]

Fighting began at Cold Harbor on May 31 when Union forces took the crossroads at Old Cold Harbor. From June 3–12, Union forces made a series of failed assaults against Lee's well-entrenched line. Although it seemed as though the Union army was caught in something of a stalemate east of Richmond, Grant—who was essentially guiding and fighting Meade's army, much to that officer's chagrin—withdrew from Lee's front and crossed a long pontoon bridge spanning the James River. With most of Lee's army north of the James, the important railroad junction at Petersburg was ripe for the taking. Why the outnumbered Confederates fighting from behind strong earthworks did not deploy mines at Cold Harbor or attempt to use them along the roads the Union army used to reach the James remains unknown.

While the Army of the Potomac maneuvered and fought north and east of Richmond, Union troops initially operating farther out on the Peninsula earlier that April, including the Army of the James under Maj. Gen. Benjamin Butler, encountered mines. Many 20-pound shells filled with canister rounds (small iron balls) and fused with friction primers were found on a road near Williamsburg. Confederates "had scattered torpedoes or shells, with friction fuses, in the road, six of which exploded in my column, the fire of the fuses making a strong light, of which the enemy took advantage to fire on the men," recalled Col. Benjamin F. Onderdonk of the 1st New York Mounted Rifles. "I wheeled into line, and gave the enemy a volley," he continued, "which caused them to leave, but they returned again and kept up a continuous fusillade on my column as it passed."

Fearful of the mines, Onderdonk decided against following the enemy into nearby woods. "I had reason to suppose their infernal machines might do me more injury than the random fire," he added. "Although the shells exploded in the midst of the horses and men, strange to say but one man and two horses were

---

3 Sheridan, *Personal Memoirs*, vol. 1, 380.

slightly wounded with pieces of shell. My men behaved as coolly as on parade, although the uncommon style of warfare was sufficient to destroy the equanimity of the best troops."[4]

Brigadier General Isaac J. Wistar, to whom Col. Onderdonk had forwarded his report, passed it on to General Butler with his own observations about Rebels in his front as well as the capture of Confederates and a wagon full of command-detonated Rebel landmines. "They are not self-acting but are discharged by cords attached," he explained, "and managed by men concealed in the woods. The commanding general," he concluded, "can infer from the above and the inclosed how far the enemy are expecting our advance by the Peninsula."[5]

Defending Richmond

When the Overland Campaign opened in early May, most observers believed that the pattern of what had taken place in the past would continue: A major battle would be fought and the Union army would retreat back above the Rapidan River. After the bloody fighting in the Wilderness, however, the Army of the Potomac moved south and east around Lee's army and continued fighting, this time at Spotsylvania Court House. This was something new, and the threat it posed to the Confederate capital could not be ignored.

On May 10, while a major, though localized, attack that temporarily pierced the front of the Army of Northern Virginia was underway at Spotsylvania, Gabriel Rains was recalled to Richmond. A month later on June 8, during the Cold Harbor phase of the campaign, Rains was named superintendent of the Torpedo Bureau. It was the zenith of his military career. Often critical of the deployment of mines during the Peninsula Campaign in 1862, the Davis

---

4 Col. Benjamin F. Onderdonk, Colonel, First New York Mounted Rifles, Report: "Expedition From Williamsburg and Skirmish at Twelve-Mile Ordinary, VA," April 27–29, 1864, *OR* vol. 33, 313. General Butler's diversionary offensive was tasked with seizing Petersburg, the important railroad and manufacturing center 25 miles below the capital, and potentially taking Richmond itself from the south. His efforts culminated in the fascinating failure called the Bermuda Hundred Campaign.

5 I. J. Wistar, Brigadier-General, Headquarters Second Division, April 29, 1864, *OR* vol. 33, 314.

administration and the Confederate high command had come to fully embrace his use of landmines.[6]

Secretary of the Navy Stephen Mallory, once lukewarm about mine warfare, informed President Davis that the Confederacy relied on naval torpedoes as an important weapon in an increasingly "defensive war." Lieutenant General James Longstreet, who in 1862 did not recognize mines "as a proper or effective method of war," was by 1864 a supporter of the technology.[7]

Thanks to Rains's high-level political connections and growing support, landmine production increased significantly. Rains now had at his disposal his own Richmond-based laboratory, the labor of others developing torpedoes-- including the Fretwell-Singer mines produced in Lavaca, Texas—and the mines made by Matthew Maury, who at that time was in Europe seeking further support for the Confederate war effort.

The cost of landmine production was offset by the collection of thousands of condemned and unexploded artillery shells, all of which could be fitted with the Rains fuse. Rains oversaw the retrieval of shells, and implemented an effective and simple arrangement for retooling and converting them into landmines. In a resource-strapped Confederacy, reconfigured and improvised mines were cheap, easy to produce, and required relatively few men to deploy them.[8]

---

6 Special Orders No. 133, "By command of the Secretary of War," JNO Withers, Assistant Adjutant-General, Adjt. and Insp. General's Office, Richmond, June 8, 1864, *OR* vol. 36, pt. 3, 882–883.

7 Stephen R. Mallory, Secretary of the Navy, to Jefferson Davis, President, April 30, 1864, *ORN* Series 2, vol. 2, 634.

8 According to modern Civil War ordnance experts Michael P. Kochan and John C. Wideman, the collecting of unexploded Union ordnance and resulting conversion to Confederate uses was relatively straightforward: "The system was simple and required no major tooling, other than the fuse plugs, which were fabricated by ordnance personnel. The sensitive primers were constructed locally from paper, chemicals and glue. The tin can cover used to increase the sensitivity radius of the fuse and to help keep the fuse moisture free, was cut with simple shears and formed by hand. . . . Once the sub-terra shells were ready to be used, they were placed in wooden crates and carried to the location of use. They were not fused with the sensitive primers until their actual emplacement. A hole was dug in the ground. The sub-terra shell was placed in the hole. The sensitive fuse primer was placed in the shell. The tin can was placed over the primer and the shell and gently pressed down until the top of the can was just above the primer. Earth was filled in around the shell and a

"These shells are now appreciated, and I now have more calls for their use than I can possibly fulfill," Rains wrote with great satisfaction to Secretary of War Seddon in a Torpedo Bureau status report that October. The shells, Rains added, "now seem to be popular with our officers and are being planted as fast as our limited means will permit, say about 100 per diem." However, he cautioned, more supplies would be needed if he was going to satisfy the growing demand. "To meet the requirements of this Bureau there exists an absolute necessity for the articles specified in the accompanying bill," he pleaded, "which cannot be obtained in the Confederacy . . . [including 1,000 primers for Wheatstone batteries and five miles of gutta-percha cable]."[9]

Rains eventually received enough of what he required for a few months of peak landmine production. In the meantime, Confederate forces defending Richmond and Petersburg in a long and brutal quasi-siege that had begun in June remained short of most resources and manpower, including trained engineers who could help design and build effective defensive fortifications.

Colonel M. R. Talcott, commanding officer of the engineers of the Army of Northern Virginia, observed that "few of the officers in the Confederate Engineers Corps had any previous practice as military engineers." As a result, the basic construction of the fortifications was carried out by "enlisted men with very little direction from the officers," leaving visiting foreign officers astonished "at seeing troops of the line performing what, to them, seemed technical engineering duties which, in their services, would be done by trained officers and men." Because of the shortages in military engineers, landmines became a weapon of choice.[10]

Engineers were more plentiful on the Union side. The most famous deployment and use of a mine during the Civil War took place on July 30, 1864, in what is known as the Battle of the Crater during the siege of Petersburg. There, Union troops under the guidance of engineers dug a 511-foot tunnel

thin layer over the top of the tin can. The device was now ready for the unsuspecting." Kochan and Wideman, *Civil War Torpedoes*, 179.

9 Gabriel J. Rains, Brigadier-General, Superintendent, Torpedo Bureau, to James A. Seddon, Secretary of War, October 29, 1864, *OR* vol. 42, pt. 3, 1,182; Rains Status Report From Torpedo Bureau, Richmond, Virginia, to Honorable James A. Seddon, Secretary of War, November 18, 1864, ibid., 1,220.

10 T. M. R. Talcott, "Reminiscences of the Confederate Engineer Service," 256–270, in Miller, *Forts and Artillery*, 257; O. E. Hunt, "Entrenchments and Fortifications," 194–218, in Miller, *Forts and Artillery*, 212.

beneath the enemy's front line, packed the lateral galleries with 8,000 pounds of gunpowder, and detonated it early in the morning.[11] The resulting explosion, designed to achieve a breakthrough in the lines for a Union attack to push through, created instead a giant smoldering crater 30 feet deep, 170 feet long, and 80 feet wide—into which thousands of soldiers jammed into a chaotic mass. The careful attack plan was squandered by miserable planning, poor communication, inept leadership, and a capable tactical response by the Confederates.[12]

Chaffin's Farm, near major transportation arteries leading into Richmond, was one of the most critical sectors in the capital's defense system. However, the fortifications hastily constructed there in 1862 during the Peninsula Campaign and the Seven Days' Battles were substandard or woefully incomplete. Repairs and reinforcement were desperately needed. A shortage of labor compounded the problem, and Robert E. Lee could not afford to use soldiers for the construction of Richmond's fortifications.[13]

The limited manpower irked Lee. In early September, for example, he complained that "rich young men are elected magistrates, etc., just to avoid service in the field." James Longstreet was also exasperated by the lack of

---

11 The term "mines" as applied to the contemporary usage of landmines derived from constructing tunnels to place explosives beneath enemy positions, such as castles and fortifications.

12 Subsequent to the "Crater" detonation, the Confederate defenders at Chaffin's Farm were eager to prevent similar mining operations. As a precaution, they constructed cavernous troughs in front of their positions, most notably at Fort Johnson. Landmines were buried every two to five feet behind the Fort Johnson trough. National Park Service waymark, Fort Johnson, Henrico County, Virginia. A "Horological Torpedo," which functioned as a time bomb using a clockwork mechanism to detonate the charge, was used about a week after the Battle of the Crater on August 9, 1864, on a barge containing Union ammunition moored at City Point, Virginia, on the James River. The explosion caused more than $2,000,000 in damage and killed at least 43 people. Henry W. Halleck, Major General, to Honorable Edwin M. Stanton, Secretary of War, June 3, 1865, *OR* vol. 46, pt. 3, 1,250.

13 E. Harrison to father, July 7, 1862, in Harrison Family Papers, VHS, in Clifford R. Dickinson, *Union and Confederate Engineering Operations at Chaffin's Bluff/Chaffin's Farm, June 1862–April 3, 1865*, Advanced Research Grant, Eastern National Park & Monument Association, Department of the Interior, National Park Service, Richmond National Battlefield Park, Richmond, Virginia, September 29, 1989, 7. William Elzey Harrison, a native of Leesburg, Virginia, was a graduate of the Virginia Military Institute with a degree in civil engineering. He would remain at Chaffin's Farm supervising construction of fortifications until October 1864, when illness forced him to take a leave of absence from the army.

A Fretwell-Singer percussion torpedo. Note the tapered tin case (13.5" x 12.25"), with a spring-loaded hammer on rod at top. This device was used during the siege of Richmond and Petersburg (June 1864– April 1865) and was probably produced in the Confederate torpedo factory in Richmond.

West Point Museum, U.S. Military Academy, New York

available manpower to build the fortifications. To alleviate the shortage of workers, Lee issued a call for a mandatory 60-day labor period for up to 5,000 slaves. Only 2,000 slaves were marshaled for this work, and some of them ran away into the Union lines.[14]

A dearth of tools and obstruction materials compounded the challenges of constructing or reinforcing the fortifications. These deficiencies resulted in weak areas in Richmond's defensive system, and gaps in the abatis throughout the outer defenses. Branches were cut for them, but many were not sharpened or properly placed simply for want of labor.

Built in August and September 1863, Fort Harrison was the major Confederate stronghold at Chaffin's Farm. Situated on a hill with a view of the James River to the south, it protected multiple approaches to Richmond just eight miles to its rear. The fort, however, suffered from immense neglect. A sand parapet needed to be reconstituted and gun emplacements lacked timber beams for stands. The abatis, meant to obstruct would-be attackers, was woefully incomplete. Rifle trenches needed to be reinforced and the trees that were left needed to be cut down to create better fields of fire.

---

14 Jones, *A Rebel War Clerk's Diary*, vol. 2, 281. Some of the major opposition to mobilizing blacks came from slave owners themselves. One wrote to Secretary of War Seddon that they (the owners) "know from past experience and observation that Negroes impressed for the fortifications are generally badly treated and suffer much." General Robert E. Lee to Secretary of War Seddon, December 11, 1864, *OR* vol. 42, pt. 3, 1,267.

General Grant tested the Richmond defensive lines in what is known as the "Fifth Offensive" from September 29 – October 2, 1864. This assault included a major push south of the James River at Poplar Spring Church (Peebles' Farm) to break key Southern supply lines, and a more limited diversionary attack north of the James at Chaffin's Bluff (Fort Harrison). The attack against Harrison resulted in the surprisingly easy seizure of the fort on the first effort, which exposed the Southern capital to potential capture. Immediately after taking Harrison, Federal troops attempted to enlarge their bridgehead by attacking forts up and down the Chaffin's Farm section of the line. The Federals pushed south toward Fort Hoke and launched uncoordinated assaults against other Confederate forts farther north, but failed to capitalize on their earlier successes and were pushed back. The grand effort farther south below Petersburg made only limited headway.[15]

After the failure of the Fifth Offensive, both sides settled back into the day-to-day deadly grind of trench warfare. Confederate soldiers beefed up their front above the James with new lines and by erecting Battery Alexander to better protect the approaches to Richmond along the nearby New Market Road. A new bastion called Fort Johnson, constructed about 1,000 yards north of Fort Harrison, marked the northern anchor of the new line to cover the gap created by the fall of the latter fort. To bolster much or all of this front, Rains ordered that torpedoes be integrated with the abatis in front of Forts Gregg, Gilmer, Johnson, and Battery Alexander. The landmines, observed Union Col. Edward Hastings Ripley, were sprinkled in "double and triple rows." A Union informant in Richmond confirmed Ripley's observation when he reported to Union Capt. J. McEntee that "[t]here are torpedoes placed in front of a number of the enemy's works."[16]

---

15 Fort Hoke was named for Confederate Maj. Gen. Robert F. Hoke of North Carolina. Fort Johnson was probably named after Confederate Maj. Gen. Bushrod R. Johnson of Tennessee. Fort Gregg was named after the commander of the famous Texas Brigade, Gen. John Gregg, who played a key role in the Battle of Chaffin's Farm and later died defending the approaches to Richmond on October 7, 1864. Fort Gilmer was named after Jeremy F. Gilmer, one of the leading Confederate engineers. For complete information on this offensive above and below the James River, see Richard J. Sommers, *Richmond Redeemed: The Siege at Petersburg: The Battles of Chaffin's Bluff and Poplar Spring Church, September 29 - October 2, 1864* (Savas Beatie, 2014).

16 Earl J. Hess, *In the Trenches at Petersburg: Field Fortifications and Confederate Defeat* (Chapel Hill, NC, 2009), 205; J. McEntee, Captain, to Major-General Humphreys, Chief of Staff, Office of the Provost-Marshall-General, Armies Operating Against

The front was further strengthened with wide and deep ditches. The mine-laced abatis were usually positioned on the glacis, or outer slope of field fortifications exterior to the ditch. Their purpose was to break the momentum of an assaulting body of troops and hold them up under close musket fire delivered from the parapet. Rains believed that landmines and abatis were natural partners that mutually reinforced defensive positions. "The glacis," he began,

> was often omitted or imperfectly made yet the abatis was always added when possible and subterra shells were found (buried among the trees) as to demoralize the assailants as to render the field work impregnable. . . . No enemy would attempt to remove abatis. Thus strengthened, and as such subterra shell is like a sentinel who never sleeps, the troops behind these report in confidence fancied security so that many men were removed for more active serve in the field from these works so guarded.[17]

Other landmines were laid between the two lines of raised earthen beds protecting that section of the defenses. Among the most common landmines used along this part of the line were unexploded 24-pound shells mounted with a custom wooden fuse plug. When they were ready to put in place, the small wooden sealing plug was easily pressed down into the large iron projectile or detached. A sensitive Rains primer was then inserted into the wooden fuse plug. After being carefully buried in the soil, the shell was topped with a sheet-metal crown.[18]

Rains also wanted torpedoes deployed "about as many feet distant as the number of inches in the diameter of the shells." An attempt was made to lay the landmines two to five feet apart in shallow holes that were then packed with soil up to the plungers found in the noses of the shells. Short planks were laid over the noses, covered with dirt, and marked with red flannel flags planted on

---

Richmond, Virginia, City Point, November 1, 1864, *OR* vol. 42, pt. 3, 472. Union forces also created new works, most notably on October 11, two weeks after seizing Fort Harrison, which they renamed Fort Burnham and reconfigured by building new fortifications and completely enclosing it. General Hiram Burnham had been killed after his brigade routed enemy skirmishers from a cornfield near Fort Harrison while leading his men into the fort. The victorious Union soldiers renamed the captured fort in his honor.

17 Herbert M. Schiller, ed., *Confederate Torpedoes: Two Illustrated 19th Century Works with New Appendices and Photographs* (Jefferson, NC, 2011), 61.

18 Dickinson, *Union and Confederate Engineering Operations*, 98.

upright rods. Just seven pounds of pressure was all that was required to explode one of these devices.[19]

The most important construction on Chaffin's Farm occurred between October 17 and November 1. During this time, Rains oversaw the deployment of nearly 1,300 landmines along this portion of the Southern line. On November 18, Rains reported that his bureau's

> efforts for the defense of this place have been directed lately to planting subterra shells between our lines of abatis at our works. . . . [P]lanted at this date 1,298 subterra shells so protected by tin covers inverted over them as thoroughly to shield them from the effect of rain and increase the area of the primer, and might thus be put at the bottom of the river without deteriorating their efficacy.[20]

Each Confederate position in the Chaffin's Farm defensive line was fortified with similar strategies for using landmines:

- The "[t]orpedoes [were] placed on the eastern side between the abatis from Battery Gregg southwards to Fort Johnson . . . and the torpedo line continued beyond Fort Johnson."[21]

- Fort Hoke: A small artillery emplacement located on a strategic low-lying knoll. It guarded the 500-yard stretch of fallow fields in the direction of Fort Harrison. A line of landmines was placed between fraise and abatis.

- Fort Johnson: Defended by a deep ditch and a heavy cordon of sharpened stakes as abatis and landmines in front. At Fort Johnson, as with the rest of the Confederate defensive line, the landmines were buried every two to five feet. Fort Johnson's deep ditch was a preventive measure. After the famous "Crater" explosion at Petersburg, both sides feared similar mining operations would occur north of the James River opposite Richmond.

- Fort Gilmer: Extensive fortification located behind a sweeping chasm. The landmine plan for Fort Gilmer placed them between fraise and the abatis. Specifically, the landmines were deployed just behind the fraise from the northern edge of Fort Gilmer south to a small earthwork named Battery Gregg along Mill Road. Abatis

---

19 Rains, *Torpedo Book*, 61.

20 Rains, Status Report to Seddon, November 18, 1864, *OR* vol. 42, pt. 3, 1,219.

21 Dickinson, *Union and Confederate Engineering Operations*, Figure 15, 90. Figure 16, p. 91 and Figure 17, 93.

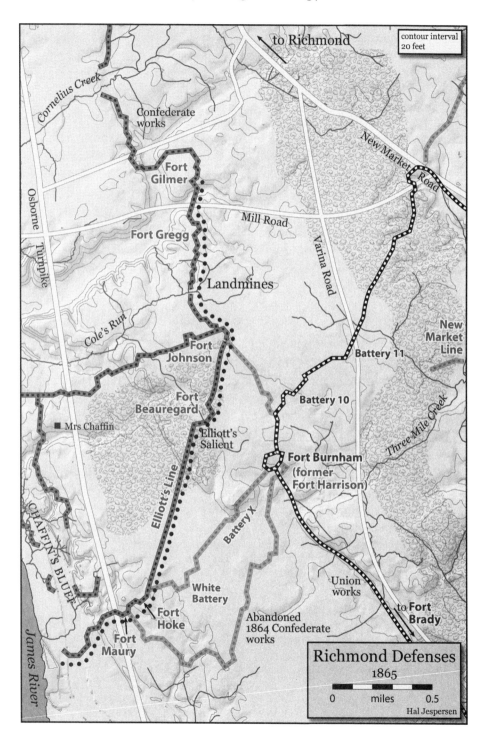

contour interval
20 feet

to Richmond

Cornelius Creek

Confederate
works

New Market Road

Fort
Gilmer

Osborne Turnpike

Fort Gregg

Mill Road

Landmines

Varina Road

New
Market
Line

Cole's Run

Fort
Johnson

Battery 11

Fort
Beauregard

Battery 10

Mrs Chaffin

Elliott's
Salient

Three Mile Creek

Elliott's Line

Fort Burnham
(former
Fort Harrison)

CHAFFIN'S BLUFF

Battery X

White
Battery

Union
works

to Fort
Brady

Fort
Hoke

Abandoned
1864 Confederate
works

James River

Fort
Maury

Richmond Defenses
1865

0   miles   0.5

Hal Jespersen

were constructed between the landmines and Fort Gilmer's walls extending north to the New Market Road. Union spies reported that "[t]here are seven torpedoes placed in front of Fort Gilmer. They are under one plank, and a weight of seven pounds on any part of the plank will explode them."[22]

Rains emphasized that only the most disciplined of soldiers should perform the hazardous duty of setting mines. "To plant the subterra shells men must be selected of staid & sober habits, and drilled to it, to prevent the possibility of accident." With more than 2,000 torpedoes planted, the Chaffin's Farm defensive line north of the James became the largest formal landmine field in the entire Civil War.[23] Rains's mines were intended to sow fear in the enemy. "[I]n fact our object is not to kill but to demoralize which a knowledge of this intended use of them is sure to do after the first exhibition of their effects," Rains explained. Reports filtered in from Union deserters that landmines were "rapidly demoralizing the [Federals]."[24]

In a notable new tactic associated with landmine warfare, many torpedoes planted in the Chaffin's farm area were carefully mapped and marked by soldiers trained in the art of minelaying, all to prevent fellow Confederates from becoming casualties of their own deadly contraptions. Small red flags, for example, were planted about three feet behind each buried shell. Each night, or when the Federals were approaching, the flags were removed, only to be replaced just before first light. In addition, pathways were created through the minefields for ease of movement. A Union intelligence report confirmed the precautions taken to mark the landmines "by little flags to prevent their own men from stepping on them; in case of an attack or necessity of falling back the

22 J. McEntee, Captain, to Major-General Humphreys, Chief of Staff, Office of the Provost-Marshall-General, Armies Operating Against Richmond, Virginia, City Point, November 13, 1864, *OR* vol. 42, pt. 3, 613–614.

23 The Chaffin Farm area front lines, including its landmine fields, became quite a curiosity for a host of Northern and Southern visitors. A party of ladies from Richmond visited the area, where one of their dogs wandered into the landmine field, and, much to everyone's delight, did not trigger any mines. "Record of the War," 3:60, Minor Family Papers, SC-UVA, ibid., 180. Also visiting the Confederate lines was a Northern reporter guided by a civilian to avoid the minefields near Fort Burnham. Minor, Trowbridge, *Desolate South*, ibid., 290.

24 Rains, *Torpedo Book*, 63; Rains, *Status Report to Seddon*, November 18, 1864, *OR* vol. 42, pt. 3, 1,219.

flags are removed. Our agent gets this from the parties who have been at work placing the torpedoes."[25]

Because the capture of a major road could bring disaster to the Confederates defending Richmond, Rains gave specific instructions on how and where to lay landmines along the various arteries leading into the Southern capital. "To check the advance of an army along a road," he directed,

> plant these shells in their front, but attached to each sensitive primer a string a foot long tied with 3 loops around the shank just under the head and upon the end of that piece of red flannel about as wide and long as the finger. When the shell is planted this piece of red flannel is brought to the surface so as to identify the spot where the shell is. . . . This precaution is necessary in case the shells have to be removed.[26]

The precautions were helpful in preventing Confederate casualties, but it could not stop all of them. Army Torpedo Bureau soldier William S. Deupree, for example, worked closely with Rains but still fell victim to his invention. Deupree, explained his superior, "accidentally fell upon one and was immediately killed in full sight of the foe, who, hearing the explosion, was attracted to the spot observing the effects."[27]

Deupree was not the only loss. Taking a shortcut back to his billet, a Confederate soldier identified only as "Burkhalter" cut through a minefield and stepped on a torpedo and triggered an explosion. "[His] shoe was a little powder-burned on the bottom and a split about an inch long, as if cut with a knife, was on the front," a doctor recalled. "This was the only injury to the shoe, and the skin was not broken on the foot, but every bone in the foot, up to several inches above the ankle, was crushed by the concussion. He refused to have the member removed, and died in about 10 days."[28]

25 Rains, *Torpedo Book*, 57. McEntee to Humphreys, November 13, 1864, *OR* vol. 42, pt. 3, 613.

26 Rains, *Torpedo Book*, 60.

27 Rains, Status Report to Seddon, November 18, 1864, *OR* 42, pt. 3, 1,219. William Stephen Deupree is buried in Richmond's Hollywood Cemetery, Section L, Lot 4, where his gravestone reads, "Killed in Secret Service CSA." Kochan and Wideman, *Civil War Torpedoes*, 42.

28 J. B. Stimson, "Three Unusual Gun-Shot Wounds," in *Southern Practitioner, An Independent Monthly Journal Devoted to Medicine And Surgery* (1900), vol. 22, 364.

As he had on the Virginia Peninsula in 1862, and again during operations around Jackson, Mississippi, in 1863, Rains ordered his men to exert care in deploying the landmines in order to avoid civilian and Confederate casualties. "Such use of these shells . . . is to be made with caution," he warned, "for fear of destruction of women, children, & non-combatants & should never be done except on roads used for military purposes."[29]

As an additional humanitarian measure, Rains noted that "[o]rdinarily the primers are not inserted until necessary on proximity of the enemy and [that] they should never be left unguarded by a sentinel on horseback, until the enemy appears. This is a general rule." Such command of the landmines themselves would ensure that they would not kill indiscriminately or injure unintentionally, while also saving military resources for their designed purpose of killing the enemy. Landmine-infested areas in the Chaffin's Farm sector were mapped as carefully as possible.[30]

Rains paid special attention to roads leading into Richmond that were the most vulnerable to Federal breakthroughs and raids. According to a Union intelligence report, "Confederate soldiers mined the approaches to the city, planting shells in the roads, and covering the 400-foot lead cords under a layer of dust. These cords were to be pulled from hiding to set off an explosion."[31]

"For the surprise of a camp by night, ordinarily the public highways must be used, and the most efficient picket guard is a sentinel and subterra shell or shells planted therein," argued a determined Rains. "On the approach of the enemy," he continued,

> the sentinel is to make his escape as secretly as possible using the shell to give the alarm, and to a certain extent to demoralize. . . . The fact of one man and a shell on each approach from the direction of an enemy securing a camp from night surprise, is sufficient of itself alone without other advantages, to establish this arm of service as an essential adjunct to an army in the field. . . . In attempts to approach a camp by an enemy at night, no surer guard can be formed than one, two, or three of these subterra shells buried in the roads of approach with a sentinel in watchful distance. When the foe

29 Rains, *Torpedo Book*, 63.

30 Ibid., 60. By mid-November, Rains had presented a detailed "diagram of the position of the subterra shells" along the Confederate lines. This is one of the few Confederate-produced landmine maps in existence. See Rains, Status Report to Seddon, November 18, 1864, *OR* vol. 42, pt. 3, 1,219.

31 John C. Babcock to Andrew Humphreys, October 20, 1864, *OR* vol. 42, pt. 3, 281–282.

comes upon them, in their loud report no mistake can be made—the garrison or camp at once aroused while the enemy becomes demoralized from the mishap.[32]

Union forces devised a tactic to counter Confederate landmines guarding the roads leading into Richmond by simply avoiding them as much as possible. Maj. Gen. Godfrey Weitzel advised subordinates "to look out for torpedoes and mines [because] [i]t is now reported that large numbers of the former are put down on Chaffin's farm and Bermuda front. Don't let your columns take the roads," he cautioned. "Keep them in the woods and bypaths. Send the cattle and old horses up the roads first."[33]

While Rains and his Army Torpedo Bureau men seeded the Chaffin's Farm front and roads heading into Richmond, naval personnel mined several rivers, including the James, Pamunkey, Chickahominy, and Appomattox.

Because of this increased Confederate usage of naval mines, Union officers ordered "thousands of their soldiers" to scan the banks of the James for both mine suppliers and the operators waiting to trigger the devices. Union Col. George H. Sharpe's spy network reported that a

torpedo party who had been doing nothing for two or three weeks, left Richmond on Saturday night with a wagon-load of torpedoes, and it was expected that they would attempt to put them in the water somewhere between the mouth of the Chickahominy and Jamestown Island. This information was obtained from an officer of the rank of captain, who had been out with the torpedo party several times before, and who, on Saturday upon being asked about some preparations for departure, gave the above reason.[34]

The arrival of a very cold and often wet winter, which turned the roads into nearly impassable ribbons of icy mud, limited further major offensive operations. Far away from the bloody stalemate being waged around Petersburg and Richmond, meanwhile, Maj. Gen. William Sherman and 60,000 Union troops marched east out of Atlanta into the deep interior of Georgia. During the

32 Rains, *Torpedo Book*, 64.

33 General E. O. C. Ord to General Weitzel, HDQRS Dept. of Virginia, Army of the James, "In the field," March 27, 1865, *OR* vol. 46, pt. 3, 212.

34 John K. Mitchell to Gabriel J. Rains, October 29, 1864, *ORN* vol. 11, 748; George H. Sharpe, Colonel, Headquarters, Army of the Potomac, Office of the Provost-Marshall-General, September 19, 1864, *OR* vol. 42, pt. 2, 912–913.

long journey to Savannah, one landmine incident in particular would draw Sherman's fury.[35]

Fort McAllister: Fifteen Minutes of Hell

After the fall of Atlanta on September 2, 1864, William Sherman's command spent some time in and around the city marshaling provisions and resting. Chasing northward after John Bell Hood's Army of Tennessee proved a fruitless endeavor, and Sherman decided on a different course. He would leave Maj. Gen. George Thomas in Nashville to handle the weakened Confederate army. Sherman, meanwhile, convinced Grant to let him drive deeper into the state, destroying Georgia's resources and the will of its people to fight as he made his way to the important coastal city of Savannah. There, he could easily and quickly resupply his army and take his men and guns north by sea to reinforce the Union forces around Richmond and Petersburg and finally end the rebellion. Sherman divided his army into two wings of two corps each with a division of cavalry operating in support, and marched southeast through the countryside destroying everything in his path useful to the Confederate war effort. "I can make the march," Sherman wrote to Grant, "and make Georgia howl." Landmines deployed along his route to Savannah, however, would make Sherman howl.[36]

The fall of Atlanta and Hood's decision to move his army north and west exposed the entire state to occupation and potential disaster. The Davis administration did everything in its power to rush troops there to reinforce the critical manufacturing cities of Augusta and Macon, both of which were almost entirely undefended and, in reality, indefensible. Lt. Gen. William J. Hardee's Department of South Carolina, Georgia, and Florida had few men and resources to allocate. Some 10,000 cavalry under Maj. Gen. Joseph Wheeler and a few

---

35 The last landmine war casualty of the Richmond campaign likely occurred on April 3, 1865, when a soldier in the 9th Vermont Infantry was killed by "the explosion of a torpedo in crossing the rebel line of works" as Union troops were occupying the capital city. See Report of Brigadier General Charles Deems, U.S. Army, commanding Third Division, Richmond, Virginia, April 3, 1865, www.sonofthesouth.net/leefoundation/richmond-campaign.htm.

36 William T. Sherman, *Sherman's Civil War: Selected Correspondence of William T. Sherman, 1860–1865*, Jean V. Berlin and Brooks D. Simpson, eds. (Chapel Hill, NC, 1999), 731.

Maj. Gen. William T. Sherman, who forced Confederate prisoners to clear out landmines. *Fort McAllister State Park Museum*

thousand state militia were on hand, but the primary Confederate opposition was entirely inadequate for the task. Nothing was going to stop Sherman's veteran juggernaut.[37]

In desperation, President Davis pressed his generals in Georgia to obstruct "roads by every practicable means" to delay Sherman's march for as long as possible. In mid-November, he conveyed to his generals fighting in Georgia that "every effort will be made, by destroying bridges, felling trees and planting subterra shells, and otherwise to obstruct the enemy." On November 18, Davis ordered Brig. Gen. Howell Cobb (who was helping organize resistance in Georgia) to contact Col. George Rains, the commander of the Augusta Powder Works and Gabriel's brother, "to furnish Cobb "with shells prepared to explode by pressure," as they "will be effective to check an advance."[38] General P. G. T.

37 Macon was a valuable military and industrial complex. Augusta was the home of the Augusta Arsenal as well as the much larger and much more important Augusta Powder Works, which produced nearly all of the gunpowder (and related products) consumed by the Confederacy. Its destruction would have ended the war within a relatively short period of time, though it was never specifically targeted for destruction. Some considered Augusta to be "the most indispensable of the South's limited number of manufacturing centers . . . [and] [i]f it was captured or destroyed, the effect on the Southern war effort would have been almost instantly fatal." See, generally, Theodore P. Savas, "Heartbeat of the Southern War Machine," pt. 1, *Civil War Times Magazine* (June 2017), 34-43, and Theodore P. Savas, "The War's Biggest Blunder," pt. 2, *Civil War Times Magazine* (August 2017), 30-35. See also, Louis A. Garvaglia, "Sherman's March and the Georgia Arsenals," in *North and South* (December 2002), vol. 6, no. 1, 20.

38 President Jefferson Davis to Col. William M. Browne, Aide-de-Camp, Augusta, Georgia, November 22, 1864, *OR* vol. 44, 880–881; President Jefferson Davis, Richmond,

Beauregard appealed to Secretary of War Seddon for "a large supply of Rains' sub-terra shells, with competent persons to employ them" for General Cobb's forces to use at Macon. Seddon, in turn, instructed Rains "to give immediate attention" to Beauregard's appeal for sub-terra shells to be sent to Cobb.[39]

That same week, James Tomb, chief engineer in the Confederate Navy, offered to use some of his torpedoes "against the enemy in their advance through Georgia." Maj. Gen. Sam Jones, the commander of a district in South Carolina, asked naval authorities to free up Tomb "for the the defense of Macon."[40]

Instead of heading for one or both of the major industrial cities, however, Sherman feinted at Macon and Augusta, dividing his paltry opposition, and drove through the soft middle toward Savannah. He reached the outskirts of the city on December 10. Lt. Gen. William Hardee, Savannah's commander, had about 10,000 men behind strong entrenchments anchored by Fort McAllister. Four days earlier Gen. Beauregard, who was now the commander of the Department of the West (a sprawling five-state area from Georgia all the way west to the Mississippi River), had ordered forces along the Savannah River "to obstruct [the approach] thoroughly with trees and torpedoes and break up roads." Iowa soldiers were especially affected. Many of the Hawkeyes "were killed or horribly mangled, or both, by torpedoes buried near the surface of the

---

Virginia, to General H. Cobb, Macon, Georgia, November 18, 1864, ibid., 865. A few days later, Davis instructed Augusta's defenders to provide the help and transportation necessary to "enable Colonel Rains to save his valuable machinery" should holding Augusta become an impossibility. President Jefferson Davis to Gen. B. D. Fry, Augusta, Georgia, November 22, 1864, ibid., 883.

39 Gen. G. T. Beauregard to Hon. J. A. Seddon, November 18, 1864, ibid., 866. In a further desperate move to provide the heavily outnumbered defenders more troops, General Beauregard also ordered the formation of a "foreign battalion of Federal prisoners" from the Florence, South Carolina, prison to help defend Savannah. After being mustered into service in December, "[t]he troops took part, grudgingly, in the defense of Savannah," but quickly mutinied after General Sherman, who was informed of their existence by Southern deserters, "sent word that if they would mutiny and desert, he would welcome them back." Those who would not mutiny "would be shot when captured." E. Cantey Haile, Jr., "John Hampden Brooks: South Carolina Soldier: Full Circle," in *North South Trader's Civil War*, vol. 19, no. 2, 43.

40 Sam Jones, Major-General, Headquarters District of South Carolina, Charleston, to General Hardee, Charleston, South Carolina, November 22, 1864, *OR* vol. 44, 885; Sam Jones, Major-General, Headquarters District of South Carolina, Charleston, to J. R. Tucker, Flag Officer, Charleston, South Carolina, November 21, 1864, ibid., 880.

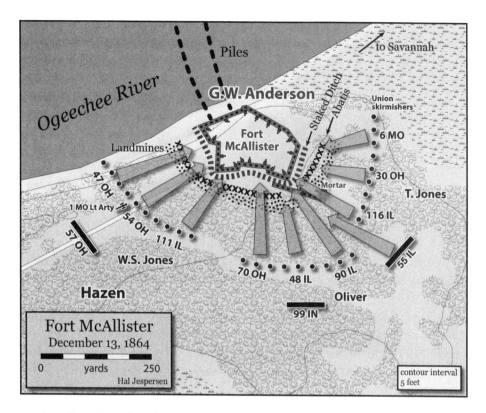

roads, railroads and paths, and at all places where men were likely to march," recalled one of the Hawkeyes. "The Iowa men had never met this kind of warfare before."[41]

Sherman himself witnessed the effects of a torpedo explosion on December 8 just east of Confederate-held Savannah. A "handsome young officer" in the XVII Corps was riding with the brigade staff when the horse he was riding detonated a victim-activated mine. The device gutted the mount and the unfortunate soldier's foot was "blown to pieces," with flesh hanging from his wounded leg. Sherman found the unfortunate officer waiting in agony for a surgeon to amputate his mangled limb. "I saw the terrible wound, and made full inquiry into the facts," recalled the angry general. "There had been no resistance at that point, nothing to give warning of danger." Confederates had planted

41 G. T. Beauregard to Maj. Gen. S. Jones, December 6, 1864, *OR* vol. 44, 934; Kochan and Wideman, *Civil War Torpedoes*, 185.

eight-inch shells in the road, "with friction-matches to explode them by being trodden on."[42]

The manner of the wound enraged Sherman. "This was not war," he fumed, "but murder." Immediately after the incident he ordered Confederate prisoners brought up "from the rear of the brigade," told his "soldiers to get a proper distance away," and "directed the prisoners with picks and spades to find the other torpedoes." According to Sherman, he "made them march in close order along the road, so as to explode their own torpedoes, or to discover and dig them up. The Rebel prisoners, he wrote, "begged hard, but I reiterated the order, and could hardly help laughing at their stepping so gingerly along the road, where it was supposed sunken torpedoes might explode at each step, but they found no other torpedoes till near Fort McAllister."[43]

Sherman's response to torpedoes was nothing new. On June 23, 1864, just before his attack against Kennesaw Mountain above the Chattahoochee River north of Atlanta, he sent a letter to Maj. Gen. James B. Stedman threatening the enemy with drastic measures. "The use of torpedoes in blowing up our [train] cars and road after they are in our possession is simply malicious," he wrote, referring to the blowing up of rail lines and trains. "It cannot alter the great problem, but simply makes trouble. Now," Sherman continued,

> if torpedoes are found in the possession of an enemy in our rear, you may cause them to be put on the ground and tested by wagon-loads of prisoners, or, if need be, citizens implicated in their use. In like manner, if a torpedo is suspected on any part of the road, order the point to be tested by a car load of prisoners, or citizens implicated, drawn by a long rope. Of course an enemy cannot complain of his own traps.[44]

Now, outside Savannah and likely with Sherman's blessing, Union commanders handled the matter the same way. When the explosive devices were found, a Federal officer reported that Confederate POWs were killed when forced to march through a mined area in front of Union columns:

---

42 William Tecumseh Sherman, *The Memoirs of General W. T. Sherman by Himself* (Bloomington, IN, 1957), 194.

43 Ibid.

44 W. T. Sherman, Major-General Commanding, HDQRS, Military Division of the Mississippi, to Maj.-Gen. J. B. Steedman, Commanding District of the Etowah, Chatta- nooga, June 23, 1864, *OR* vol. 38, pt. 4, 579.

We had quite a number of rebel prisoners who had been escorted along under guard. . . .
[o]fficers and soldiers had to march ahead of us. During the first ha[lf] mile three more
exploded killing two Johnnies and wounding several more or less. No more were found
then. But Genl. [William] Hardee was informed under flag of truce and notified of the
measures we had taken to discover the torpedoes.[45]

A newspaper correspondent accompanying Sherman's army to Savannah
reported prisoners "removed two of these treacherous, death-dealing
instruments." Soon thereafter, Sherman noted a sudden lack of torpedoes in the
road. "By some coincidence," he added sarcastically, "no more explosions took
place." Whether the lack of mines was because the Confederates knew their
captured comrades were being used to clear them is not known with certainty,
but there is little doubt what Sherman believed.[46]

Sometimes prisoners were not on hand and Sherman's own men were
ordered to clear mines. One company, reported the *New York Times*, took on the
dangerous task in a "delicate and careful manner." The soldiers found four
mines, each about 18 inches long and eight inches in diameter with percussion
or friction fuses barely beneath dust in the road. "When a horse with an iron
shoe or a man with a solid tack heel shoe stepped upon it," according to an
account, "there was almost sure to be an explosion carrying death to those
nearby."[47]

On December 9, Sherman established his headquarters in Pooler, just east
of Savannah, and began laying the groundwork to assault the city. Some of
Sherman's troops advancing to Pooler reported landmine casualties. "Here we
mined the road," admitted a Confederate soldier responsible for the Pooler
torpedoes,

placing some bomb shells in the road which just at this point was a plank road; a few
planks were lifted, some percussion shells were place[d] under these planks & about
one quarter of a mile away just at the other edge of the swamp we had our artillery ready
& when the first bomb exploded, our artillery, which until then was out of sight,

45 John Henry Otto, David Gould, and James B. Kennedy, *Memoirs of a Dutch Mudsill:
The "War Memories" of John Henry Otto, Captain, Company D, 21st Regiment Wisconsin
Volunteer Infantry* (Kent, OH, 2004), 311.

46 "Sherman's March: Journal of an Eye-Witness," *New York Times*, December 23, 1864,
3; Sherman, *Memoirs*, 194.

47 Ibid.

wheeled into line & opened on their Cavalry column which was in advance. They were thrown into great confusion & rout.[48]

Although the Federals significantly outnumbered Savannah's garrison, the city's defenses were formidable. The most important fortification was Fort McAllister, 12 miles south of the city on the Ogeechee River. Like other coastal forts on the Eastern seaboard, it was built to protect American coastlines from foreign enemies attacking from the Atlantic Ocean. It was not designed to stop large infantry attacks from the landward side, though its defenses in that quarter had been bolstered in advance of Sherman's approach. His army needed supplies, Admiral Dahlgren's fleet was waiting offshore with everything he needed, and Sherman was not a patient man. If McAllister fell, Sherman would control the river, his army could be resupplied, and Savannah would soon be his.[49]

On December 12, Sherman issued orders for a division of infantry under William B. Hazen to assault the fort, which was defended by a small 250-man force of Georgians commanded by Maj. George W. Anderson. Ever since word of Sherman's approach reached Savannah's defenders, the Georgians had been diligently improving Fort McAllister's works, particularly those on the westward land side. To create an unobstructed field of fire, trees were cut within a half-mile on the southwest side. Any Union attackers would also encounter a wall of sharpened branches directed upward and outward, and a deep dry moat. "The fort was an enclosed work," explained Sherman,

> and its land-front was in the nature of a bastion and curtains, with good parapet, ditch, *fraise*, and *chevaux-de-frise*, made out of the large branches of live-oaks. Luckily, the rebels had left the larger and unwieldy trunks on the ground, which served as a good cover for the skirmish-line, which crept behind these logs, and from them kept the artillerists from loading and firing their guns accurately.[50]

48 John Williams Green, Albert Dennis Kirwan, and Kent Masterson Brown, *Johnny Green of the Orphan Brigade: The Journal of a Confederate Soldier* (Lexington, KY, 2002), 179.

49 The Fort McAllister State Park showcases one of the best-preserved earthwork fortifications of the Confederacy. In the 1930s, the site was owned by industrialist Henry Ford, who was instrumental in the initial efforts to preserve and restore the fort as a historical monument for future generations. Ownership of the fort later passed to the International Paper Company, which in turn deeded the land to the State of Georgia.

50 Sherman, *Memoirs*, 199.

Fort McAllister Landmine, Fort McAllister
State Park Museum. *Author*

Lacking a sizable infantry garrison and proper field artillery, the defenders relied on their ingenuity, including innovative landmine deployment. The weapons were comprised of eight-inch shells "planted in a row" about three feet apart along the fort's western approaches. The shells were attached to the ends of sections of railroad rails or ties so when someone stepped on any part of the tie, the shell would explode. The shells themselves "had a flattened section inside, opposite the fuse hole, that gave the shell a firm base that would direct the force of the explosion upwards into the air rather than dissipating its force into the ground." These shells were available "because the mortar would be of little use in a land assault across the rear, [and] they were an ideal source to be converted into torpedoes."[51]

Under the direction of naval engineer James Tomb, defenders embedded landmines on roads from Savannah to Fort McAllister, including along the main causeway linking Genesis Point to the mainland. Pickets guarding the fort's perimeter expected landmines to detonate when Federal scouts approached. Unfortunately, wrote commander Anderson, they were "unaware that Federal scouts had already arrived in the tree line on the opposite side of the causeway and had spotted them."[52]

51 Brig. Gen. R. Delafield, Chief of Engineers, U.S. Army, Washington, DC, October 8, 1865, *OR* vol. 44, 61; Roger S. Durham, *Guardian of Savannah: Fort McAllister, Georgia, in the Civil War and Beyond* (Columbia, SC, 2008), 125.

52 George W. Anderson, Jr., "General Outline of the Fall of Fort McAllister," in Anderson Papers, Georgia Historical Society, Savannah, Georgia; Strong Report, quoted in Durham, *Guardian of Savannah*, 142.

Before dawn on December 13, Federal cavalry on King's Bridge, the causeway leading to McAllister, captured a group of Confederate pickets. On their march back to the Union lines, the prisoners filed to the extreme edge of the road to the fort. When asked why they did so, one of the POWs offered a one-word reply: "Torpedoes." After revealing the locations of the mines, the prisoners were forced to dig up the weapons. Federal soldiers advancing along the causeway to form for the impending attack against the fort were informed by sentries about additional landmine locations. As a result, no Federals were injured by the mines.[53]

Hazen's division was well aware of the minefield and needed several hours to get into position to attack. At 4:45 p.m., Hazen ordered the assault. In what was surely a surprise to both sides, the fort was in Union hands by 5:00 p.m. For the attackers, however, it was fifteen minutes of hell.

The Federals rushed over and past challenging, and often deadly, man-made defenses. The attacking formation was thrown out of alignment by a network of slashed timber. The Confederates deployed "every conceivable obstruction known to military skill and ingenuity," admitted Union Lt. Col. William E. Strong, including fallen trees, three rows of abatis, two rows of *chevaux-de-frise*, and a massive ditch. Those, however, were mere inconveniences compared to the mines waiting for them. Perhaps as many as 150 eight-inch shells converted to landmines lay buried just below the surface. The pressure of a man's foot was all it took to detonate one of these dreadful weapons.[54]

The landmines blew "many men to atoms," reported Hazen. Lieutenant Colonel Strong agreed with the general. "Many a gallant soldier was mutilated and fairly torn to pieces." Soldiers wrote of the fear and horror they faced in the landmine field. Private James S. Horner of Company D, 30th Ohio, attacked with the rest of Col. Theodore Jones's brigade on the right side of the line. During the charge, Horner jumped over a pile of fresh earth, as did another man on his right. "But the man behind him struck the cap of the torpedo as he ran," Horner recalled, "and it exploded and blew off his foot above the ankle joint.

53 Report of Brig. Gen. William B. Hazen, U.S. Army, commanding Second Division, HDQRS, Fifteenth Army Corps, Savannah, Georgia, January 9, 1865, *OR* vol. 44, 110.

54 Strong, "The Capture of Fort McAllister," 413; Reports of Capt. Orlando Poe, Corps of Engineers, U.S. Army, Chief Engineer, Military Division of the Mississippi, to Brig. Gen. R. Delafield, Chief of Engineers, U.S. Army, Washington, DC, October 8, 1865, *OR* vol. 44, 61.

When I heard the report of the shell I looked back and saw the poor fellow as he fell back in the hole the torpedo made when it exploded."[55]

Sergeant Lyman Hardman, also with the 30th Ohio, stepped on a landmine and the blast threw him violently to the ground. "I had arrived near the edge of small ditch around a mortar bed when I exploded a torpedo that had been placed in the ground by stepping on it," wrote the sergeant. When he recovered from the shock, Hardman discovered his left shoe had been blown off by the explosion, his foot badly burned, and his bones shattered. The iron fragments and powder blast also cut and burned his hand, face, and ears, and temporarily swelled his eyes shut.[56]

Private Charles C. Degman of Company F of the 70th Ohio, Col. John Oliver's brigade, was in the center of the assaulting line. Degman recalled that "at least five boys in blue [were] torn into fragments and scores hurled to the ground" of an explosion crater. Charles Bateman of Degman's company lost both his legs to a "cruel torpedo." He was near death a few days later when one of his comrades, Pvt. Michael Murray, visited Bateman to check on his condition. "I . . . found him still living," he recalled, "but there was no hope or possibility of his living. . . . He was torn to pieces from his stomach downward, all his bowels was mashed." According to another Union soldier, "some 50 yards from the fort we crossed a line of torpedoes buried in the sand and John [Compton], stepping on one of them, was instantly killed. His body was mangled almost beyond recognition."[57]

Newspaper reporters were shocked by what they saw. A *New York Times* correspondent wrote that as he and other reporters "arrived near the line where nearly all our killed and wounded lay, and where our assaulting line had wavered, we were soon investigating this new line of warfare. The scene was

---

55 Report of Brig. Gen. William B. Hazen, January 9, 1865, *OR* vol. 44, 110; Strong, "The Capture of Fort McAllister," 413; Saunier, *A History of the Forty-Seventh Regiment*, 365.

56 Hardman was transported to a New York City hospital at David's Island and in June 1865 was discharged from military service. Durham, *Guardian of Savannah*, 155. Thomas T. Taylor, diary, December 13, 1864, in Taylor Papers, Ohio Historical Society, Columbus, Ohio; S. P. Bonner to Mrs. Taylor, December 15, 1864, Major Taylor's Service Records, National Archives, Washington, DC; Hardman, Service and Pension Records, as quoted in Durham, *Guardian of Savannah*, 190.

57 Durham, *Guardian of Savannah*, 155.

awful," he continued, "and our men were horribly mutilated, for they had been torpedoed and literally blown to pieces."[58]

Sherman, who had observed the assault from Dr. John R. Cheves's house two and a half miles away across the Ogeechee River, remembered that "[t]he assault had been made by three parties in line, one from below, one from above the fort. . . . All were simultaneous, and had to pass a good abatis and line of torpedoes, which actually killed more of the assailants than the heavy guns of the fort, which generally overshot the mark." "I have seen many gallant assaults made on fortified positions, but none like that," reflected Lt. Col. Strong regarding the charge on Fort McAllister. "Not a straggler in sight. Every officer and enlisted man in that grand division proved himself a soldier and a hero."[59]

Major General Oliver O. Howard witnessed a horrendous scene the night the fort was captured. An ambulance led by a team of mules detonated a torpedo. "Mules, ambulance, and men were blown to pieces," Howard recalled. "This sight indicated to us something of the dangers which our brave men had had to encounter."[60]

Two weeks after the capture of Fort McAllister, a Union physician wrote about how the landmines had terrorized and delayed the Federals. "[T]he major part of the casualties occurred from the torpedoes, which were placed in and about the works," Dr. D. L. Huntington recalled. "The wounds thus inflicted were generally of a grave nature." General Hazen reported Federal losses at 24 killed and 110 wounded, while Dr. Huntington listed them at "12 killed and 90 wounded." Two color bearers of the 48th Illinois were killed by landmines.[61]

After the victory, Sherman boarded a gunboat to visit Fort McAllister with his victorious troops. After dining with Hazen in a nearby house, Sherman

---

58 "From the Diary of a Private, Operations in the Capture of Fort McAllister Slaughter of Union Soldiers by Buried Torpedoes," *New York Times*, June 11, 1893.

59 Report of Maj. Gen. O. Howard, U.S. Army of the Tennessee, Savannah, Georgia, December 28, 1864, *OR* vol. 44, 72; Fort McAllister, historical marker, Bryan County, Georgia, Georgia Historical Commission/Department of Natural Resources; Sherman, *Memoirs*, 199.

60 Durham, *Guardian of Savannah*, 169.

61 Report of Asst. Surg. David L. Huntington, U.S. Army, Acting Medical Director, Medical Director's Office, HDQRS, Department and Army of the Tennessee, Savannah, Georgia, December 25, 1864, *OR* vol. 44, 79; Report of Brig. Gen. William B. Hazen, January 9, 1865, ibid., 111; Report of Colonel John Oliver, Fifteenth Michigan, Infantry, commanding Third Brigade, Savannah, Georgia, January 6, 1865, ibid., 122.

walked to the fort. A sentinel warned him to be careful, for the ground outside the fort was "full of torpedoes." During Sherman's walk a torpedo exploded, he later wrote, "tearing to pieces a poor fellow who was hunting for a dead comrade."[62]

Angered once again by the enemy's use of landmines, Sherman ordered Confederate prisoners to remove them. Engineers, who probably planted the landmines, were at times tapped for this potentially deadly duty. Under the supervision of Union officers, a 16-man detail of POWs removed the unexploded anti-personnel devices. A Union veteran recalled watching Confederates removing mines "on their knees until long into the night."[63]

Although the War Department had ordered prisoners to be treated humanely, Sherman believed that he was protecting his men by using POWs to clear landmines. "It was, I think, a much better show of tenderness for me to have the enemy do this work than to subject my own soldiers to so frightful a risk," he noted. The Confederates, Sherman reasoned, knew where the torpedoes were buried. "The fact that every torpedo was safely removed," he wrote, "showed my reasoning was right." Sherman continued to justify his actions by writing that "[p]risoners should be protected, but mercy is not a legitimate attribute of war. Men go to war to kill or get killed if necessary and should expect no tenderness."[64]

With Fort McAllister captured and a supply line opened, Sherman prepared for the siege and capture of Savannah. Instead of making a determined stand, however, General Hardee evacuated the city by marching across the Savannah River on a pontoon brigade on December 19-20. On December 23, Sherman sent a telegram to President Lincoln: "I beg to present you, as a Christmas gift, the city of Savannah, with 150 guns and plenty of ammunition; also, about 25,000 bales of cotton."[65]

---

62 Sherman, *Memoirs*, 199.

63 Confederate landmines marker, south side of Fort McAllister, erected in 1963 by the Georgia Historical Commission; Lloyd Lewis, *Sherman: Fighting Prophet* (New York, NY, 1932), 462; "Missouri Batteryman tells of the Capture of Fort McAllister," *National Tribune*, February 20, 1896.

64 Lewis, *Sherman: Fighting Prophet*, 462.

65 Noah Andre Trudeau, *Southern Storm: Sherman's March to the Sea* (New York, NY, 2008), 508.

About five weeks later Sherman would once again be on the march, this time north into the Carolinas, where he would once again encounter more "infernal devices."

Chapter 5

1864–65: Desperation

On January 28, 1865, blue-clad soldiers led by Maj. Gen. William Sherman crossed the Savannah River near Sister's Ferry and entered South Carolina. The recent capture of Savannah and Fort McAllister had raised his soldiers' spirits and boosted morale across the Northern states. Sherman's veterans in the right wing of his army were marching along back roads in the first state to secede from the Union. As it always did, danger lurked ahead.

Before long, wary soldiers wise to the tactics of their enemy spotted small wooden pegs in the road—a telltale sign of landmines just beneath the surface. Unsure of the route Sherman's advance would assume, Confederates had left the markers in place in case they wanted to retrieve the mines for use elsewhere. Ironically, the act may have saved the lives of Yankees. "Had it not been that the enemy had marked the localities where they had planted their destructive engines of—we cannot call it 'civilized'—warfare, it would have been very difficult to have removed them with safety from our path," wrote a *New York Times* correspondent from South Carolina.[1]

Near a bridge built over the Savannah River by Federal engineers, the rumble of supply wagons and artillery caissons was occasionally interspersed

1 "Operations in the Interior. Additional Particulars of the Movement," *New York Times*, February 17, 1865, 1.

with the distinctive heavy boom of mines exploding in the distance. The entire area was infested. Around "forty of these villainous inventions were discovered in the mud" and were removed by Union sappers without incident, explained a reporter. Some concealed underwater near where the line of march crossed the banks may have drifted downstream during recent flooding and entangled themselves in timber and branches. Though out of position, the waterborne weapons were still deadly.[2]

"The frequent explosion of torpedoes, concealed under the water and drifting, subjected the working parties to considerable danger, and several men were killed and wounded by these infernal machines," complained Bvt. Maj. Gen. Jefferson C. Davis, the Union's XIV Corps commander. According to the *New York Times*, the killed and wounded were from Bvt. Maj. Gen. Alpheus Williams' XX Corps, which had "to circumvent a five mile long swamp" and take a road well known to Confederate soldiers. Because it was the only open route for the Federals, Confederates "filled the road with torpedoes."[3]

Union troops, rank and file and officers alike, could not conceal their anger about mine warfare. "Planting torpedoes for the defense of a position is legitimate warfare," argued Maj. Gen. Henry Slocum, "but our soldiers regarded the act of placing them in a highway . . . as something akin to poisoning a stream of water; it is not recognized as fair or legitimate warfare." The killing and wounding of soldiers by these devices was "unfortunate for that section of the State," Slocum added. Confederate Brig. Gen. Alfred Iverson, on duty in North Carolina during the closing months of the war, confirmed the XX Corps torpedo casualties at Sister's Ferry a few days later.[4]

As Sherman's juggernaut carved a path through South Carolina, the demoralized and heavily outnumbered Confederates opposing them proved no

---

2 Ibid. The article was written by the *New York Times* correspondent reporting from Sister's Ferry on February 4, 1865.

3 Report of Bvt. Maj. Gen. Jefferson C. Davis, U.S. Army, Commanding Fourteenth Army Corps, of Operations, January 20–March 23, Headquarters, Fourteenth Army Corps, Goldsborough, North Carolina, March 28, 1865, *OR* vol. 47, pt. 1, 429; "Operations in the Interior," 1.

4 Henry W. Slocum, Major-General, "Sherman's March From Savannah to Bentonville," in *Battles and Leaders of the Civil War*, vol. 4, 684; Alfred Iverson, Brigadier-General, to Lieutenant Hudson, Acting Assistant Adjutant-General, February 1, 1865, *OR* vol. 47, pt. 2, 1,077.

match for the Yankees. Initially, there was little to stop Sherman besides local militia forces of old men, young boys, and injured veterans.[5]

In early February, when Sherman's left wing crossed the Savannah River into South Carolina, several soldiers were killed and injured by landmines planted in the road near the landing area. Cavalry commander Maj. Gen. Judson Kilpatrick was livid at their use and swore to soldiers near the blast site, "There'll be damn little for you infantrymen to destroy after I've passed through that hell-hole of secession." Within hours of crossing into the Palmetto State the Union army began wreaking havoc. Houses, barns, and mills were burned and plundered, some in direct retaliation for the use of landmines. "Indeed, our columns were not fairly upon the 'sacred soil' of South Carolina," reported a New York newspaper correspondent,

> before Sherman's veterans began to ply the torch, and plunder right and left as they rushed along, seeming, as it were, to feel instinctively that the generous treatment accorded Georgia—a State that seceded with evident reluctance, was ill-bestowed upon South Carolina, where the monster of Secession first drew the breath of life.[6]

Although it may not have seemed like it to Sherman's men, the Confederate Army Torpedo Bureau's situation by this stage of the war was especially dire. In addition to a lack of trained men and fighting materials, it faced significant logistical challenges. Captain Garnett McMillian, the commander of the torpedo men in the Carolinas, struggled to keep pace with what was becoming a a relatively rapid Confederate retreat. Transportation for his landmine supplies was spotty at best, hampering operations and limiting opportunities for the deployment of mines. The captain explained the frustrating situation he faced in a letter he penned to Gabriel Rains.

On February 12, Southern cavalry commander Lt. Gen. Wade Hampton ordered Captain McMillian to mine a causeway 11 miles outside Columbia, the state's capital. The route was bordered by an "impenetrable morass" that channeled the approach of the enemy and thus made it ideal for mine

---

5 G. T. Beauregard, Rock Hill, South Carolina, to General R. E. Lee, Richmond, February 21, 1865, *OR* vol. 47, pt. 2, 1,238.

6 Lewis, *Sherman: Fighting Prophet*, 489; "Retribution," *Burlington* (VT) *Daily Times*, March 22, 1864.

deployment. "With all possible dispatch," McMillian recalled, "I made ready for the work."[7]

At 7:00 a.m. the next morning, McMillian waited for transportation to arrive to carry him and his materials to the causeway. Hours passed, and his promised ride failed to appear. About noon, McMillian was loaned a "lady's ambulance" to transport his deadly cargo to its destination. By the time he arrived near the causeway, however, the target was in Federal control. The mines "fell into the hands of the enemy," admitted the frustrated officer. An equally exasperated Rains blamed the Confederate quartermaster's incompetence for "not furnishing transportation." General Hampton "is now wanting me with him," McMillian complained in the letter to Rains, "but nothing can be done without means." After this episode, Hampton downplayed the impact the landmines would have had at the causeway. "The shells there would have impeded [the Federals'] march on that road," he rationalized, "but would not have seriously delayed them."[8]

The devastation of the state was punctuated with the burning of much of Columbia on February 17, 1864, an event that remains controversial. Union troops soon occupied all of the state's major cities, including Charleston, where General Beauregard issued orders on February 15 to evacuate the city's remaining troops and supplies. Charleston had withstood assaults from the sea for years, but a major inland threat proved too much. Once the city fell, the victorious Union troops found equipment used in mine manufacturing and assembly in private homes. Federals discovered 13 mines in one house and 32 in another, as well as "all the conveniences for making more." Rains and his teams did not need a factory to manufacture their "infernal machines," but the discovery of mine-making supplies inside private dwellings served to further enrage the enemy. "South Carolina has since paid the penalty of a resort to this low and mean spirit of warfare," was how one Federal officer put it.[9]

---

7 Garnett McMillian, Captain in Charge of Subterra Defense, Charlotte, North Carolina, to Brig. Gen. G. J. Rains, Chief Torpedo Bureau, March 1, 1865, *OR* vol. 47, pt. 2, 1,299.

8 McMillian to Rains, March 1, 1865, *OR* vol. 47, pt. 2, 1,299; Wade Hampton, Lieutenant-General From Headquarters Cavalry, April 1, 1865, ibid., 1,300.

9 Sherman was blamed for burning a large swath of Columbia, but it is apparent from sources that have appeared since the war that there were multiple causes for the conflagration. Beauregard to Lee, February 21, 1865, ibid., 1,238; Snyder, "Torpedoes for the Confederacy," 42; Report of Bvt. Maj. Gen. Jefferson C. Davis, March 28, 1865, ibid., pt. 1, 429.

Fort Fisher: Cut off in North Carolina

A few weeks after the capture of Fort McAllister, preparations began for an ocean-based attack against Fort Fisher, the South's most formidable coastal bastion. Fort Fisher guarded Wilmington, North Carolina, the Confederacy's only open port on the Atlantic and a favorite harbor for blockade-runners traveling from Europe, Canada, and the Caribbean islands. These ships smuggled in military supplies and other necessities to a deprived Confederacy and departed with cotton and tobacco for European markets. The capture of Wilmington would cripple the already teetering Confederacy and speed the demise of the Southern war effort.[10]

Fort Fisher's importance to the Confederacy was highlighted in a confidential message from U.S. Assistant Secretary of War Charles A. Dana to Lt. Gen. Ulysses Grant regarding what he had been told by a secret agent. "If Fort Fisher fell," Dana explained, he was advised

> it would be their [the enemy's] policy to hold Wilmington at all hazards, even if they have to give up both Petersburg and Richmond, for Wilmington was of more importance to them than the other places. It would be hard even to live without Wilmington. Richmond was not necessary to Wilmington, but Wilmington was indispensable to Richmond. These were his very words, but whether they were his own conclusions or the substance of information received from Richmond, my informant can't tell.[11]

Fort Fisher was commanded by Col. William Lamb, who had arrived there in the summer of 1862. Since that time, Lamb had significantly strengthened the garrison's defenses, overseeing the construction of a nine-foot palisade backed by a series of 15 mounds that hosted 25 large coastal guns. The main defensive fortifications were shaped in an upside down "L" pattern, with a towering 43-foot mound called the "Northeast Bastion" at the angle. The massive sand fort ran along the ocean and land face near the end of a narrow peninsula between the sea and the Cape Fear River.

10 Chris E. Fonvielle, Jr., *The Wilmington Campaign: Last Rays of Departing Hope* (Savas Publishing, 1997), 615. Fonvielle's award-winning work remains the definitive study of Fort Fisher and the later fall of the city of Wilmington.

11 C. A. Dana, Assistant Secretary of War, to Lieutenant-General Grant, "Confidential. Washington, January 18, 1865," *OR* 46, pt. 2, 170.

Lamb ordered torpedo specialists from Richmond to install a command-detonated minefield of 24 improvised water torpedoes in front of the land-face palisade. The weapons covered an area from the river to the beach along the northeast bastion side, the most likely location for an ocean-based Federal assault. The torpedoes, connected to galvanic batteries by a network of underground wires, could be detonated from inside the fort.[12]

After the fort fell, Cyrus B. Comstock, a Union lieutenant colonel and chief engineer, provided a detailed description of the minefield in a letter to Brig. Gen. Richard B. Delafield:

> [The network contained] three sets of double wires, each wire apparently intended to fire five or more torpedoes. A single wire running to a group of torpedoes was branched to each, in the expectation, apparently, of having battery power sufficient to fire the whole group, and, in addition, some of these groups were connected with each other, thus giving (with sufficient battery power) a choice of positions in the work to fire the group from.[13]

Union intelligence reports placed the landmine field about 200 yards in front of the palisade. The torpedo field, which Comstock described as an "elaborate system," included 20-inch shells, large boiler-iron cylinders, and buoy-shaped vessels. Comstock's information was right. The Confederates "received a supply of wire, acids, battery, and electrical appliances through the blockade from Europe," with which they intended to construct mines to seed all around the fort. The result was a large minefield complex, explained R. O. Crowley, an electrician with the Torpedo Bureau. "Among the apparatus received from Europe was a lot of Wheatstone exploders and Abels fuses." Crowley continued:

> With these we hastily prepared several copper tanks of a capacity of one hundred pounds of powder, planted them about three feet deep in the sand on the land side of the

---

12 Specifically, Civil War torpedo experts believe that the Fort Fisher landmines were Type 19s, converted Type 6-size water torpedoes. Kochan and Wideman, *Civil War Torpedoes*, 187.

13 Lieutenant Colonel, Brevet Brigadier-General, and Chief Engineer Cyrus B. Comstock, U.S.A., Headquarters U.S. Forces, Fort Fisher, to General Richard B. Delafield, Chief of Engineers, January 23, 1865, *OR* Series 2, vol. 46, pt. 2, 215-217.

fort, about three hundred yards in front, and led the wires in trenches to the traverses of the fort. This was done in expectation of an assault by the Federal land forces.[14]

Part of the defense included "a torpedo right on the bar, the entrance there being very narrow." However, the arrival of Union vessels forced the Confederates to abandon this plan.[15]

Lamb's defensive improvements were strong enough to repulse land- and sea-based artillery assaults from December 23–27, 1864. The Federals even detonated an explosives-laden ship near the fort an effort to damage the large sand walls and to act as a signal for the start of a massive naval bombardment. The creative, if ineffective, stunt was coordinated by Maj. Gen. Benjamin Butler and Adm. David Porter, but the subsequent amphibious assault was unsuccessful despite being supported by one of the war's heaviest bombardments.

The Federals launched a second and final attack on January 13. The land and naval assaults comprising the Second Battle of Fort Fisher made it the largest combined sea and land engagement of the Civil War. General Grant appointed Maj. Gen. Alfred Howe Terry—commander of the XXIV Corps of the Army of the James—to replace the discredited Butler. Cooperating fully with Terry, Porter ordered a two-and-a-half-day naval bombardment on the land- and sea-face fortifications. He focused especially on the land-face artillery positions on the parapets and palisade wall.[16]

Union warships rained artillery shells across Fisher's land front. Once the naval shelling ended on January 15, a land assault by 3,300 soldiers against the weakened land-face fortifications got underway. The partial destruction of the palisade, including nearly all its guns, put more pressure on the minefield to serve its intended purpose. During the assault, however, the landmines failed to explode. The giant naval shells had cut the wires of the command-detonated mines. The fort's electrician frantically tried to detonate the underground explosives, to no avail. "[I]t was discovered that the heavy shells, plowing up

14 Ibid.; R. O. Crowley, Formerly Electrician of the Torpedo Division, C.S.N., "The Confederate Torpedo Service," *Century Magazine* (June 1898), vol. 56, 295.

15 Crowley, "The Confederate Torpedo Service," 295.

16 The day before, on January 12, nearly 60 warships of Admiral David D. Porter's flotilla set out from Beaufort, North Carolina, to Fort Fisher and prepared to launch a massive bombardment.

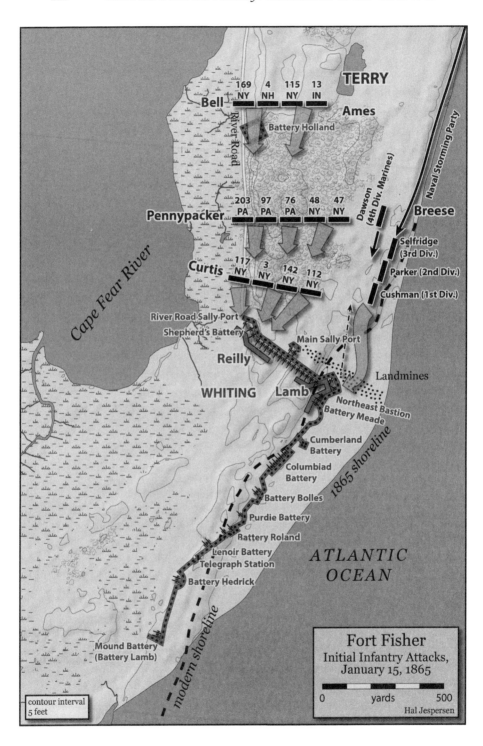

TERRY

169 4 115 13
NY NH NY IN

Bell

Ames

River Road

Battery Holland

Naval Storming Party

203 97 76 48 47
PA PA PA NY NY

Pennypacker

Dawson (4th Div. Marines)

Breese

117 3 142 112
NY NY NY NY

Curtis

Selfridge (3rd Div.)

Parker (2nd Div.)

Cushman (1st Div.)

Cape Fear River

River Road Sally Port

Shepherd's Battery

Main Sally Port

Reilly

Landmines

WHITING   Lamb

Northeast Bastion

Battery Meade

Cumberland Battery

Columbiad Battery

1865 shoreline

Battery Bolles

Purdie Battery

Battery Roland

Lenoir Battery

Telegraph Station

ATLANTIC OCEAN

Battery Hedrick

Mound Battery
(Battery Lamb)

modern shoreline

Fort Fisher
Initial Infantry Attacks,
January 15, 1865

0   yards   500

Hal Jespersen

contour interval
5 feet

the ground in front, had utterly destroyed all our wires," lamented Crowley some years later, "so that the plan of exploding the 100-pound tanks on shore failed entirely." At the time, however, the defenders were unaware of the damage to the minefield.[17]

"The accidental cutting of four out of the six wires leading from the work was a piece of good fortune, which probably saved us from severe loss and demoralization," Comstock recalled. In part because of the malfunctioning minefield on the landward side, Union forces reached the fort and, after a few hours of heavy fighting, captured it.[18]

"We have no heart to enter late details," a North Carolina newspaper reported afterward, "nor to comment on this disastrous defeat." Northern news sources were more than happy to comment on the victory, which they rightly hailed as one of the greatest of the war. "Glorious!" and "Fort Fisher Carried by Storm!!" trumpeted the front page of the *Washington Evening Star*.[19]

The morning after the surrender, Northern victory celebrations were tempered by a massive explosion in Fort Fisher's magazine. "A volume of smoke and sand rose fifty feet in the air, enveloping and hiding from view the whole of the immense work for four or five minutes," the *New York Times* reported on January 19. "It was at once apparent that the magazine had exploded, and that it must have been accompanied with great loss of life." Nearly 200 men on both sides were killed in the explosion. Some thought the blast was caused by a Confederate torpedo, but an official inquiry blamed careless Union soldiers, sailors, and marines. Apparently drunk, some of them fired their weapons while carrying torches through the magazine, a deadly combination that triggered the explosion.[20]

During the weeks that followed the loss of Fort Fisher, Confederate garrisons in the Cape Fear coastal region abandoned their posts, thus shutting down the final outside delivery channel available to Southern forces defending

---

17 Crowley, "The Confederate Torpedo Service," 295.

18 Comstock, to Delafield, January 23, 1865, *OR* Series 2, vol. 46, pt. 2, 215-217; also see *ORN* 11, 591. The latter half of Comstock's letter is a sketch of the landmine with a description of the sketch.

19 *The Confederate* (Raleigh, NC), January 25, 1865; *Washington Evening Star*, January 17, 1865.

20 Nathaniel J. Burton, "A Discourse Delivered January 29th, 1865 in Memory of Robert H. Gillette," 1865, 15.

Richmond and Petersburg. On February 22, more than a month after occupying Fort Fisher, Union forces marched unchallenged into Wilmington after crossing the Cape Fear River and capturing Fort Anderson. Confederates retreated inland to reorganize and to continue defending what was left of Southern-controlled North Carolina.

As losses mounted across the Confederacy, embattled state and regional leaders struggled to retain their control. The desperate Confederates increasingly resorted to more improvised defensive tactics, with mines playing an important role.

Mobile Bay: Damn the Torpedoes!

With the capture of New Orleans by Federal forces in the spring 1862, nearby Mobile, Alabama, became the hub for many Confederate blockade-runners operating out of the Caribbean. The city was the primary seaport for cotton exports, which provided critical financing for the Southern war effort. It was also in the cross hairs of the Union Army and Navy.

The Confederates significantly strengthened Mobile's defenses in 1862. Fifteen redoubts strung out within an unbroken line of earthworks were built west of the city. In July 1863, after the fall of Vicksburg and Port Hudson, another line of fortifications was constructed west of Mobile. To the east, 5,000 Confederates were posted across Mobile Bay and the Blakeley River at Spanish Fort and Fort Blakeley, with the river itself acting as a natural barrier.

On February 15, 1864, Gabriel Rains was ordered to Mobile by Secretary of War James Seddon and Gen. Joseph E. Johnston. There, he would serve under Lt. Gen. Leonidas Polk, his former classmate at West Point and the commander of the Department of Alabama and East Mississippi. Rains was assigned to supervise deployment of naval mines in Mobile Bay and to make the bay impenetrable to Union vessels.[21]

Rains's daunting task was made all the more difficult by a lack of universal support. Officers in Mobile, especially local commander Maj. Gen. Dabney H. Maury (the nephew of naval mine expert Matthew Maury) remained

---

21 Special Orders No. 38, February 15,1865, *OR* vol. 32, pt. 2, 738; Gabriel J. Rains to James A. Seddon, August 15, 1864, *OR* vol. 39, pt. 1, 433-434; Richard Lancelot Maury, *A Brief Sketch of the Work of Matthew Fontaine Maury During the War, 1861-1865* (Richmond, VA, 1915), 28.

A Confederate Fretwell-Singer naval mine, on display at the Fort Morgan State Historic Site Museum. *Author*

unconvinced of his mine warfare skills and perhaps even of the value of the deadly devices themselves. Maury's negative impression of Rains had been formed during Rains's brief and rather hectic sojourn there in the summer of 1863 before he was quickly called away to Charleston. Rains, who had arrived exhausted and in desperate need of men and resources, had had little time to accomplish anything and had come across as something of a scattered madman. "General Rains has gone away with his gimcracks: he was not at all practical; everything I received from him was vague and visionary," Maury had complained that summer to Joe Johnston. "He was here about a week and did not commence work." And so it was that when Rains arrived a second time, Maury greeted the North Carolinian's arrival with open skepticism.[22]

Opposing Rains and the defenders of Mobile was Adm. David G. Farragut, the commander of the West Gulf Blockading Squadron. Farragut's orders were clear: conquer Mobile Bay. Praised for his capture of New Orleans and other exploits along the Mississippi River, Farragut was a popular selection to take

22 Report from Maj. Gen. Dabney H. Maury, Headquarters of the Gulf Mobile, Alabama, to General Joseph E. Johnston, August 23, 1863, *OR* vol. 26, pt. 2, 180. Dabney was the nephew of renowned electronic torpedo perfectionist Commodore Matthew Fontaine Maury, who had developed and implemented the first Confederate water torpedoes in 1861 before heading to London.

another Confederate seaport. His force included 14 wooden ships and the ironclads *Chickasaw, Manhattan, Winnebago* and *Tecumseh*.[23]

By August 1864, Mobile Bay's defenses were in good shape, strengthened by hundreds of Fretwell-Singer naval mines manufactured in Mobile and placed in the mouth of the bay by an Army Torpedo Bureau detachment stationed at Fort Morgan. In addition to naval torpedoes, an attacking force would have to contend with Fort Morgan's big guns and a small but determined naval squadron of three gunboats and the formidable ironclad CSS *Tennessee*.[24]

The Confederate strategy was simple: Defend incursions by Union vessels at the mouth of the bay with naval mines and the firepower from Fort Gaines on the western side of the mouth, and Fort Morgan on the eastern side. Forty-six mines, more dependable than those placed in the water in 1862, were deployed on the western side of the mouth of the bay.[25] Union ships passing between the minefield and Fort Morgan would be exposed to artillery fire at short range from a pair of 7-inch Brooke rifles, six 4.10-inch rifles, several 32-pounders, and rifle fire from sharpshooters.[26]

While planning was underway for the attack, Union commanders discovered what they believed to be a crucial tactical mistake in the harbor's defenses. Union personnel watched a Confederate vessel passing near Fort Morgan. A channel, marked by a buoy 160 yards from the Fort Morgan shore, had been left open for the CSS *Tennessee* and other Confederate ships.[27]

The Confederates believed Fort Morgan's guns could repel any ships attempting to pass this opening. Farragut's long experience against fixed positions informed him otherwise. Sensing an opportunity, the admiral ordered his captains to prepare for action. Before getting underway early on the morning of August 5, he instructed that smaller wooden vessels be fastened to larger

---

23 Congress created three new naval ranks, including full admiral, especially for David G. Farragut, the son of Jorge Farragut, a Spanish-born mariner and hero of the American Revolution.

24 "Report of Submarine Operations, February, 1865, at Mobile" and "Property Return of Submarine Defenses of Mobile, Jan.-Feb., 1865," in Records of the Confederate Engineers, Record Group 109, National Archives; Perry, *Infernal Machines*, 184-185.

25 Craig L. Symonds, *The Civil War at Sea* (Oxford, England, 2012), 181.

26 Dabney H. Maury, Major-General, Commanding, Headquarters District of the Gulf, Mobile, Alabama, September 26, 1864, *OR* 39, pt. 2, 786.

27 Ibid.

wooden ships so the latter could serve as a protection from Fort Morgan's artillery. He also ordered the ironclads to take up a position on the starboard side of the attacking columns closest to Fort Morgan on the eastern side of the channel, i.e., *away* from Confederate naval torpedo defenses. According to a Confederate report, the attacking Union ships "passed within 800 yards of Fort Morgan." The well-planned naval assault, however, did not quite go as Farragut had planned.[28]

The ironclad USS *Tecumseh* led the Union fleet into battle about 7:00 a.m. on the channel's eastern edge. The warship was cruising northwest of Fort Morgan intent on engaging the CSS *Tennessee* when it was rocked stem to stern by a massive explosion. Unbeknownst to the *Tecumseh's* crew, the powerful ironclad had struck a Fretwell-Singer mine. "She was blown clear of the water and in the air quivered like a thing of life," recalled a shocked 22nd Alabama soldier watching from Fort Morgan. "Then, in a bare second, it seemed, she disappeared beneath the waters forever." Witnesses saw about a dozen survivors where the ironclad had gone down. In midst of the battle, several vessels rushed to pluck them from the water. It was, admitted the Alabamian, "one of the bravest things I believe that ever characterized a naval fight." Up until that time no one believed a simple naval mine could sink an ironclad. The *Tecumseh's* fate ended that notion when she quickly went to the bottom of Mobile Bay with nearly all of her 120 sailors. It was the deadliest naval mine incident of the entire war.[29]

Among those who died in the disaster was the vessel's 51-year-old captain, Tunis Craven, described by one who knew him as a "brave, true-hearted and most skillful officer." Craven and *Tecumseh* pilot John Collins were both in the conning tower above the turret, and both realized almost immediately that the warship was sinking. The only way out was a narrow opening. Both reached it at the same time. Craven turned to Collins and offered, "You first, sir." The pilot

28 F. S. Barrett, Second Lieutenant, in charge of Torpedoes, to Lieut. J. T. E. Andrews, Acting Assistant Adjutant-General, Mobile, August 20, 1864, *OR* 39, pt., 2, 785-786.

29 F. S. Barrett, Second Lieutenant, in charge of Torpedoes, to Lieut. J. T. E. Andrews, Acting Assistant Adjutant-General, Mobile, August 20, 1864, ibid., 785-786; *National Tribune*, February 23, 1911; Crowley, "The Confederate Torpedo Service," 300. By way of comparison, the timer bomb explosion at City Point on August 9, 1864, killed 58 Union sailors, soldiers, and staff; "The Naval Battle of Mobile Bay," *Montgomery Advertiser* (Montgomery, AL), January 16, 1905.

slipped through and escaped, but just as he exited, the vessel fell away under him, taking Craven with it.

"Our gallant captain's intention was to butt the ram [*Tennessee*] and fire the two solid shot at the same time," survivors said in a statement published in a Boston newspaper, "but [before] he could give the order to revolve the turret, a torpedo or infernal machine exploded under us, causing the water to rush up into the berth-deck and turret chamber, where nothing but confusion and despair reigned."[30]

Some speculated the ironclad had been sunk by the explosion of its own spar torpedo, but that suggestion was quickly dismissed. Rains reported to President Davis that the *Tecumseh* "was sunk by a torpedo," and there was "no evidence that her magazine was penetrated" by cannon fire. Confederate Secretary of the Navy Stephen Mallory had "no doubt she [*Tecumseh*] was sunk by a torpedo." Farragut believed the same thing.[31]

Torpedo or not, the Union admiral disregarded the now very obvious and deadly risk and ordered his remaining flotilla into the bay with words that would be forever famous: "Damn the torpedoes, full steam ahead!" he is said to have yelled from the deck of his wooden flagship USS *Hartford*. A little more than three hours later, the Union ships had taken Mobile Bay, the ironclad *Tennessee* was captured, and the battle was at an end. Beleaguered Fort Morgan would surrender on August 23 after a two-week siege. The city itself would not fall until April 12, 1865—three days after General Lee's surrender in Virginia.[32]

On August 6, Farragut issued General Order 12 thanking his officers and crewmen for their gallantry in the recent fighting. The order read as follows:

It has never been his good fortune to see men do their duty with more courage and cheerfulness; for, although they knew that the enemy was prepared with all devilish means for our destruction, and though they witnessed the almost instantaneous annihilation of our gallant campaign in the *Tecumseh* by a torpedo and the slaughter of

30 *Liberator* (Boston, MA), September 9, 1864.

31 G. J. Rains, Brigadier-General, Superintendent, Torpedo Bureau, Richmond, Virginia, October 21, 1864, *OR* vol. 39, pt. 1, 431-432. S. R. Mallory, Secretary of the Navy, Navy Department, October 26, 1864, *OR* vol. 39, pt. 1, 432; General Order No. 12, issued by Admiral Farragut from his flagship on August 6, 1864.

32 Union losses numbered two ships, about 166 killed (between 83 and 93 on the sunken *Tecumseh*), 170 wounded, and four captured. Confederate losses were 12 killed, 20 wounded, and Adm. Franklin Buchanan, of the CSS *Tennessee*, captured.

their friends, mess-mates and gun-mates on our decks, still there were no evidences of hesitation in following their Commander-in-Chief through the line of torpedoes and obstructions, of which, we knew nothing except from the exaggerations of the enemy, who had given out "That we should all be blown up as certainly as we attempted to enter."[33]

As was to be expected, there was plenty of blame and finger-pointing on the Confederate side as to who was responsible for the catastrophe. In his after-action report, Lt. F. S. Barrett, in charge of the deployed naval mines for the Mobile Bay command, described what he believed to have been a mortal blunder and the adverse results that followed. "By the course they [Union ships] took running in," he began, "it is evident they were well informed as to the location of the torpedoes we had planted, as they kept well in on the east side of the channel where we had not, that part being left open by orders of the Chief of Engineer Department for our steamers to pass in and out. . . . The enemy evidently," Barrett continued:

by observing blockade steamers running in (one having done so after daylight that morning), were well informed of this open space in the channel free from torpedoes, as they steamed in through it from 200 to 300 yards farther to the eastward than vessels usually do in coming in from the outer bay. Had their object been not to avoid them they certainly would not have exposed themselves to the fire of Fort Morgan at such short range, when by keeping farther to the westward, with the same depth of water, they would have avoided the short range of its guns and necessarily the accuracy of its gunners.[34]

After the Union victory, Gabriel Rains reported his discontent with the Mobile officers and their obstruction of the implementation of his torpedo plan for Mobile Bay. "I had sixty-seven torpedoes planted where this one [the one that sank the *Tecumseh*] acted . . . to close the main channel," he complained to Secretary of War Seddon, "[b]ut my instructions and wishes were frustrated after I left, the place left open and the enemy made use of it." Rains, perhaps feeling some vulnerability, vigorously pointed out that his previous use of mines in Charleston Harbor had kept that important city protected. Union forces

---

33 General Orders NO. 12, General Order of Rear Admiral Farragut, U.S. Navy. U.S. Flagship Hartford, Mobile Bay, August 6, 1864.

34 Barrett to Andrews, August 20, 1864, *OR* vol. 39, pt. 2, 785-786.

could not pass through mines, he insisted, and they were also "unable to remove them."[35]

With Fort Morgan's surrender 18 days after the Battle of Mobile Bay, the Union had halted blockade-running into and out of Mobile, relieved the exhausted blockading fleet from its tiresome duty, and prepared the way for operations against the city of Mobile itself, which would be undertaken early in 1865.[36]

Mobile: "A Fiery Path"

The loss of the bay and access to the sea made it clear to the defenders that Mobile itself would soon be next. Confederates there under Lt. Col. Victor von Sheliha, Dabney Maury's chief engineer in the Gulf District, prepared to repel a land attack. Throughout 1864, von Scheliha, a native of Berlin, Prussia (modern-day Germany) supervised construction of imposing fortifications around the city, ensuring that all routes were obstructed and covered by artillery fire. He also coordinated the deployment of mines on land and in the waterways that could be used as avenues of attack by supporting naval forces.

Von Scheliha's efforts were remarkable considering he lacked almost everything he needed to mount a successful defense. Equipment of all sorts was in short supply, and consistent leadership was wanting. Defenders even lacked gunpowder for mines, which delayed their deployment. Most importantly, his undermanned labor force was exhausted and demoralized. On November 27, 1864, three months after the bay fell to Farragut, von Scheliha wrote to the Engineer Office in Mobile that "precious time is being lost for want of labor."[37]

The Confederate garrison suffered from a high desertion rate, especially among its soldiers from Alabama. The situation was so bad that Maj. Gen. Maury preferred non-Alabama troops. "It seems to me important that no more Alabama troops be sent here if others can be found equally available," he had advised Gen. Joseph E. Johnston as early as August 1863. "The weak-kneed influence is now working in the two regiments which now make my garrison,

35 General Rains, Communication with James Seddon, August 15, 1864, *OR* vol. 39, 433.

36 For a general history of the Mobile operations, see Paul Brueske, *The Last Siege: The Mobile Campaign, Alabama 1865* (Casemate, 2018).

37 Y. Sheliha, Lieutenant-Colonel and Chief Engineer, District of the Gulf, to Engineer Office, Mobile, Alabama, November 27, 1864, *OR* vol. 45, pt. 1, 1,249-1,250.

and in the past two or three nights more than twenty desertions have occurred, due, I believe, to the despondency of their friends at home."[38]

Slave labor was also in short supply. Alabama Governor John Gill Shorter wrote to sheriffs and jailors in the state requesting their assistance in returning runaway slaves to fortification construction sites. Frustrated by these and other mounting concerns, an exhausted von Scheliha submitted his resignation in August of 1864. It was refused.[39]

To counter Union naval support for impending Federal land operations, naval mines were planted by Confederates in the inlets and bayous of Mobile by October 1864. Seventeen 30-pound Singer torpedoes, for example, were anchored in the channel of Burns Bayou.[40]

In late December, the Confederate weekly operations report for the defense of Mobile noted that 10 Fretwell-Singer torpedoes were laid in 12 to 20 feet of water along the eastern bank of Bay Minette, with "four Rains torpedoes continuing the line." Additionally, naval mines were scattered from small boats in the Tombigbee River just above its junction with the Alabama River. Finally, the "floating batteries *Huntsville* and *Tuscaloosa* [were] scuttled to obstruct the Spanish River." Union naval forces attempted to neutralize Confederate naval mines with various counter-mining operations.[41]

Mobile had long been considered a major Union target. Luckily for the city, the military situation was not advantageous for an attack until early 1865. By

---

38 Maury to Johnston, August 23, 1863, *OR* vol. 26, pt. 2, 179.

39 Caldwell Delaney, *Confederate Mobile* (Mobile, AL, 1971), 78. Ultimately, at the end of the year von Scheliha took six months leave to return to Bohemia to recuperate from sickness, and "the work of supervising the torpedo defenses at Mobile fell to Lieutenant J. T. E. Andrews." See Scheliha to Engineer Bureau, August 16, August 18, August 20, 1864, in Vol. 7, Letters Received, Confederate Engineers, Scheliha, Military Service Record in Carded Files; Perry, *Infernal Machines*, 184.

40 Weekly report of operations for the defense of Mobile, Alabama, during the week ending October 15, 1864, Engineer Office, Mobile, Alabama, submitted by Saml. H. Lockettt, Colonel and Chief Engineer Department of Alabama, Mississippi, and East Louisiana, *OR* vol. 39, pt. 3, 841.

41 Weekly reports of operations for the defense of Mobile during the week ending December 24, 1864, ibid., Vol. 45, pt. 2, 735; Thatcher to Welles, April 15, 1865, *ORN* vol. 22, 95-96. For example, a Union report dated March 29, 1865, regarding the naval mine clearance operations in the waters near Spanish Fort stated: "Last night's work developed a large number of infernal machines (submerged), and there are probably many more between us and the enemy's works." Ibid., vol. 49, pt. 1, 730.

then, Richmond and Petersburg had been under siege for six months and their defenders were barely hanging on. In the Western Theater, Confederates were still reeling from the loss of Mobile Bay and the catastrophic defeat of John Bell Hood's Army of Tennessee at Franklin and Nashville in late 1864. Atlanta had fallen, Georgia had been ravaged, and Savannah was in Union hands. By the turn of the calendar to 1865, Mobile's defenses had been strengthened by almost 10,000 soldiers who had once served in Hood's army.

On January 18, U. S. Grant ordered Maj. Gen. Edward R. S. Canby, commander of the Army of West Mississippi, to capture Mobile, Selma, and Montgomery, Alabama. Grant sent troops to help Canby, and who by March had 45,000 men operating on the gulf coast.

Although plagued by desertions and a shortage of labor, Confederates managed to construct three lines of defensive fortifications dotted with some 300 heavy artillery pieces on the western side of Mobile Bay. In an effort to avoid them, Canby decided to attack Mobile from the bay's eastern shore. His goal was to capture Spanish Fort and Fort Blakeley, both of which were east of the Tensaw River.

The land movements by Canby against Mobile's eastern defenses were part of a two-pronged attack. The first got underway on March 17 when the Union XVI Corps sailed on transports to get into position on the eastern shore, and the XIII Corps set out on a hazardous overland march from Fort Morgan. The two corps rendezvoused at Danley's Ferry in the vicinity of Spanish Fort, and Canby's command began siege operations against Spanish Fort on March 27.

Canby's second column of 13,000 Union men moved northward to appear as if it was heading toward Montgomery. At the railroad track at Pollard, Alabama, some 50 miles north of Pensacola, Florida, the column turned west toward the Tensaw River and then south to confront Fort Blakeley. A Union cavalry brigade from the Pensacola column overran an outpost of Confederate infantry at Blakeley on the afternoon of April 1. The next day, while Robert E. Lee's lines around Petersburg, Virginia, were breaking under heavy attacks, serious skirmishing began when Union infantry and light artillery moved into position opposite Blakeley's fortifications just five miles north of Spanish Fort.

Spanish Fort was the southernmost heavily fortified position of Mobile's eastern defenses. Stretching three and a half miles in a semicircular formation, it comprised of numerous artillery positions protected by natural obstacles like ravines, and by manmade obstructions including 205 Rains landmines. Trees near the fort had been cut to offer good fields of fire. The fortifications needed work, for they had been "hastily rebuilt forts [batteries] remaining from the days

Spanish Fort. *History Museum of Mobile*

of Spanish rule." The fort was under the command of Brig. Gen. Randall L. Gibson and manned by 2,100 men from Arkansas, Georgia, and Louisiana.[42]

Federals approaching Spanish Fort by land from Donaldson's Mill admired the beautiful pine forests through which they marched. When they identified clumps of tilled soil along their march—obvious signs of landmines—they detonated the devices with gunshots. "More infernal machines," reported one soldier, were discovered as they drew closer to their destination. "From the 22nd of March until the 3d of April," wrote John Scott of the 32nd Iowa, "the roadsides were filled with torpedoes, buried in the ground so that if man, horse or wagon should step on or pass over one so as to strike the plug, it would explode and scatter the missiles of death in every direction."[43]

Of Canby's 45,000 soldiers, 32,000 were deployed against Randall Gibson's understrength garrison in Spanish Fort. Canby's first target was Fort

42 "Report of Submarine Operations, February 1865, at Mobile" and "Property Return of Submarine Defenses of Mobile, Jan.-Feb., 1865," Perry, *Infernal Machines*, 184-185; "Last Civil War Battle Fought at Spanish Fort: 95 Years Ago Today," in *Mobile Press Register*, April 9, 1960.

43 John Scott, "Compiled and Published," *Story of the Thirty-Second Iowa Infantry Volunteers* (Nevada, IA, 1896), 333-334.

McDermott, a large battery position on the highest point of Spanish Fort's defensive line—its southernmost end. Its 200 defenders had planted landmines in front of their south- and east-facing defensive positions.

The following day more than 50 torpedoes were discovered by Union operations designed to find and clear the devices. Elsewhere, a captured "rebel officer who was posted in the torpedo planting [was] placed in charge of a force of rebel prisoners [and] given the contract of taking out the explosives and stacking them in pyramidal form," observed one eyewitness.[44]

Some mines at Spanish Fort were placed around non-defensive positions, such as watering areas. Other landmines were planted in front of the fortifications and along roads leading into and around the fort's defenses. Such landmine-laying tactics had not been used since the Yorktown fighting in 1862. Samuel W. Gross, a Union doctor serving in the front lines of the fighting at Spanish Fort, compared the deployment of landmines to the enemy's use of the weapon at Yorktown in the spring of 1862. "In the outer defenses of Mobile, and especially about Spanish Fort, in April, 1865," he began,

> the Confederates had planted an immense number of percussion shells, of from eight to fifteen inches in diameter, which were very harassing to our troops, so much so that it was even highly dangerous to take the horses to water. The loss of life and the number of injuries were large. The first instance of the employment of such measures during the war occurred after the evacuation of Yorktown, upon occupation of which place many of our troops were killed and wounded.[45]

Despite the widespread use of landmines, the Confederates were only able to hold Spanish Fort for 13 days until April 8, when Federal siege guns and mortars opened a massive bombardment. Late that day and early the following morning, with the Union lines only 30 yards from Fort McDermott, Gibson ordered all the guns spiked and the garrison evacuated. Some of the Confederates managed to escape by boat across the bay to Mobile or by walking along a narrow path, sometimes through waist-deep muddy water, to reach

---

44 Ibid.; Scott, *Story of the Thirty-Second Iowa Infantry Volunteers*, 335.

45 S. W. Gross, "On Torpedo Wounds," in *American Journal of the Medical Sciences* (1866), vol. 51, 370.

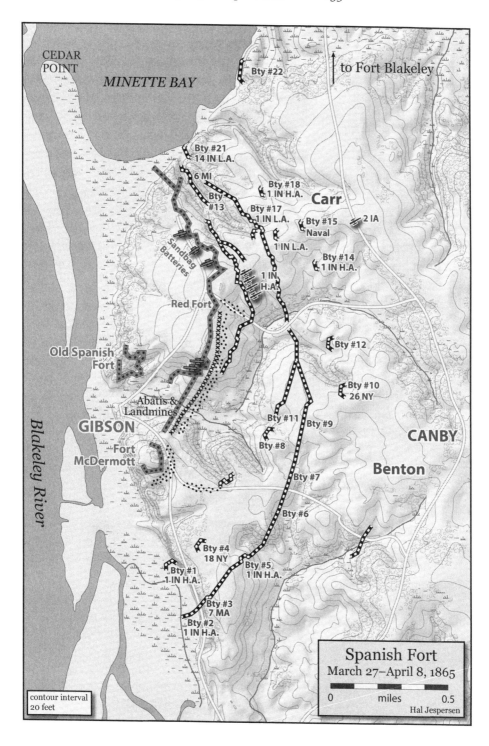

CEDAR POINT

MINETTE BAY

Bty #22

to Fort Blakeley

Bty #21
14 IN L.A.

6 MI

Bty
#13

Bty #18
1 IN H.A.

Carr

Bty #17
1 IN L.A.

Bty #15
Naval

2 IA

1 IN L.A.

Sandbag
Batteries

1 IN
H.A.

Bty #14
1 IN H.A.

Red Fort

Bty #12

Old Spanish
Fort

Bty #10
26 NY

Abatis &
Landmines

GIBSON

Bty #11

Bty #9

CANBY

Bty #8

Fort
McDermott

Benton

Bty #7

Blakeley River

Bty #6

Bty #4
18 NY

Bty #1
1 IN H.A.

Bty #5
1 IN H.A.

Bty #3
7 MA

Bty #2
1 IN H.A.

contour interval
20 feet

Spanish Fort
March 27–April 8, 1865

0   miles   0.5

Hal Jespersen

Confederate land mine detonator from the Battle of Blakeley (14"83)

Landmine detonator that was found at Fort Blakeley and is now on display at the The History Museum of Mobile. Mobile, Alabama. *Author*

friendly positions to the north. During the operation, mines killed and wounded several Federals.[46]

On March 31, about one week before Spanish Fort fell, the second column of Union troops that had been marching toward Mobile from Pensacola, Florida, arrived near Fort Blakeley and laid siege to the bastion. They were soon joined by additional Union forces invigorated by the occupation of Spanish Fort.

Fort Blakeley was the last significant Confederate defensive position on the eastern side of Mobile Bay. It was also much stronger than Spanish Fort. Fort Blakeley was built on the banks of the Tensaw River five miles north of Spanish Fort. It was an expansive affair comprised of red clay trenches, breastworks, and rifle pits joined by nine strong redoubts mounting 41 artillery pieces of various calibers. The fortification started on a bluff next to the river and stretched for three miles in a semicircle that ended on high ground close to the Tensaw. Abatis of felled trees had been positioned 50 yards in front of the works. Defenders assured clear fields of fire by cutting trees for several hundred yards in front of each redoubt, and stumps had been left in place to create chaos for any attacking enemy troops.

Expecting an overwhelming attack, the defenders strengthened their positions by deploying hundreds of landmines made from 10-, 12-, or 24-pound artillery shells. The weapons were planted in front of the fortifications and on other approaches to the garrison.

On April 1, about half a mile from Fort Blakeley, the 2nd Illinois Cavalry suffered two torpedo casualties. One of the troopers was mortally wounded "so

---

46 Michael F. Beard, "Mobile: The Overland Campaign, March–May 1865," in *Damn the Torpedoes? The Official Guide to the Civil War Trail: Battle of Mobile Bay* (undated). Gross, "On Torpedo Wounds," 370. It is estimated that total Confederate losses at Spanish Fort were 93 killed and 350 wounded; Federal losses in the assault were 232 killed and 1,403 wounded.

near the enemy's works that he could not be brought off by his comrades," recalled one of his officers.[47]

Another torpedo exploded near brigade commander Charles Gilbert and his staff. Scott of the 32nd Iowa recalled hearing "a sudden crash like the bursting of a shell in our front." Instantly Gilbert, his aides, and other soldiers close by were "enveloped in a cloud of dust and smoke." A horse had stepped on the triggering mechanism of a torpedo planted near the root of a stump, Luckily for those closest to the blast, the flying iron only killed two horses and left several others with non-mortal wounds.[48]

The defenders employed what were now fairly standard tactics to impede the Federal advance. Telegraph wire had been strung from stump to stump. Rows of sharpened abatis dotted the area. Ditches in front of redoubts were filled with brush and briars. "A wire is trenched about one foot from the ground so as to catch our feet when we try to jump over the ditch," observed William R. Eddington of the 97th Illinois. "And between our line and the Rebels is a quarter of a mile of ground all planted full of torpedoes over which we must pass to get to them." The Union soldiers carefully dug out some of the landmines. A member of an Iowa regiment recalled seeing unearthed 13-inch torpedo shells neatly stacked.[49]

The Confederates planted landmines around and within the rows of abatis in front of Redoubt No. 4. The sharpened branches were woven together with wire that was attached to the plugs of the landmines. It was as ingenious as it was deadly. Simply moving through the obstructions was likely to detonate the shells. In the days before the enemy appeared, a Confederate doctor recalled how the men planted torpedoes in front of the "sooty marsh" near their defensive line, which was powerfully constructed. "We cut down great trees, rolled the trunks over the mouth, then put a layer of brush and dirt; then came

---

47 Lt. Col. A. B. Spurling, Commanding, Second Illinois Cavalry, Correspondence to Capt. John. F. Lacey, Assistant Adjutant-General, April 2, 1865, *OR* 49, pt. 1, 311.

48 Ibid., 130; Scott, *Story of the Thirty-Second Iowa Infantry Volunteers*, 334-335.

49 W. R. Eddington, *Memoir*, 46, unpublished manuscript at http://macoupincty-genealogy.org/war/edding/html, copy at Fort Blakeley State Park archives. Eddington served in the 97th Illinois, 2nd Brigade, 2nd Division, 13th Corps. Scott, *Story of the Thirty-Second Iowa Infantry Volunteers*, 335.

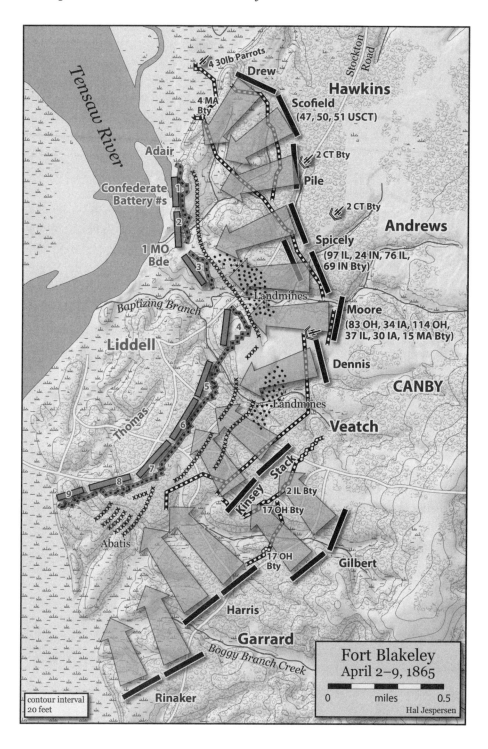

Fort Blakeley
April 2–9, 1865

Hal Jespersen

0   miles   0.5

contour interval
20 feet

The Augusta Powder Works in Augusta, Georgia, produced all the gunpowder used for the Mobile operations, including the landmines at Fort Blakeley, Beverly M. DuBose III Collection, Atlanta, Georgia. *Author*

another layer of heavy logs crosswise, then a layer of brush and dirt, until thereof was 6 to 8 feet thick," he wrote.[50]

In preparation for the siege, the Federals dug rifle pits in advanced positions to support the impending infantry assault. The two- or three-man pits, often extending from or attached to the main line of trenches, served as an early warning in case the defenders launched night sorties. As the Federals crept closer to Confederate positions, they frequently encountered 12- and 24-pound cannon balls with pressure-triggering devices.[51]

On April 9, the same day Robert E. Lee's Army of Northern Virginia was surrendering at Appomattox, the return artillery fire from inside Fort Blakeley slackened significantly. Union commanders worried that the enemy was planning to evacuate the fort and escape, as some of the Spanish Fort garrison had done. These Confederates, however, were expecting an imminent attack and were "conserving ammunition." Their prudence was justified, for a late-afternoon attack was indeed planned. About 5:00 p.m., drums sounded and the Federal soldiers organized for the advance. "We had just got our coffee for supper," one of them recalled. "We set down in our tents, grabbed our guns and fell in line and they rushed us up to the front and into the rifle pits. In a few minutes we got orders to charge."[52]

50 "The Defense of Mobile: Dr. Stephenson's Interesting Narrative, State of Alabama, Department of Archives and History," Federal project S 51-F 2-8 (Fort Morgan assignment).

51 Andrews, *History of the Campaign of Mobile*, 225; Scott, *Story of the Thirty-Second Iowa Infantry Volunteers*, 335.

52 Trudeau, *Like Men of War*, 403; Camille Corte, "Historic Fort Blakeley: Hawkins' Division of 6,000 Black Troops," March 24, 2016, www.blakeleypark.com/73rdUSCT. htm, accessed March 24, 2016; Eddington, *Memoir*, 47.

Sixteen thousand Federal troops attacked from south to north, with the center of the assault aimed against Redoubts 3 and 4. As they crossed a huge ravine, soldiers began "calling out warnings of 'torpedo!' as they ran." A captain's leg was blown off below the knee, sending a portion of the appendage 50 feet in the air, recalled one of the attackers. "I had not gone far when a man next to me on my left stepped on a torpedo with his left foot," recalled the 97th Illinois' William Eddington. "I grabbed him as he fell, but I could not hold him."[53]

The attackers pushed through barriers of felled trees and branches, abatis, and ankle-high trip wires. "The field over which the charge had been made," wrote Sgt. Sidney T. B. Marshall of the 83rd Ohio with understandable exaggeration, "had been planted with many thousand torpedoes, or 'subterra shells,' as the Confederates termed them, but not one had been stepped on by any of our regiment."[54]

Colonel Hiram Schofield described the high spirits of the troops as they charged across the minefields toward the Confederate positions. The ground over which they advanced was flat, wet, and "very unfavorable for the health and comfort of the men," explained the colonel. Yelling soldiers rushed through abatis and over torpedoes, "several of which exploded." Still, continued Schofield, "the spirit and enthusiasm of the troops could not be excelled. Men actually wept that they were placed in reserve and could not go with their comrades into the thickest of the fight."[55]

Sgt. Andrew Lafayette Swap of the 37th Illinois was knocked down when a landmine exploded near him, but survived to tell the tale. "I had been jumping from one to another of the logs that had been felled, with sharpened stakes sticking up, to impede our advance," Swap recalled. "On all open ground between the enemy's line and ours . . . they had planted torpedoes to blow us up.

---

53 Hansen and Nicolson, *The Siege of Blakeley and the Campaign of Mobile*, 21; Eddington, *Memoir*, 47.

54 T. B. Marshall, *History of the Eighty-Third, Ohio Volunteer Infantry, The Greyhound Regiment* (Cincinnati, OH, 1912), 160-167.

55 Report of Col. Hiram Schofield, Forty-Seventh, U.S. Colored Infantry, Commanding Second Brigade, of Operations, HDQRS, Second Brigade, First Div., U.S. Colored Troops, Blakely, Alabama, April 11, 1865, *OR* 45, pt. 1, 291-292.

A wire extended from them which being stepped upon or against, exploded them."[56]

Many were not as fortunate. According to one Union officer, "quite a number of men were killed or wounded by the explosion of torpedoes, which were exploded by stepping upon them." Iowan Scott explained that everyone did their best to avoid the devices. "[N]otwithstanding all of the precautions taken," he added, "a number of lives were lost by the exploding of the torpedoes."[57]

Sergeant Henry W. Hart of the 2nd Connecticut Light Artillery, who participated in the attack, complained the landmines were "not civilized." The vicinity of the fort, he recalled in a descriptive letter to his wife, was "filled with torpedoes." He saw three types: 6-, 8-, and 10-inch spherical shells, "the same as those fired from cannon." Each had "a cap and primer arrangement which ignites and bursts the shell with the lightest touch." Some were planted in clusters of 12, connected to a trip wire. When triggered, the grouping created a massive explosion.

Hart was counting mines planted in a cluster when he discovered that his right foot was just three inches from a triggering device. Nearby he spotted a pile of 20 mines that had not been buried. According to his best guess, nearly 1,000 mines had been deployed near the fort or on roads leading to it. Some had been exposed by recent rains.[58]

Sergeant Hart recalled a soldier who lost his left leg and was also "wounded in his privates" by a landmine explosion. He lived for three long and agonizing hours. A triggered torpedo blew off the leg of a captain who had just stepped from a rifle pit during a charge. Another soldier, wrote the Connecticut artillerist, lost both his legs and had "his parts . . . all blown off" by a mine. "In 9 cases out of 10 a person stepping on one of them is killed," he concluded. "Our men suffered more by these devilish things than by the reb fire. They was

56 Diary of 1st Sgt. Andrew Lafayette Swap, 37th Illinois Infantry, Third Brigade, Second Division, copy at Fort Blakeley State Park Archives.

57 Report of Col. Hiram Schofield, April 11, 1865, *OR* vol. 45, pt. 1, 291-292; Scott, *Story of the Thirty-Second Iowa Infantry Volunteers*, 339.

58 Henry W. Hart to his wife, written near Blakeley, April 10, 1865, History Museum of Mobile, Mobile, Alabama.

exploding all the time during the charge. The wonder is they did not fall back, such a fiery path is too much."[59]

Several brigades of United States Colored Troops (U.S.C.T.) also participated in the attack. With red cloths tied to their muskets as a symbol of revenge, they shouted "Fort Pillow!" during their advance—a reference to what many believed had been a massacre of surrendered black troops at Fort Pillow, Tennessee, on April 12, 1864. A landmine killed one man and wounded 13 more in the 51st U.S.C.T. One report noted that a company in the 51st regiment had six men "severely wounded by the explosion of one of the enemy's subterra shells."[60]

Despite the landmines and other defenses, the attack on Fort Blakeley was over in less than 30 minutes. With the Federals at the ramparts, some defenders retreated into nearby woods. Those who remained surrendered or were killed or wounded. Confederate casualties included 75 dead, 455 wounded, and some 3,000 captured, together with 40 heavy guns. Many of the defenders attempting to escape by jumping into the river drowned in the attempt. Federals losses totaled 150 dead and 650 wounded.[61]

Confederate prisoners led the way through torpedo fields as they were taken to a U.S.C.T. camp. One of their guards, Pvt. Josias Lewis of the 47th U.S.C.T., lost his leg to a torpedo explosion near the camp.[62]

---

59 Ibid.

60 Scott, *Story of the Thirty-Second Iowa Infantry Volunteers*, 340. Union soldiers, including United States Colored Troops, were defending Fort Pillow in Tennessee when Maj. Gen. Nathan Bedford Forrest attacked the installation. More than 300 black troops were killed, with witnesses claiming some Confederates yelled "no quarter!" and others claiming the troops had surrendered. See also Andrews, *History of the Campaign of Mobile*, 201; Report of Col. A. Watson Webber, Commanding Regiment, Fifty-First U.S. Colored Infantry, of operations April 1-9, to Lieut. T. Sumner Green, Actg. Asst. Gen., 2nd Brig., 1st Div., U.S. Colored Troops, April 11, 1865, Fort Blakely, *OR* vol. 44, pt. 1, 295.

61 Mike Bunn, Director, Historic Blakeley State Park, "Battle of Fort Blakeley, " www.en cyclopediaofalabama.org/article/h-3718, accessed January 24, 2019; Carl Zebrowski, "Frozen in Time: A Ghost Town and the Efforts of an Unflappable Organizer Have Kept Alabama's Fort Blakeley in Pristine Condition," *Civil War Times, Illustrated* (December 1994); Diary of 1st Sgt. Andrew Lafayette Swap, Fort Blakeley State Park Archives.

62 Report of Col. Hiram Schofield, April 11, 1865, *OR* vol. 45, pt. 1, 291-292; Andrews, *History of the Campaign of Mobile*, 201; Hansen and Nicolson, *The Siege of Blakeley and the Campaign of Mobile*, 43.

After the fighting, Union officers took precautions to protect their men from landmines by placing guards near the minefields. As evening fell on April 9 not a musket or cannon was fired, but explosions still reverberated along the lines. Soldiers searching for fallen comrades were triggering more mines, as were careless Federals who had been celebrating their victory with alcohol. According to one Ohio soldier, "the sharp report of exploding landmines continued to echo through the night, spilling the victor's blood."[63]

"We captured 15,000 prisoners with all their guns and war equipment of every kind, even their commissary whiskey," recalled a proud William Eddington of the 97th Illinois, who likely was expressing what he had been told. The number, however, was a gross exaggeration. "Some of our boys imbibed a little too freely of the latter thereby losing their heads and running over the torpedoes."[64]

Union officers had no compunction about ordering the prisoners to clear the mines. Two were killed in the effort. "Amen," spat a Union soldier when told of their demise. Harvey Dowd, who fought with Company A, 114th Ohio, recalled how the "Rebs had torpedoes planted in the Ground," that they killed "several men," and that the officers "Got the Rebs digging up their torpedoes around the post at [Fort Blakeley]."[65]

The fact that the prisoners were made to uncover their own dirty work was of great interest to the men who had just endured the minefields and lost comrades to the blasts. After the battle, wrote Sidney Marshall of the 83rd Ohio, "the enemy were compelled to locate, cap, and dig them up, under a penalty of being marched in a body, back and forth until all had been exploded." Another Union soldier noted that "[f]or two days after this, the rebel prisoners" were ordered "to remove the torpedoes. Those that could not dig out they exploded with a stick, lying back away from them to avoid the explosion."[66]

63 Diary of 1st Sgt. Andrew Lafayette Swap; Woods, 96th Ohio, 123, in Chester Hearn, *Mobile Bay and the Mobile Campaign: The Last Great Battles of the Civil War* (Jefferson, NC, and London, England, 1998), 200.

64 Eddington, *Memoir*.

65 Hart to his wife April 10, 1865; H. U. Dowd, Company A, 114th Ohio, diary, Jackson County Historical Society (Independence, MO); Perry, *Infernal Machines*, 186-187.

66 Marshall, *History of the Eighty-Third, Ohio Volunteer Infantry*, 160-167; Diary of 1st Sgt. Andrew Lafayette Swap.

Once Fort Blakeley fell, the Federals shelled the marshland batteries of Fort Huger and Fort Tracy before crossing the Tensaw and Mobile rivers into Mobile itself. With the destruction of those two batteries, Union naval vessels cleared the waterways of mines and brought up the gunboats. The fall of Spanish Fort, Fort Blakeley, and Batteries Huger and Tracy convinced Dabney Maury that further defense of Mobile was futile and he ordered the city and its remaining defenses evacuated.[67]

Mobile was declared an open city on April 12 and the remaining Confederate garrison retreated with the intention of joining remnants of the Army of Tennessee in North Carolina. The Union had taken possession of Richmond on April 2. The fall of Mobile on April 12 meant the last major urban area in the Confederacy was now in Union hands.

North Carolina: The Final Countdown

In a last-gasp attempt to avoid disaster, Secretary of War James Seddon ordered Gabriel Rains and his Army Torpedo Bureau agents to travel to North Carolina in early spring 1865 and use their mines in the best way possible. By that time the prospect for achieving anything worthwhile, however, was long past.[68]

Although Jefferson Davis believe further resistance was a viable option, it was clear to nearly everyone else that the Southern Confederacy had reached its end. Lee's Army of Northern Virginia was trapped in the Richmond-Petersburg trenches, and John B. Hood's Army of Tennessee had been nearly destroyed, its remnants now under Joe Johnston's command in North Carolina. The ability to feed, clothe, and arm them was becoming more difficult by the day. The presence of two Union armies camped in North Carolina only added to the woes faced by the crumbling Southern nation.

---

67 Lt. Commander Thos. B. Huger, C.S.N., was killed on the CSS *McRae* in the Battle of New Orleans on April 25, 1862. Battery Huger was named in his honor. Battery Tracy was named after Brig. Gen. Edward D. Tracy, who had been killed at Port Gibson on May 1, 1863, during the Vicksburg Campaign. Canby to War Department, *OR* vol. 39, pt., 1, 98; Thatcher to Welles, April 15, 1865, *ORN* vol. 22, 92.

68 Special Orders No. 43. Adjut and Insp. General's Office, Richmond, By Command of the Secretary of War, JNO Withers, Assistant Adjunct-General, February 21, 1865, *OR* vol. 47, pt. 2, 1,239.

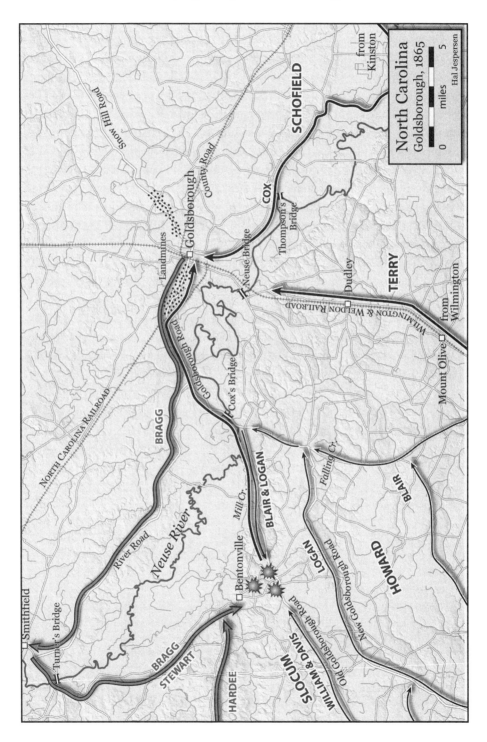

On March 8, 1865, Sherman's soldiers left South Carolina and tramped into the Old North State, where they aimed to consolidate with Maj. Gen. John Schofield's army, recently bolstered by Maj. Gen. Alfred Terry's newly christened X Corps. On the Atlantic coast, Terry's forces had captured Fort Fisher on January 15, and, together with Schofield, took Wilmington on February 22. To stop the Federals, Joe Johnston (who had been recommended by Gen. Robert E. Lee and reappointed to command in the field on February 25, 1865), had a rag-tag command that included remnants from the Army of Tennessee, and various elements from the Carolinas and the District of the Gulf. The 58-year-old Johnston knew there was little he could do. His best option was to defeat one of the Union armies (Sherman or Schofield) before they could combine against him.[69]

Back in his home state, Gabriel Rains now had to decide on a strategy. It was not the first time he was called to defend North Carolina. In October of 1864, he had sent his men and landmines to the state at the request of Maj. Gen. William H. C. Whiting "to guard land approaches at certain places," including Goldsboro. As a result of that experience, Rains had written Secretary Seddon in the fall of 1864, his landmines "are now appreciated, and I now have more calls for their use than I can possibly fulfill."[70]

Between October of 1864 and early 1865, however, Confederate fortunes plummeted. On March 2, Brig. Gen. Laurence S. Baker requested that Richmond provide him with more landmine support. Rains is "wanted here immediately," he pleaded, "with all torpedoes on hand." His message was confirmed later that day by Archer Anderson, assistant adjutant general to Maj. Gen. Robert Hoke, who confirmed the "[t]orpedo man in Richmond has been telegraphed for."[71]

---

69 Terry was promoted to major general after the capture of Fort Fisher. In March, Terry's Fort Fisher Expeditionary Corps was combined with other forces from various divisions and brigades and renamed X Corps.

70 Message from Gabriel J. Rains, Brigadier-General, Superintendent, Torpedo Bureau, Richmond, Virginia, to Hon. James Seddon, Secretary of War, October 29, 1864, *OR* vol. 42, pt. 3, 1,181-1,182. In 1869, the spelling of Goldsborough was officially changed to Goldsboro, though most modern Civil War histories use the latter spelling.

71 L. S. Baker, Brigadier-General to Doctor Fretwell, Goldsborough, North Carolina, March 2, 1865, *OR* vol. 47, pt. 2, 1,315; Archer Anderson, Assistant Adjutant-General to General Hoke, Rockfish Creek, Goldsborough, March 2, 1865, *OR* vol. 47, pt. 2, 1,315. Baker had also requested land torpedoes two years earlier for use in North Carolina.

With his troops woefully outnumbered and resources of every kind in short supply, it was Johnston who, on March 7, asked Secretary Seddon to send Rains and his Army Torpedo personnel and landmines to his home state, this time to support defensive positions around Kinston. His views on mines had changed since the early days around Yorktown. In addition, Seddon also sent John Fretwell, whom he introduced as "an expert with Singer torpedoes," to Brig. Gen. Baker at Goldsborough, who had requested "something more for success."[72]

While Rains was making his way to North Carolina, Johnston's motley army was further threatened by Schofield's and Terry's joint advance north from Wilmington. Schofield was determined to advance his rail lines from Kinston to Goldsboro and unite with General Sherman's command, and had tasked Maj. Gen. Jacob Cox to lead the way. Several skirmishes occurred while scattered Confederate forces fought small actions as they retreated northward in the face of a powerful enemy. On March 7, Gen. Braxton Bragg and some 8,500 Confederates blocked Cox's route east of Kinston. Bragg, who had been an aggressive general throughout the war, attacked and made some headway, but the Federals eventually rebuffed his assault. Skirmishing followed for the next few days. The request for landmine and commensurate technical support was too late to help. Bragg retreated in the face of growing enemy pressure and left Kinston in Union hands one week after the call for torpedoes reached Richmond.[73]

Reeling from overwhelming Union forces on multiple fronts, the remaining Confederates retreated to Goldsboro, planting mines in the roads leading out of Kinston to slow their pursuers. Union soldiers marched with extra caution. One Federal who had fought at Kinston wrote in his memoirs that "the principal source of apprehension was the turnpike to Goldsboro being full of torpedoes, a fact that was discovered by a detachment of the 12th Cavalry, which was pushed

---

72 Gen. Joseph E. Johnston, Fayetteville to Brig. Gen. Gabriel Rains, Greensborough, March 7, 1865, ibid., 1,336; Letter from James A. Seddon, Confederate Secretary of War, from Wilmington, North Carolina, undated, Calhoun County Museum Archives, accessed January 10, 2017; Baker to Fretwell, March 2, 1865, ibid., 1,315. In November 1864, Rains had sent "Dr. Fretwell, to Brigadier-General Baker at Goldsboro to support his defenses with torpedo operations." See *OR* 42, pt. 3, 1,220.

73 For the best study on this important late-ware action, see generally, Wade Sokolosky and Mark A. Smith, *"To Prepare for Sherman's Coming": The Battle of Wise's Forks, March 1865* (Savas Beatie, 2015).

out on that road toward Mosley Hall on a scout." The "infernal traps, he continued,

> were percussion shells set on the end in a hole in the ground, covered with a piece of tin and dirt. Horse, man or cannon wheel pressing on the spot where one of them was concealed was certain to be blown to pieces. A horse and rider were blown up by one of them within sight of our entrenchments. A New Hampshire man at length cleared the road of these deadly traps by going out alone and ferreting them out. [74]

General Cox confirmed the use of torpedoes on the roads leading to Goldsboro. "In addition to the obstacles presented by the flood and fallen timber (most of which was under water)," reported Cox,

> we found torpedoes buried in the road, many of which exploded, killing and wounding several soldiers. The rest of the Cavalry are scouting on the Goldsboro and Snow Hill roads some six miles out. They found one torpedo in the road, which exploded and killed one horse, and they are now searching for others supposed to be planted thereabouts. [75]

This move toward Goldsboro confirmed to Johnston that Sherman's immediate goal was not to capture the state capital at Raleigh, but to take the vital rail junction at Goldsboro. Confederates under Lt. Gen. William H Hardee made a stand at Averasboro on March 16, but were finally driven out of their lines and retreated. His defensive action, however, had held up the Union march for two full days. [76]

Three days later near Bentonville, Johnston's reinforced army of nearly 22,000 men stood in the path of Sherman's 60,000 troops marching to Goldsboro. In what was perhaps Johnston's boldest move of the war, he attacked one of Sherman's wings and drove it back some distance. Heavy fighting followed and the Confederates eventually fell back to their original position. Two days of mostly light skirmishing and on one occasion heavy

---

74 Henry Hall and James Hall, *Cayuga in the Field: A Record of the 19th N.Y. Volunteers* (Auburn, NY, 1873), 263, 280.

75 D. Cox, Major-General, Commanding, to Capt. William A. Lord, Aide-de-Camp, Headquarters, Department of North Carolina, from Headquarters, District of Beaufort, Kinston, North Carolina, March 15, 1865, *OR* 47, pt. 2, 853.

76 Ibid., 852.

fighting followed before Johnston retreated. The Battle of Bentonville was too little, too late, and served nothing except to increase the names on casualty rolls. Johnston's forces regrouped at Smithfield.

With Lee's surrender on April 9 at Appomattox Courthouse in Virginia, Johnston was left to face the potential combined might of Grant and Sherman. Instead, he surrendered to Sherman on April 26, 1865, at James Bennett's house near Durham. Given the extent of his command by that time, it was the largest body of troops to surrender during the war. The mass capitulation effectively ended the conflict in the eastern United States.

Chapter 6

Mine Warfare: A Lasting Legacy

After the close of the Civil War, the two men most responsible for the Confederacy's extensive yet still little-known mine warfare campaign led very different lives.

Matthew Fontaine Maury was informed the war was over while in Havana, Cuba, in transit from England to the United States with a consignment of torpedo equipment. Disappointed by the outcome he settled in Mexico, where he served as "Imperial Commissioner" for Emperor Maximilian. He encouraged and implemented an immigration plan to bring former Confederates to Mexico. These potential immigrants, he informed the royal family of Mexico, were "subjects of high importance . . . worthy of careful consideration," and who increase the country's prosperity.[1]

After arriving in Mexico Maury pledged to help resettle "10,000 of those noble [Carolinian] families who left their desolated houses to the victors and sought refuge like me of true pluck in a foreign land." He also encouraged his son-in-law to emigrate to Mexico.[2]

---

1 Virginia Military Institute Archives, https://archivesspace.vmi/respositories/3/593, accessed January 21, 2019; Matthew Maury to Empress Carlota of Mexico, January 18, 1866, Matthew Fontaine Maury Papers, VMI Archives, Manuscript #00103.

2 Matthew Maury to son-in-law, S. Welford Corbin, January 1, 1866, Matthew Fontaine Maury Papers, VMI Archives, Manuscript #00103.

Maury expressed in letters that he was pleased with pace of "colonization" in Mexico by former Confederates, but in reality he was not. The immigration effort, which was decried by many including Robert E. Lee, failed. "The thought of abandoning the country, and all that must be left in it, is abhorrent to my feelings," Lee scolded Maury in September 1865, "and I prefer to struggle for its restoration, and share its fate, rather than to give up all as lost."[3]

By early 1866 Maury had returned to England, where he explored the use of steam agricultural machinery. Two years later he took advantage of a general amnesty offered to former Confederates and returned to his homeland. In his native Virginia, Maury promoted the state's agricultural resources and served as a professor of physics at the Virginia Military Institute in Lexington. During this period he lived part-time in Richmond, where his mine research had flourished during the brief life of the Confederacy.[4]

Maury died at age 67 at his home in Lexington on February 1, 1873. His last words were "All's well"—a nautical term for calm sea conditions. He was buried near Presidents James Monroe and John Tyler in Richmond's Hollywood Cemetery. At the time of his passing Maury was riding a crest of popularity. A year before his death, the estimated sales of his book *The Physical Geography of the Sea* exceeded $125,000.[5]

During much of his professional life Maury was venerated around the globe, mostly for his navigational work, which shortened by many months the voyage from the eastern seaboard of the United States to California and Australia. He was awarded many honors, including France's Cross of Commander of the Legion of Honor, Austria's and Prussia's Grand Medals of Sciences, and Russia's Order of St. Ann. At VMI, a building on the school's historic parade ground is named in his honor.[6]

*   *   *

3 Rev. John William Jones, *Personal Reminiscences, Anecdotes, and Letters of Gen. Robert E. Lee* (New York, NY, 1874), 206.

4 Matthew Maury to son-in-law, S. Welford Corbin, May 13, 1868, Matthew Fontaine Maury Papers, VMI Archives, Manuscript #00103.

5 Matthew Maury to daughter Diana Maury Corbin, July 26, 1871, Matthew Fontaine Maury Papers, VMI Archives, Manuscript #00103.

6 "The Late Professor Maury," *Buffalo Courier*, February 4, 1873, 1.

"What became of Gen. Rains after the close of the war we do not know," observed an obituary. Although Gabriel Rains's postwar life isn't always completely transparent, and he did not write what would have been a potentially fascinating memoir, significant information exists about his postwar career.[7]

The former general lived for many years in Augusta and Atlanta. In 1868, he was working as "an analytical chemist of high merit" for a local fertilizer company. While in Augusta he would have visited often with his brother George, who had operated the Augusta Powder Works during the war and who remained in Augusta to teach in the medical college. In 1873, Gabriel, his wife, four children, and two servants moved from Augusta to Aiken, South Carolina. There, they lived in one home and ran a boardinghouse in another while Gabriel became headmaster of the Aiken Academy. The family was active in St. Thaddeus Episcopal Church. By 1880, from causes unknown, Rains's wife Mary Jane, was an invalid.[8]

Rains intended to set up a fertilizer company in Charlotte, but the venture never came to fruition. Any failures he endured did not dampen his enthusiasm for, or interest in, mine warfare. Representatives of foreign countries approached him regarding his work, and though one account claims he had developed a new system that would revolutionize warfare, no evidences exists that anything came of it or that he ever worked for a foreign power.

Although he did not write his memoirs, he did publish an article in the *Southern Historical Society Papers* in 1877 entitled simply, "Torpedoes." The text offered a general history of his use of mines as early as 1839-40 in Florida against the Seminoles, and ran through their use during the late war. "Ironclads are said to master the world," he penned, "but torpedoes master the ironclads." He wasn't wrong.

In 1879, Gabriel provided information on his wartime work to former President Jefferson Davis, who was finishing up his memoir on his role in the conflict. Rains' information included the number of torpedoes he had placed in harbors, rivers, and other locations. As far as he was concerned, the evidence was clear: The weapon was more successful for river and harbor defense than it had been on land. According to Rains, his mines had sunk 58 Union ships. A

---

7 "Death of Gen. G. J. Rains," 2; South Carolina Historical Society, Gabriel J. Rains papers, 1840–1865, https://beta.worldcat.org/archivegrid/collection/data/37521848.

8 Waters, *Gabriel Rains and the Confederate Torpedo Bureau*, 93.

thankful Davis used this information in *The Rise and Fall of the Confederate Government* (1881).[9]

Rains died on August 6, 1881, of a heart condition in Aiken, South Carolina and was buried there with military honors in St. Thaddeus Episcopal Church Cemetery. His marriage to wife Mary Jane, who would die two years later in 1883, produced seven children. Sevier Rains, who had followed in his father's footsteps to West Point, was serving as an officer in the U.S. Army when he was killed by the Nez Perce at Craig's Mountain in Idaho in 1877.[10]

Two years before Rains's death, former Union admiral David D. Porter had nothing good to say about his deadly invention. "We showed during the war either a want of intelligence in not using torpedoes," he began,

> or an excess of humanity and a rash of confidence in easily overcoming a vigilant and energetic foe, a confidence which was not justified by our experience as the war went on. . . . It is only since the year 1861 that it [the torpedo] has been generally adopted as an engine of war, a tardiness in great measure due to false sentimentality which until a recent period banned the torpedo as an inhuman and unchristian means of destroying the enemy.[11]

*   *   *

The leading Lavaca torpedo men led quiet lives after the war. Before turning in their parole papers to Federal officials, Edgar Singer and John Fretwell destroyed many of the wartime records relating to their torpedo work to "avoid prosecution for war crimes." Singer died in 1874 in Marlin, Texas, close to where his daughters resided. After retiring from medical practice, Fretwell operated a hotel for five years before moving to Galveston in 1872. About a year later he moved to Mobile, Alabama, where he married his second wife. Fretwell died in abject poverty on April 16, 1885. The Masonic Grand Lodge of Texas contributed $50 to pay for his funeral. He is buried in Mobile's Magnolia Cemetery.[12]

---

9 Ibid., 94-96.

10 Ibid., 97.

11 Ibid., 96.

12 Don Barnhart, "Masonic Saboteurs," *Warriors of the Lone Star State*, April 20, 2016, http://warriorsofthelonestar.blogspot.com/2016/; "A Page From Rich Calhoun History,"

Innovation and Improvisation

At the start of the Civil War, the disparity in military manpower, materiel, and weaponry between the North and South was significant. The gap widened in the Union's favor as the war progressed, forcing the Confederate war industry to innovate and improvise. That was especially true with land and water mines.

With a significant advantage in resources and industry, and because it was mainly on the offensive, the Union had neither the desire nor the necessity to develop mine warfare. Unlike the South, Northern harbors or fortifications were rarely threatened. Fueled by only a handful of key figures, a desperate Confederacy developed and embraced mines as weapons of defensive warfare to delay advancing Federal armies and to defend its land fortifications and harbors.

A variety of medieval-style wooden obstructions worked well to slow and imperil attackers—something any military could make. Layers of these obstructions constituted the most important defensive feature of fortified lines in front of parapets and trenches. Sometimes the Confederates did not have the time or the labor, especially later in the war, available to construct adequate defensive fortifications at multiple locations simultaneously. Because of a lack of engineers, resources, and/or time, Confederate defenders often had to be creative in constructing fortifications, which included the use of improvised landmines made from unexploded ordnance.

The Confederacy's use of landmines was initially controversial and considered by many to be unfair and immoral. The arguments against landmine use—at least on the Confederate side—dissipated relatively quickly, however, and mines came to be viewed as a legitimate, highly effective, low-cost weapon and methodology of war. Opposition within the Confederacy's high command, especially by Gen. Joseph E. Johnston and Lt. Gen. James Longstreet, abated as the war progressed as Confederates became increasingly desperate to defend their shrinking territory.

Besides a shortage of war materials and manpower, especially compared to their enemies, Confederates found the need for alternative weapons of defense

---

Calhoun County Museum Archives; Calhoun County Museum, web post, February 19, 2004, www.ancestry.com/boards/localities.northam.usa.states.texas.counties.Calhoun/260 .1/mb.ashx, accessed January 19, 2019; Mark K. Ragan, *Building the Hunley and Other Secret Weapons of the Civil War* (College Station, TX, 2015), 186.

even more critical because they had been ill prepared for war at its onset. The Union controlled its own ordnance arsenals. In contrast, the Confederacy had to negotiate with its member states, which controlled the U.S. arsenals and armories they had seized upon secession. In addition, the South lacked munitions and weapons production facilities. As one scholar put it, "At the outset of the Civil War not a gun or gun-carriage, and, excepting during the Mexican War, not a round of ammunition had been prepared in the States of the Confederacy for fifty years. They were forced to improvise all of the vast paraphernalia necessary for war."[13]

During the war, Confederate military personnel developed the world's first landmine warfare doctrine and designated landmine bureaucracy, known as the Army Torpedo Bureau. Led by Brig. Gen. Gabriel Rains, a creative and innovative military engineering officer, the bureau offered a new and prophetic philosophy of modern, technological landmine warfare. The Confederate high command ultimately embraced Rains's maxim that "deception is the art of war, and landmines were appropriate weapons to conduct a war."[14]

Even while Southern fortunes waned, the expertise of its mine personnel improved. It wasn't until January 1863, however, that torpedoes became truly reliable in the field. The Confederacy's efforts were aided by the invention of the Rains fuse, the innovative engineering technology of the Fretwell-Singer torpedoes, and the creation of the Torpedo Bureau, along with the industrial manufacture of landmines as opposed to improvising them on the fly.

Even when the Torpedo Bureau was created, the organization itself was relatively decentralized. Typically, a single officer (or sometimes two) would oversee landmine deployment, implementing tactical plans involving the use of home guard units, members of the public, and slave laborers. In such cases, the Torpedo Bureau men had wide discretion in how they deployed mines.

Once given an order to use landmines, lower-ranking Confederate officers and their troops were able to improvise, usually in a spontaneous act of self-preservation, with adequate time to deploy the mines against often overwhelming Federal forces. The result was the varied deployment of

13 McIntosh, "The Confederate Artillery: Its Organization and Development," 56-70 in Miller, *Forts and Artillery*, 57.

14 Rains, *Torpedo Book*, 61. Rains' book consists of 100 pages of longhand notes and 29 drawings. It also includes newspaper clippings that Rains assembled after the Civil War. Waters, "Deception is the Art of War," 29. The original *Torpedo Book* prepared by Rains for President Davis is stored at the American Civil War Museum in Richmond.

Table 1: Landmine Types and Tactical Uses During the Civil War						
	Command	Trip Wire	Pressure	Nuisance	Delay	Defense
Battery Wagner, South Carolina			X			X
Jackson, Mississippi			X		X	
Fort Blakeley, Alabama		X	X			X
Fort Esperanza, Texas			X			X
Fort Fisher, North Carolina*	X					X
Fort Gilmer, Virginia			X			X
Fort Griffin, Texas	X					X
Fort Harrison, Virginia			X			X
Fort Johnson, Virginia			X			X
Fort McAllister, Georgia			X			X
Fort McDermott, Alabama**			X			X
Fort Sumter, South Carolina			X			X
Georgia (southeastern region, late 1864)***			X		X	
North Carolina (southeastern region, early 1865)			X		X	

* Friction primers were commonly used to fire artillery pieces up to the end of the 19th century.

** Fort McDermott is considered an extended fortification of Spanish Fort's defenses, where Confederates had also deployed nuisance mines. They were placed at a watering hole some distance from the fort's immediate defenses. To avoid double counting, the deployment of these nuisance landmines is placed in the column for Spanish Fort rather than for Fort McDermott alone.

*** Although General Sherman wrote that he believed the devices that took the leg of one of his officers during their March to the Sea were "nuisance landmines," they are not listed as such in this chart because most likely the Southern defenders used them as a delaying weapon so that they could re-calibrate their own defensive strategy and gain additional time.

Table 1: Landmine Types and Tactical Uses During the Civil War (continued)						
	Command	Trip Wire	Pressure	Nuisance	Delay	Defense
Port Hudson, Louisiana****	X		X			X
Richmond (roads leading into city, 1865)	X					X
Sister's Ferry, Georgia-South Carolina border			X		X	
Spanish Fort, Alabama			X	X		X
Williamsburg, Virginia			X		X	
Yellow Tavern, Virginia		X			X	

**** Port Hudson is the only known Civil War location where command-detonated and victim-activated landmines were used, and, as far as can be determined, it is also the only place in the world where both command- and victim-activated landmines were used in the same location.

increasingly sophisticated explosive devices and innovative landmine warfare tactics near fortifications and on main invasion routes.

The Confederates developed two ways to detonate a landmine: victim-activated and command-controlled. Victim-activated (also known as contact-detonated) mines were the easiest to detonate because victims inadvertently triggered them. They were made by coupling a shell and a percussion cap or, later in the war, a purposefully manufactured detonator. In a postwar memoir about his combat experience, Union surgeon S. W. Gross described the victim-activated landmines as

> simply large shells arranged with levers connected with a percussion fuze and sunk below the surface of the ground in the supposed path of an assailing party. A pressure of the foot upon the concealed lever was sufficient to explode the shell, resulting in effects similar to the bursting of a like projectile under ordinary circumstances.[15]

15 These landmines are also referred to in the literature as self-detonating devices. Gross, "On Torpedo Wounds," 370.

As the first and only head of the Torpedo Bureau, General Rains invented a pressure-sensitive fuse that was much more reliable than previous designs. The Rains fuse could be dialed or set to the slightest pressure, which was eventually stabilized at seven pounds.[16]

Victim-activated landmines, including many with the Rains fuse, were used as reinforcing defensive devices in such fortifications as Battery Wagner, South Carolina; Fort Blakeley, Alabama; Fort McAllister, Georgia; Spanish Fort, Alabama; the forts at Chaffin's Farm, Virginia, and places such as Jackson, Mississippi, and Williamsburg and Yorktown, Virginia. (They were utilized less successfully between Kinston and Goldsboro, North Carolina, in March 1865.)

The second type of landmine—which was infrequently used—was a command-detonated device (see Table 1). These were activated by human control through a priming charge with an electrical current or pull wires that would cause a friction-sensitive mixture to ignite. This system required some manner of connection between the person firing the device and the device itself.

Although they gave the operator more control, command-detonated landmines could be hampered because of a lack of materials, faulty technology, and inadvertent cutting of the wires by artillery fire or other means. In this friction-primer system, a wire was pulled through a small tube (usually copper) filled with an explosive substance (usually fulminate of mercury) and small grain black powder, which, in turn, created a spark that ignited the powder; the main charge of black powder was then ignited.[17]

Prisoners of War

As a countermeasure to landmines, Union commanders marched prisoners of war ahead of their own troops to identify or detonate landmines deployed by

---

16 To a lesser extent, Confederate landmines also employed the Girardey percussion fuse, which was fabricated for the contact detonation of artillery shells. The fuse worked by placing a "serrated piece of a common artillery primer in the front of the fuze so that upon contact, the reaction was identical to that of the friction primer . . . anyone stepping on it detonated the shell." Examples have been recovered in South Carolina. See Charles H. Jones, *Artillery Fuses of the Civil War* (Alexandria, VA, 2001), 129, as quoted in Kochan and Wideman, *Civil War Torpedoes*, 186.

17 Although landmines were inexpensive to create, there was a certain complexity about them that had to be mastered for them to be fully (and reliably) useful.

Location	Confederate POWs Forced to Clear Landmines Immediately After the Fighting Ended	Confederate POWS Forced to March at Head of Federal Columns on Known Landmine-infested Roads
Fort Blakeley, Alabama	X	
Fort McAllister, Georgia	X	
Georgia (southeastern region, late 1864)	X	X
Spanish Fort, Alabama	X	
Yellow Tavern, Virginia	X	X
Yorktown, Virginia	X	

Table 2: Prisoners of War Clearance Operations Chart

other Confederates or Southern sympathizers (see Table 2). Landmine warfare outraged Union generals such as Philip H. Sheridan and William T. Sherman, and Federal officers frequently took revenge by ordering Confederate soldiers to dig up the landmines. If they refused, they risked execution. In at least six post-fighting situations, Federal forces pressed POWs to clear their own landmines, with occasionally fatal results.[18]

Unexploded Landmines and Civilian Casualties

Throughout the long war, Confederate soldiers harvested unexploded ordnance rounds by either seizing stockpiles on battlefields or by collecting and re-purposing the ordnance from within their own defensive perimeters, which was then used as their ordnance or was converted into landmines. Sometimes these unexploded shells were "shipped to an arsenal for refitting with copper

---

18 Some of the other Federal responses to Confederate landmines, including targeting civilians for retribution and burning their homes, today are prohibited under international law. The Federals also used marksmen as another counter-landmine measure to "clear a torpedo by shooting the fuse and exploding it." Schneck, "Foreword," in Kochan and Wideman, *Civil War Torpedoes*, xiv–xv.

time fuse adapters and sometimes resorted and/or converted from shell to case shot."[19]

Surprisingly, few civilian casualties were caused by landmines, either during or after the war.[20] A possible reason is that most landmines were laid away from crowded inhabited areas.[21] In fact, most Civil War landmines were used at forts that, by coincidence, are some distance from today's urban areas. Many of the forts were purposefully constructed away from the cities they were used to protect—they were designed to provide a first-tier defense so cities could buy time "for the transportation of more defensive forces and/or the 'calling out' of a militia defensive force."[22]

Some of the unrecovered unexploded ordnance inflicted civilian casualties. A Union prisoner being held in a Charleston jail, for example, witnessed unexploded ordnance clearance casualties:

> I saw two men and a Negro boy who had been killed while uncarthing one of our shells. They tried to break off the copper ring with an axe! The thing burst, tearing them to pieces. I hear that several boys have been killed in this way—they pay dearly for their stupidity.[23]

19 Fired artillery shells did not always detonate for a wide variety of reasons. "Field recoveries," in *North South Trader's Civil War*, vol. 35, no. 6, 17. Jack W. Melton, Jr., "Accurate Projectile Names," in *North South Trader's Civil War*, vol. 35, no. 6, 56.

20 Jack W. Melton, Jr., "Accurate Projectile Names," in *North South Trader's Civil War*, vol. 35, no. 6, 56. There were also cases in which innocent civilians, or noncombatants, were injured and killed by landmines. Confederate POWs were injured and killed while clearing mines, and Union soldiers were killed after battles in which those landmines were deployed. Confederate POWs cleared most—but not all—the mines. For a few decades after the war, landmines killed and injured Southerners as they walked through woods or flower-filled fields once defended by Confederate infantry. Hearn, *Mobile Bay and the Mobile Campaign*, 200. Nineteenth-century newspaper headlines in the Mobile area regarding the finding of unexploded ordnance and landmines, included "Old Shells Unearthed Here at Civil War Battery Site," "Civil War Munitions Dump Found in Mobile," and "Old Shell Found in Yard."

21 Notable exceptions include landmine use in Jackson, Mississippi; Williamsburg and Yorktown, Virginia; and on the roads around Goldsboro and Kinston, North Carolina.

22 John R. Weaver II, *A Legacy in Brick and Stone: American Coastal Defense Forts of the Third System, 1816–1867* (McLean, VA, 2001), 33.

23 Sneden, *Eye of the Storm*, 283. More recently, in 2008, a relic restorer in Chester, Virginia, was killed in his driveway working on a live artillery round.

Thankfully, civilian casualties from this type of ordnance and landmines were low during and after the war. From 1958 through 2008, for example, there were only two known fatalities due to disarming Civil War ordnance.[24] One of the reasons is the distance between the forts that used mines and the major urban areas. Mobile is 16 miles from Fort Blakeley, Port Lavaca is 29 miles from Fort Esperanza, Richmond is nine miles from Fort Johnson, Savannah is 30 miles from Fort McAllister, and Wilmington is 19 miles from Fort Fisher. The distances involved reduced the chances for civilians to come into contact with the unexploded mines.[25]

Insurgency

One of the notable aspects of landmine use during the Civil War was their lack of employment by guerilla or insurgent forces (although some may well have wanted to use them). Landmines could have been used on a larger scale by irregular forces, but they were not. Most likely this was because the Confederate Army kept the limited number of landmines solely for its own purposes. Improvised landmine production involving the conversion of artillery shells was simply too time consuming and too burdensome for guerilla forces, who were usually on the move.

Union intelligence reported in an October 1864 letter to Secretary of War Edwin Stanton that Confederate sympathizers operating in the North were planning to ship landmines to guerillas fighting in Missouri, which by this time was firmly under Union control. One witness, a former Rebel guerilla, noted

---

24 According to the leading publication for Civil War relic hunters, "There have been scant few other explosions and injuries, most recently the July 2006 incident that injured Lawrence Christopher of Dalton, Georgia." Stephen W. Sylvia, "Publisher's Forum: Look Out for Baseballs," in *North South Trader's Civil War*, vol. 33, no. 2, 7.

25 Shortest route among existing roads, which likely may have existed during the Civil War. Since Fort Esperanza was situated on an island, it is not possible to drive to Port Lavaca, so the value is a rough estimate if driving were possible to the closest mainland city (Port O'Connor, Texas) and beyond to Port Lavaca. The fort is located on the eastern shore of Matagorda Island. Its eastern walls were destroyed after an 1868 storm eroded the shoreline. By 1878 the rest of the nine-foot-high, 20-foot-thick, turf-covered walls had eroded away, but the shore was accreting again. The outlying emplacements and rifle pits can still be traced in some areas. Formerly located on the north end of Morris Island. Tides and time have long since removed all traces of Battery Wagner. Today, Morris Island stands uninhabited and desolate, a silent testament to the bloody fighting.

that a pro-Southern "Order" possibly had 340,000 sympathizers there, who possessed "6,000 muskets and 60,000 revolvers, besides private arms. . . . A statement was made by Hunt, grand commander of Missouri, before his arrest to a fellow-member, that shells and all kinds of munitions of war, as well as *infernal machines*, were manufactured for the order at Indianapolis [emphasis added]."[26]

Other Regions

Many locations that seemed ideal for the use of landmines were never seeded with them. The defenders at Vicksburg, for example, did not use torpedoes even though the extended fortifications and siege operations carried on there seemed ideal for their employment. Landmines were not used in Florida, even though water-based mines had been used successfully against Federal vessels in the northeastern part of the state. Florida's remote location, the difficulty of shipping mines there, and resource shortages may have played a part in their non-use, but the most likely reason was because Florida was a backwater, and there were only so many experienced torpedo-men available; higher priorities elsewhere required their attention.[27]

Landmines did not change the outcome of a single major battle, although they did delay pursuing Federals and give Confederates time to escape at Yorktown and Williamsburg, Virginia, and Jackson, Mississippi. Even in the presence of minefields, Union troops managed to carry out several successful assaults by digging trenches across the fields, including at Battery Wagner outside Charleston.[28]

---

26 In addition, there was "the late discovery in Cincinnati of samples of hand-grenades, conical shells, and rockets, of which 1,000 were about to be manufactured, under a special contract, for the Order of the Sons of Liberty, which goes directly to verify such a statement." Detailed report based upon the mass of testimony furnished to me from different sources in regard to the secret associations and conspiracies against the Government, formed principally in the Western States by traitors and disloyal persons, Union & Confed. Correspondence, Orders, Etc., Relating to Prisoners of War and State From April 1, 1864 to December 31, 1864, *OR* vol. 51.

27 My thanks to Dr. Daniel Schafer, author of *Thunder on the River*, about the Civil War in northeastern Florida, for this observation.

28 At Battery Wagner, Union engineers breached the Confederate minefields by digging trenches and saps toward the fortifications.

America's Buried History: Research Challenges

Several research challenges confronted the completion of *America's Buried History*, notably a dearth of Confederate records. Many of the Confederates involved in landmine development and deployment did not keep records at all for fear of being put to death as a war criminal if they were captured. The Union high command and many junior Federal officers did not look favorably on those who used landmines, and some ordered that captured Confederate soldiers involved in these operations be executed. Union naval officer H. H. Bell, a commodore in charge of the West Gulf Blockading Squadron, made the fate of mine operators perfectly clear: "Persons employed on torpedoes deserve no quarter, and none should be given them." General Sherman felt almost as strongly about their use. During the Atlanta Campaign, he instructed one of his subordinate generals that, "if torpedoes are found in the possession of an enemy to our rear, you may cause them to be put on the ground and tested by wagon-loads of prisoners, or, if need be, citizens implicated in their use.[29]

Another reason for the lack of records is that most of the few that were maintained were destroyed, intentionally or otherwise. The Army Torpedo Bureau's work files were burned at the end of the conflict during the hasty evacuation of Richmond on April 2, 1865.[30] Because the copying and dissemination of landmine instruction and training manuals was discouraged, few such documents were created in the first place. It will be recalled that, in May 1863, before leaving Richmond for Vicksburg, Rains asked President Davis if his mine manual could be published. Davis objected to its publication—a decision with which Rains subsequently agreed—because it would give away important wartime secrets. "[N]o printed paper could be kept

---

29 June 23, 1864, HQ, Military Division of the Mississippi, at Big Shanty. U.S. Steam Sloop Pensacola, off New Orleans, LA, Nov. 25, 1863, from H. H. Bell, Commodore, Commanding West Gulf Blockading Squadron, *ORN* vol. 20, 697. Not one of the operators or inventors was ever punished for having used torpedoes. In fact, some joined their former enemies and demonstrated their secrets. Sherman to Steedman, June 23, 1864, *OR* vol. 38, pt. 4, 579.

30 It is reported that Secretary of State Judah P. Benjamin destroyed the files during the Confederate government's evacuation of Richmond. Kochan and Wideman, *Civil War Torpedoes*, 34; Snyder, "Torpedoes for the Confederacy," 45.

secret," replied Davis, and "your invention would be deprived of a great part of its value if its peculiarities were known to the enemy."[31]

Colonel M. R. Talcott, who commanded the Army of Northern Virginia's engineer troops, believed that some of the records that were not burned or otherwise destroyed had "been removed when Richmond was evacuated; but what became of them will probably never be known, except that some, if not all, of the maps fell into the hands of private individuals." As a result, many of the books, essays, and other writings by the Confederate engineers "must be largely, if not wholly, [recalled] from memory, owing to the loss of records pertaining to this branch of the Confederate military service."[32]

Postscript: America's Buried History

By the end of the Civil War, the Confederates had developed the technical forerunners of many modern landmine and fuse types. Their mines employed victim-activated and command-detonated fuses. Other landmine-related innovations included their deployment to cover retreating forces, the use of nuisance mines to inflict casualties behind enemy lines, and the creation of various types of improvised and manufactured landmines.

After the war, Federals under the supervision of Maj. Gen. Richard Delafield launched a project to study Confederate mine warfare. As an American observer during the Crimean War, Delafield had seen the Russians use mines in 1854. He appointed a research team, including Capt. Peter S. Michie, to examine Southern landmines and find out other information about the weapons. Their work was organized and presented in book form in 1866 as *Torpedoes: Their Invention and Use, From the First Application to the Art of War to the Present Time.* Later, as an instructor at West Point, Michie took some of the Confederate mines he examined to the academy, where today an

---

31 Davis to Rains, June 3, 1863, *OR* vol. 52, pt. 2, 487; ibid., vol. 18, 1,082; Dunbar Rowland, *Jefferson Davis, Constitutionalist: His Letters, Papers and Speeches*, 10 vols. (Jackson, MS, 1923), vol. 5, 504.

32 T. M. R. Talcott, "Reminiscences of the Confederate Engineer Service," in Miller, *Forts and Artillery*, 270.

impressive museum includes one of the world's best collections of Civil War mines.[33]

Landmines would not be used on a widespread basis again until World War I, and American military forces deployed mines again during World War II. Unfortunately, the deadly legacy of landmines would become a global humanitarian crisis by the end of the 20th century, killing or maiming more than 26,000 people per year, primarily civilians.[34]

In 1993, according to estimates by the United Nations, there were 105 million landmines planted in 62 countries—which would have been roughly "one mine in the ground per every 50 people on earth." According to the Nobel Peace Prize-winning coalition International Campaign to Ban Landmines,

> The time delay from deployment to detonation detracted from mines' appeal and contributed to its reputation as the weapon of the inferior. This notion lived on with subsequent mine-equipped conflicts around the world, but was only combated after years of post-conflict suffering. Landmines from WWII persisted and killed in the decades following and are still active and dangerous in the 21st century.[35]

After years of international negotiations, victim-activated antipersonnel landmines were banned in 1997, and most of the world's governments would still be abiding by the prohibition decades later.

33 W. R. King, *Torpedoes: Their Invention and Use, From the First Application to the Art of War to the Present Time* (Washington, D.C., 1866).

34 U.S. Department of State Bureau of Political-Military Affairs, *Hidden Killers*. This was the first report to estimate the magnitude of the landmine threat in terms of numbers of mines laid and numbers of mine-related deaths and injuries.

35 Jack H. McCall, Jr., "Infernal Machines and Hidden Death: International Law and Limits on the Indiscriminate Use of Land Mine Warfare," *Georgia Journal of International and Comparative Law*, vol. 24, 1994, 242; Donovan Webster, "One Leg at a Time," *New York Sunday Times Magazine* cover story, *New York Times*, January 23, 1994; International Campaign to Ban Landmines: www.icbl.org.

Glossary

Abatis: Limbs and trees arranged as an obstacle to attacking enemy troops, with branches and limbs usually sharpened and pointed toward the enemy. This technique was widely used during the Civil War because the material to make it was cheap and abundant.

Army Torpedo Bureau: A secret Confederate military organization authorized in 1862 to produce explosive devices and landmines, headed by Brigadier General Gabriel James Rains.

Blockade-runners: Ships that carried cotton, tobacco, and other goods out of Southern ports to foreign harbors, and and returned with supplies needed by the Confederacy. The Southern ports were blocked or "blockaded" by the Union Navy, hence the name.

Breastworks: Barriers consisting of dirt, sand, rocks, and/or logs to protected soldiers from enemy fire.

Cheval-de-frise (**plural**: *chevaux-de-frise*): A medieval defensive obstacle consisting of a portable frame (sometimes simply a log) covered with long iron or wooden spikes or in some cases, actual spears. These were intended to act as an anti-cavalry obstacle, but could also be moved quickly to help block a breach in another barrier. (*Cheval-de-frise* means "Frisian horse.") Having little cavalry of their own, the

German ethnic Frisians relied heavily on such anti- cavalry obstacles. The term is often generically used for any spiked obstacle, and was used widely during the latter months of the Civil War.

Command-detonated mine: An explosive device consisting of a wire connected to a buried mine that explodes when a trigger is pulled by the operator.

Contact-detonated mine: A mine that explodes when touched, often because of a chemical reaction within the device itself that triggers the explosive. Also known as a victim-activated mine.

Earthen parapet: A barrier behind which troops fought.

Earthworks: A field fortification made of dirt or sand, often mixed with logs and sometimes topped with head logs to better protect the men fighting from behind them.

Fraise: A barrier made of inclined or horizontal wooden stakes.

Glacis: A bank of earth sloping down from a fortification or all to keep attackers under the fire of defenders.

Gutta percha: A substance similar to the look and feel of rubber used to coat wires of command-detonated naval mines or water torpedoes.

Improvised explosive device (IED): A bomb made of military (artillery shells) or non-military components (barrels or kegs), generally simple to make and easily hidden from the enemy.

Infernal device: A term commonly used by the Federals to refer to weapons such as landmines and torpedoes.

Landmine: An explosive device designed to be placed under, on, or near the ground, where it is exploded by the presence, proximity, or contact of a person. These are designed to incapacitate, injure, or kill people and horses, and destroy property, such as wagons or artillery pieces. These were used widely by Confederates during the Civil War. Often made with an artillery shell or iron container, gunpowder, a fuse, and a detonation source. Landmines were used primarily to defend fixed positions and to delay attackers or pursuers. They were also referred to during the Civil War as "infernal devices," land torpedoes, or sub-terra shells.

Primer: The device within a mine, torpedo, or other explosive device that holds explosives until they are detonated.

Redan: A fortification made of two parapets constructed in an arrow or V-shaped formation, which allows troops inside to fire into the flanks of an oncoming army.

Redoubt: A fortification that is small and often temporary and serves as a first line of defense against advancing enemy.

Sapper: A specialized engineer or soldier trained to dig trenches while under fire from an enemy fighting behind fortifications, such as those at Port Hudson and Battery Wagner. Saps were usually dug in a zigzag manner to offer protection while approaching an enemy fortification.

Sortie: The use of troops to disrupt a pending enemy attack, often by diverting power and resources away from the intended target.

Spar torpedo: A naval weapon that involved attaching an explosive device to the end of a long pole. Detonation usually resulted when the explosive device came into contact with an enemy vessel.

Subterra (sub-terra) shell: An explosive device hidden discreetly below the ground usually designed to detonate on contact. Another term used for a contact-detonated landmine or land torpedo.

Torpedo: An explosive weapon used by the Confederacy to defend against and to delay enemy forces in land or sea warfare. Another term used for landmines.

Torpedo boat or ram: An armored naval vessel (such as the CSS *David* off Charleston, SC) with a long torpedo spar attached used for ramming enemy ships.

Trip wire: A wire stretched close to the ground, designed to trigger an explosive device or entangle or slow enemy troops and horses.

United States Colored Troops (U.S.C.T.): Some 178,000 African-Americans—many of whom were former slaves—volunteered to fight in the U. S. Army during the last three years of the war, approximately 40,000 of whom died in service. They were prohibited from joining until July 1862. Because rank advancement was limited for the black soldiers, white officers led the regiments. Contrary to many expectations, they displayed tremendous courage in every engagement, including those where the Confederate employed landmines, such as at Port Hudson, Battery Wagner, Chaffin's Farm, and Fort Blakely. By the end of the war, the U.S.C.T. accounted for 10 percent of the Union army.

Victim-activated mine: A mine triggered by a trip wire or by pressure from contact by an enemy force. Also known as a contact-detonated mine.

Water torpedo: Another term used to refer to a naval or water mine, like the one that sunk the USS *Tecumseh* in Mobile Bay in 1864.

Bibliography

Newspapers

Buffalo Courier

Caledonian (St. Johnsbury, Vermont)

Daily Times (Burlington, Vermont)

Mobile Press Register

New York Times

New York Times Magazine

Port Lavaca Wave (Lavaca, Texas)

Richmond Dispatch

Richmond Enquirer

St. Francisville Democrat (St. Francisville, Louisiana)

The Buffalo Commercial

The Burlington Free Press

The Confederate (Raleigh, North Carolina)

The Liberator (Boston, Massachusetts)

The Montgomery Advertiser

The National Tribune

The Newbernian (New Bern, North Carolina)

Washington Evening Star

Washington Union

Wisconsin Daily Patriot

Primary Source Reports

The Medical and Surgical History of the War of the Rebellion, Appendix to Part I Containing Reports of Medical Directors, and Other Documents edited under the direction of Surgeon General Joseph K. Barnes, U.S. Army.

J. B. Brown, "Extracts From a Narrative of His Services From the Outbreak of the Rebellion to June 29, 1863."

W. E. Waters "Extract From a Narrative of his Services Medical Staff." Congressional Series of United States Public Documents. Government Printing Office, 1866.

R. Delafield. "Report on the Art of War in Europe in 1854, 1855, and 1856."

Gilmore, Q. A. Report of Maj. Brooks, "Engineer and Artillery Operations Against the Defenses of Charleston Harbor in 1863."

Human Rights Watch. "Landmines: A Deadly Legacy." Arms Project of Human Rights Watch & Physicians for Human Rights, 1993.

Records of the Confederate Engineers, Record Group 109, National Archives.

J. W. Mallet and O. E. Hunt. "The Ordnance of the Confederacy."

   "Report of Submarine Operations, February, 1865, at Mobile."

   "Property Return of Submarine Defenses of Mobile, January–February, 1865."

U.S. State Department. *Hidden Killers: The World's Landmine Problem*, 3rd ed. Washington, DC: Bureau of Political-Military Affairs, November 2001.

United States War Department. *The War of the Rebellion: A Compilation of the Official Records of the Union and Confederate Armies*, 128 vols. Washington, DC: U.S. Government Printing Office, 1880–1901.

United States War Department. *Official Records of the Union and Confederate Navies in the War of the Rebellion*, 31 vols. Washington, DC: U.S. Government Printing Office, 1894–1922.

Primary Source Memoirs, Reminiscences, Diaries, and Letters

Alexander, E. P. "Sketch of Longstreet's Division-Yorktown and Williamsburg," *Southern Historical Society Papers* Volume 10, nos. 1 and 2 (January and February 1882).

Anderson, George W., Jr. "General Outline of the Fall of Fort McAllister." Anderson Papers. Georgia Historical Society, Savannah, GA.

Atkinson, H. B. Civil War in Calhoun County Diary of H. B. Atkinson, New Canton, IL. Calhoun County Museum Archives, Port Lavaca, TX.

Bushnell, Well A. Memoirs. Palmer Regimental Papers. Cleveland, OH: Western Reserve Historical Society, n.d.

Corte, Camille. "History of the 73rd U.S.C.T."

Davidson, Hunter. "Electrical Torpedoes as a System of Defence," *Southern Historical Society Papers* 2 (1876).

Dowd, H. U. Diary. Manuscript in the Jackson County Historical Society, Independence, MO.

Eddington, W. R. "My Civil War Memoirs and Other Reminiscence's."

Foster, Alonzo. "Reminiscences and Record of the 6th New York Vol. Cavalry." Brooklyn, NY. (1892).

Fretwell, J. R. Enlistment File. Calhoun County Museum Archives, Port Lavaca, TX.

Hart, H. W. Letter From Union Sgt. H. W. Hart, 13th Corps, Andrews 2nd Division, 2nd Conn. Battery, to His Wife. April 10, 1865. Written "Near Blakely." Notation on envelope. May 28, 1865. History Museum of Mobile, Mobile, AL.

Howard, Oliver Otis. *Autobiography of Oliver Otis Howard, Major-General, United States Army*. New York, NY: Baker & Taylor, 1908.

International Campaign to Ban Landmines. "A History of Landmines."

———. "Landmine Monitor 2015."

Jones, J. Williams. *Southern Historical Society Papers* 14 (1886).

Johnson, Benjamin W. "After Action Report on the Battle at Fort Desperate," September 12, 1863.

Lafayette, Andrew Swap. Personal Diary. Fort Blakeley State Park Archives, AL.

Locke, Fred T., assistant adjutant-general to Fitz John Porter, in "Confederate Use of Subterranean Shells on the Peninsula," in *Battles and Leaders of the Civil War*, vol. 2, The Century Company, 1884.

Marshall, T. B. Sidney O. *History of the Eighty-Third Ohio Volunteer Infantry*. September 12, 1912.

Maury, Dabney. Letter to Jefferson Davis, December 25, 1871. History Museum of Mobile, Mobile, AL.

Maury, Matthew Letter to Empress Carolota of Mexico, January 18, 1866. Matthew Fontaine Maury Papers VMI Archives Manuscript #00103.

———.Letter to son-in-law, S. Welford Corbin, January 1, 1866. Matthew Fontaine Maury Papers VMI Archives Manuscript #00103.

———.Letter to son-in-law, S. Welford Corbin, May 13, 1868. Matthew Fontaine Maury Papers VMI Archives Manuscript #00103.

———. Letter to daughter Diana Maury Corbin, July 26, 1871. Matthew Fontaine Maury Papers VMI Archives Manuscript #00103.

Maury, Richard L. Notes. *Southern Historical Society Papers*.

Palfrey, John C. "The Capture of Mobile, 1865." Papers of the Military Historical Society of Massachusetts, Boston, MA, 1910.

Porter, David. "Special Orders No. 185. U.S. Mississippi Squadron, Flag-Ship Black Hawk, Alexandria, LA," March 21, 1864.

Prescott, Royal B. "The Capture of Richmond." Civil War Papers: Boston, MA.

Rains, General Gabriel J. "Torpedoes," Southern Historical Society Papers 3 (May and June 1877).

Rives, Alfred L. Letter to Lt. Gen. E. Kirby Smith, September 15, 1863. History Museum of Mobile, Mobile, AL.

Rowland, Dunbar. *Jefferson Davis, Constitutionalist: His Letters, Papers and Speeches*, 10 vols. Jackson, MS, 1923.

Seddon, James A. Letter from Wilmington, NC. Calhoun County Museum Archives. Port Lavaca, TX, n.d.

Sheliha, V. Confederate Engineer Bureau, Letters, August 16, 18, and 20, 1864, in Sheliha, Military Service Record in Carded Files, vols. 7, 7 1/2. History Museum of Mobile, Mobile, AL.

Sheridan, Philip Henry. *Personal Memoirs of P. H. Sheridan, General, United States Army*. New York: Charles L. Webster, 1888.

Taylor, Thomas T. Diary. Taylor Papers, Ohio Historical Society, Columbus, OH.

Tidball, John Caldwell. *Manual of Heavy Artillery Service: For the Use of the Army and Militia of the United States*. Washington, DC: James J. Chapman, 1891.

"The Defence of Mobile: Dr. Stephenson's Interesting Narrative, State of Alabama," Department of Archives and History, Federal project S 51-F 2-8.

Books

A Biographical History of Fremont and Mills Counties, Iowa. Chicago, IL: Lewis Publishing Company, 1901.

Allen, Stanton P. *Down in Dixie: Life in a Cavalry Regiment in the War Days, From the Wilderness to Appomattox.* Boston, MA: D. Lothrop Company, 1893.

Andrews, Christopher Columbus. *History of the Campaign of Mobile: Including the Cooperative Operations of Gen. Wilson's Cavalry in Alabama.* New York, NY: D. Van Nostrand, 1889.

Bacon, Edward. *Among the Cotton Thieves.* Detroit, MI: The Free Press Steam Book and Job Printing House, 1867.

Bell, Jack. *Civil War Heavy Explosive Ordnance: A Guide to Large Artillery Projectiles, Torpedoes, and Mines.* Denton, TX: University of North Texas Press, 2003.

Blake, Henry. *Three Years in the Army of the Potomac.* Boston, MA: Lee and Shepard, 1865.

Brainerd, Wesley, and Ed Malles. *Bridge Building in Wartime: Colonel Wesley Brainerd's Memoir of the 50th New York Volunteer Engineers.* Knoxville: University of Tennessee Press, 1997.

Brooke, George M. *John M. Brooke: Naval Scientist and Educator.* Charlottesville: University of Virginia Press, 1980.

Burton, E. Milby. *The Siege of Charleston, 1861–1865.* Columbia: University of South Carolina Press, 1970.

Campbell, R. Thomas. *Hunters of the Night: Confederate Torpedo Boats in the War Between the States.* Shippensburg, PA: Burd Street Press, 2000.

Chenery, William H. *The Fourteenth Regiment Rhode Island Heavy Artillery: (colored) in the War to Preserve the Union, 1861–1865.* Providence, RI: Snow & Farnham, 1898.

Clark, Walter. *Histories of the Several Regiments and Battalions From North Carolina, in the Great War 1861–'65*, vol. 5. Raleigh, NC: E. M. Uzzell, 1901.

Cullum, George W. *Biographical Register of the Officers and Graduates of the US Military Academy at West Point, N.Y., From Its Establishment, in 1802, to 1890, With the Early History of the United States Military Academy.* Boston, MA: Houghton, Mifflin, 1891.

Cunningham, Edward. *The Port Hudson Campaign 1862–1863.* Baton Rouge: Louisiana State University Press, 1963.

Davis, Jefferson. *The Rise and Fall of the Confederate Government.* New York, NY: D. Appleton, 1881.

De Forest, John William. *A Volunteer's Adventures: A Union Captain's Record of the Civil War.* New Haven, CT: Yale University Press, 1946.

Delaney, Caldwell. *Confederate Mobile: A Pictorial History.* Haunted Book Shop, 1971.

Denison, Frederic. *Shot and Shell: The Third Rhode Island Heavy Artillery Regiment in the Rebellion, 1861–1865. Camps, Forts, Batteries, Garrisons, Marches, Skirmishes, Sieges, Battles, and Victories; also, The Roll of Honor and Roll of the Regiment.* Providence, RI: For the Third R.I.H. art. Vet. Association, 1879.

Dickey, Luther S. *History of the Eighty-Fifth Regiment, Pennsylvania Volunteer Infantry, 1861–1865.* New York, NY: J. C. & W. E. Powers, 1915.

Dickey, Thomas S., and Peter C. George, *Field Artillery Projectiles of the American Civil War.* Atlanta, GA: Arsenal Press, 1980.

Durham, Roger S. *Guardian of Savannah: Fort McAllister, Georgia, in the Civil War and Beyond.* Columbia, University of South Carolina Press, 2008.

Eldridge, D. *The Third New Hampshire and All About It.* Boston, MA: Press of E. B. Stillings and Co., 1893.

Evans, Clement A. *Confederate Military History*, vol. 4. Atlanta, GA: Confederate Publishing Company, 1899.

Fonvielle, Chris E., Jr. *The Wilmington Campaign: Last Rays of Departing Hope.* Mechanicsburg, PA: Stackpole Books, 2001.

Foreman, Grant. *Advancing the Frontier, 1830–1860*, vol. 4 of Civilization of the American Indian Series. Norman: University of Oklahoma Press, 1933.

Grady, John. *Matthew Fontaine Maury, Father of Oceanography: A Biography, 1806–1873.* Jefferson, NC: McFarland & Company, 2015.

Gragg, Rod. *Confederate Goliath: The Battle of Fort Fisher.* New York, NY: HarperCollins, 1991.

Grattan, John W. *Under the Blue Pennant: Or Notes of a Naval Officer*, edited by Robert J. Schneller Jr. New York, NY: Wiley, 1999.

Green, John Williams. *Johnny Green of the Orphan Brigade: The Journal of a Confederate Soldier*, edited by A. D. Kirwan. Lexington: University of Kentucky Press, 2002.

Guiworth, Warren H. *History of the First Regiment (Massachusetts Infantry).* Boston, MA: Walker, Fuller, 1866.

Hall, Henry, and James Jabez Hall. *Cayuga in the Field: A Record of the 19th N.Y. Volunteers.* Auburn, NY: Published by authors, 1873.

Hannaford, P. A. *The Young Captain Richard C. Derby, Fifteenth Reg. Mass. Volunteers, Who Fell at Antietam.* Boston, MA: Degan, Estes & Company, 1865.

Hansen, Roger B., and Norman A. Nicholson. *The Siege of Blakeley and the Campaign of Mobile.* Blakeley, AL: Historic Blakeley Press, 1995.

Hastings, Earl C., and David S. Hastings. *A Pitiless Rain: The Battle of Williamsburg, 1862.* Shippensburg, PA: White Mane Publishing Company, 1997.

Hattaway, Herman, and Archer Jones. *How the North Won: A Military History of the Civil War.* Champaign: University of Illinois Press, 1991.

Hays, Gilbert Adams. *Under the Red Patch: Story of the Sixty-Third Regiment, Pennsylvania Volunteers 1861–1864.* Pittsburgh: Sixty-Third Pennsylvania Volunteers Regimental Association, 1908.

Hearn, Chester G. *Mobile Bay and the Mobile Campaign: The Last Great Battles of the Civil War.* Jefferson, NC: McFarland & Company, 1998.

Hess, Earl J. *Field Armies and Fortifications in the Civil War: The Eastern Campaigns, 1861–1864.* Chapel Hill: University of North Carolina Press, 2005.

Hess, Earl J. *In the Trenches at Petersburg: Field Fortifications and Confederate Defeat.* Chapel Hill: University of North Carolina Press, 2009.

Hewitt, Lawrence Lee. *Port Hudson, Confederate Bastion on the Mississippi.* Baton Rouge: Louisiana State University Press, 1987.

Jewett, Albert, Henry Clay, and Grace Jewett Austin. *A Boy Goes to War.* Bloomington, IN: publisher unidentified, 1944.

Johnson, Robert Underwood, and Clarence Clough Buel. *Battles and Leaders of the Civil War*, vol. 2. New York, NY: Castle Books, 1956.

Jones, Charles H. *Artillery Fuses of the Civil War.* Alexandria, VA: O'Donnell Publications, 2001.

Jones, John Beauchamp. *A Rebel War Clerk's Diary at the Confederate States Capital*, vol. 1. Philadelphia, PA: J. B. Lippincott & Co., 1866.

———. *A Rebel War Clerk's Diary at the Confederate States Capital*, vol. 2. Philadelphia, PA: J. B. Lippincott & Co., 1866.

Jones, Rev. John William Jones, *Personal Reminiscences, Anecdotes, and Letters of Gen. Robert E. Lee*, New York: D. Appleton and Company, 1874.

Kelly, Jack. *Gunpowder: Alchemy, Bombards and Pyrotechnics: The History of the Explosive That Changed the World*. New York, NY: Basic Books, 2004.

King, William Rice. *Torpedoes: Their Invention and Use From the First Application to the Art of War to the Present Time*. Washington, DC: no publisher, 1866.

Kochan, Michael P., and John C. Wideman, *Civil War Torpedoes: A History of Improvised Explosive Devices in the War Between the States*, 2nd ed. Paoli, PA: Keystone Press, 2011.

Konstam, Angus. *Confederate Submarines and Torpedo Vessels 1861–65*. Oxford, UK: Osprey, 2004.

Lewis, Charles Lee. *Matthew Fontaine Maury: The Pathfinder of the Seas*. Annapolis, MD: U.S. Naval Institute, 1927.

Lewis, Lloyd. *Sherman: Fighting Prophet*. Lincoln: University of Nebraska Press, 1993.

Linderman, Gerald. *Embattled Courage: The Experience of Combat in the American Civil War*. New York, NY: Simon & Schuster, 2008.

Long, A. L., and Marcus J. Wright. *Memoirs of Robert E. Lee: His Military and Personal History, Embracing a Large Amount of Information Hitherto Unpublished*. New York, NY: J. M. Stoddart & Company, 1886.

Mahon, John K. *History of the Second Seminole War, 1835–1842*. Gainesville: University of Florida Press, 1967.

Miller, Francis Trevelyan. Editor, *Forts and Artillery: The Photographic History of the Civil War*. New York, NY: Castle Books, 1957.

Needham, Joseph. *Science and Civilization in China, vol. 5: Chemistry and Chemical Technology, part 7: Military Technology; The Gunpowder Epic*. Cambridge, UK: Cambridge University Press, 1986.

Nosworthy, Brent. *The Bloody Crucible of Courage: Fighting Methods and Combat Experience of the Civil War*. New York, NY: Carroll & Graff, 2003.

Otto, John Henry, David Gould, and James B. Kennedy. *Memories of a Dutch Mudsill: The "War Memories" of John Henry Otto, Captain, Company D, 21st Regiment Wisconsin Volunteer Infantry*, edited by David Gould and James B. Kennedy. Kent, OH: Kent State University Press, 2004.

Patrick, Rembert W. *Jefferson Davis and His Cabinet*. Baton Rouge, LA: Louisiana State University Press. 1976,

Perry, Milton F. *Infernal Machines: The Story of Confederate Submarine and Mine Warfare*. Baton Rouge: Louisiana State University Press, 1965.

Rains, Gabriel J., *Torpedo Book, as published in Confederate Torpedoes: Two Illustrated Nineteenth Century Works with New Appendices and Photographs*, edited by Herbert M. Schiller. Jefferson, North Carolina: McFarland & Company, 2011.

Ragan, Mark K. *Building the Hunley and Other Secret Weapons of the Civil War*. College Station, TX: Texas A&M University Press, 2015.

Rhea, Gordon C. *To the North Anna River: Grant and Lee, May 13–25, 1864*. Baton Rouge: Louisiana State University Press, 2005.

Ripley, Edward Hastings. *Vermont General: The Unusual War Experiences of Edward Hastings Ripley, 1862–1865*, edited by Otto Eisenschiml. New York, NY: Devin-Adair, 1960.

Roe, Alfred S. *The Fifth Regiment Massachusetts Volunteer Infantry in Its Three Tours of Duty 1861, 1862–'63, 1864*. Boston, MA: Fifth Regiment Veteran Association, 1911.

Roman, Alfred. *The Military Operations of General Beauregard in the War Between the States, 1861 to 1865: Including a Brief Personal Sketch and a Narrative of His Services in the War With Mexico, 1846–8*, vol. 2. New York, NY: Harper & Brothers, 1884.

Rutherford, Kenneth R. *Disarming States: The International Movement to Ban Landmines*. Santa Barbara, CA: Praeger Security International, 2011.

Sanford, George Bliss. *Fighting Rebels and Redskins: Experiences in Army Life of Colonel George B. Sanford: 1861–1892*, edited by Edward R. Hagemann. Norman: University of Oklahoma Press, 1969.

Saunier, Joseph A., ed. *A History of the Forty-Seventh Regiment, Ohio Veteran Volunteer Second Brigade, Second Division, Fifteenth Army Corps, Army of Tennessee*. Hillsboro, OH: Lyle Printing Company, 1903.

Sears, Stephen W. *The Civil War Papers of George C. McClellan*. Boston, MA: Houghton Mifflin Harcourt, 1989.

Schafer, Daniel L. *Thunder on the River: The Civil War in Northeast Florida*. Gainesville: University Press of Florida, 2010.

Scharf, John T. *History of the Confederate States Navy: From Its Organization to the Surrender of Its Last Vessel*. New York, NY: Rogers & Sherwood, 1887.

Scott, H. L. *Military Dictionary: Comprising Technical Definitions; Information on Raising and Keeping Troops; Actual Service, Including Makeshifts and Improved Matériel; and Law, Government, Regulation, and Administration Relating to Land Forces. 1861*. Reprint, New York, NY: Greenwood Press, 1968.

Scott, John. *Story of the Thirty-Second Iowa Infantry Volunteers*. Nevada, IA: published by author, 1896.

Sherman, William Tecumseh. *The Memoirs of General W. T. Sherman by Himself*. Bloomington, Indiana University Press, 1957.

———. *Sherman's Civil War: Selected Correspondence of William T. Sherman, 1860-1865*, Jean V. Berlin and Brooks D. Simpson, editors, Chapel Hill, NC: University of North Carolina Press, 1999.

Smith, David. *Sherman's March to the Sea 1864: Atlanta to Savannah*. London, UK: Bloomsbury, 2012.

Sneden, Robert Knox. *Eye of the Storm: A Civil War Odyssey,* edited by Charles F. Bryan Jr. and Nelson D. Lankford. New York, NY: The Free Press, 2000.

Symonds, Craig L. *The Civil War at Sea*. New York, NY: Oxford University Press, 2012.

Thatcher, Joseph M., and Thomas H. Thatcher. *Confederate Coal Torpedo: Thomas Courtenay's Infernal Sabotage Weapon*. Fredericksburg, VA: Kenerly, 2011.

Trudeau, Noah Andre. *Like Men of War: Black Troops in the Civil War, 1862–1865*. Edison, NJ: Castle Books, 2002.

Waters, W. Davis, and Joseph I. Brown. *Gabriel Rains and the Confederate Torpedo Bureau*. Durham, NC: Monograph Publishers, 2014.

Weaver, John R. II. *A Legacy in Brick and Stone: American Coastal Defense Forts of the Third System, 1816–1867*. McLean, VA: Redoubt Press, 2001.

Wheeler, Richard. *Sword Over Richmond: An Eyewitness History of McClellan's Peninsula Campaign*. New York, NY: The Fairfax Press, 1986.

Wise, Stephen R. *Gate of Hell: Campaign for Charleston Harbor, 1863*. Columbia: University of South Carolina Press, 1994.

Youngblood, Norman. Westport, CT: Praeger Security International, 2006.

Book Chapters

Beard, Michael F. "Mobile: The Overland Campaign, March–May 1865," in "Damn the Torpedoes?" in *The Official Guide to the Civil War Trail: Battle of Mobile Bay*. Undated.

Lamb, Colonel William. "The Defense of Fort Fisher," in *Battles and Leaders of the Civil War*, vol. 4. New York, NY: The Century Co., 1884.

Locke, Fred T. Assistant Adjutant-General to Fitz John Porter, Director of the Siege, and Colonel Edward C. James, of the Engineer Corps. Letter to editors and published in "Confederate Use of Subterranean Shells on the Peninsula," in *Battles and Leaders of the Civil War*, ed. Robert Underwood Johnson, Clarence Clough Buell (The Century Company, 1884), vol. 2.

McIntosh, David Gregg. "The Confederate Artillery—Its Organization and Development," in Francis Trevelyan Miller, editor, *Forts and Artillery: The Photographic History of the Civil War*. New York, NY: Castle Books, 1957.

Moore, Mark A. "William Lamb, the Malakoff, and the Viability of Fort Fisher: A Comparative Analysis of the Capture of the South's Largest Earthen Fortification, and the Fall of Sebastopol During the Crimean War," in *The Wilmington Campaign and the Battles for Fort Fisher*. Cambridge, MA: Da Capo Press, 1999.

Savas, Theodore "The Best Powder Mill in the World: Rains and His Mission," 20-30, in C.L. Bragg, Gordon A. Blaker, Charles D. Ross, Stephanie A. T. Jacobe and Theodore P. Savas, *Never for Want of Powder: The Confederate Powder Works in Augusta, Georgia*. University of South Carolina Press, Columbia, 2007.

Slocum, Henry W. Major-General, "Sherman's March From Savannah to Bentonville," in *Battles and Leaders of the Civil War*, Volume I of 4 Volumes, Editors, Robert Underwood Johnson and Clarence Clough Buel, Editorial Staff, Century Magazine. (New York: The Century Co., 1885.

Talcott T. M. R., "Reminiscences of the Confederate Engineer Service," in Francis Trevelyan Miller, editor, *Forts and Artillery: The Photographic History of the Civil War*. New York, NY: Castle Books, 1957.

Journal Articles

Alexander, General E. P. "Sketch of Longstreet's Division: Yorktown and Williamsburg." *Southern Historical Society Papers*. Vol. 10. 38.

Association of Defenders of Port Hudson, "Fortification and Siege of Port Hudson." *Southern Historical Society Papers* (January–December, 1886), vol. 14.

Breeding, Lynda Sue. "The Singer Family of Calhoun County, Texas, The Road Home." *Calhoun County Historical Commission* 1, no. 2 (June 2002).

Garvaglia, Louis A. "Sherman's March and the Georgia Arsenals." *North and South* 6, no. 1 (2002).

Goos. S. W. "On Torpedo Wounds." *American Journal of the Medical Sciences* 51, no. 102 (1868).

McCall, Jr., Jack H. "Infernal Machines and Hidden Death: International Law and Limits on the Indiscriminate Use of Land Mine Warfare." *Georgia Journal of International and Comparative Law*, Volume 24, 1994.

Porter, David D. "Torpedo Warfare." *North American Review* 127, no. 264 (1878).

Stimson, J. B. "Three Unusual Gun-Shot Wounds." *Southern Practitioner, An Independent Monthly Journal Devoted to Medicine and Surgery* 22 (1900).

Strong, William E. "The Capture of Fort McAllister, December 13, 1864" *The Georgia Historical Quarterly*, vol. 88, no. 3. (Fall 2004).

Waters, W. Davis. "Deception Is the Art of War: Gabriel J. Rains, Torpedo Specialist of the Confederacy." *North Carolina Historical Review* 66, no. 1 (1989).

Magazine Articles

Bradshaw, Tim. "Union Veteran Made Living Selling Relics on Morris Island." *North South Trader's Civil War* 24, no. 2, 1997.

Crowley. R. O. Formerly Electrician of the Torpedo Division, C.S.N., "The Confederate Torpedo Service." *Century Magazine* 56, June 1898..

Deal, Gary. "54th Massachusetts Ring." *North South Trader's Civil War* 27, no. 6, 2001.

Durham, Roger. S. "The Saga of Sherman's Campaign Hat." *North South Trader's Civil War* 35, no. 3, 2001.

Farrant, Don. "When Yankee Ships Patrolled the Georgia Coast." *North South Trader's Civil War* 17, no. 3, 1990.

Gaidis, Henry L. "Confederate Ordnance Dream: General Josiah Gorgas, CSA, and The Bureau of Foreign Supplies." *North South Trader's Civil War* 10, no. 1, 1982.

Garcia, Pedro. "Last Bastion of the Confederacy." *Civil War Quarterly*, 2017.

Haile, E. Cantey, Jr. "John Hampden Brooks: South Carolina Soldier: Full Circle." *North South Trader's Civil War* 19, no. 2, 1992.

Harris, Charles S. "Relics of Shiloh." *North South Trader's Civil War* 15, no. 2, 1988.

Harper's Weekly, March 29, 1862. 203.

"Infernal Machines in the Mississippi." *Scientific American*, April 1862.

Jones, Robert. "Exploded Fort Huger Cannon." *North South Trader's Civil War* 36, no. 1, 2012.

Melton, Jack W., Jr. "Accurate Projectile Names." *North South Trader's Civil War* 35, no. 6, 2011.

Nowlin, S. H. "Capture and Escape of S. H. Nowlin, Private Fifth Virginia Cavalry." *Southern Bivouac*, October 1883.

Pinkney, Roger. "Iron Angel of Death." *Civil War Times*, October 1999.

Ragan, Mark K. "Singer's Secret Service Corp: Causing Chaos During the Civil War." *Civil War Times*, November/December 2007.

Rossbacher, Nancy D. "Richmond Defenses Under Siege." *North South Trader's Civil War* 15, no. 5, 1988.

Robbins, Peggy. "Bomb Brothers." *Civil War Times*, August 1997.

Savas, Theodore P. "Heart of the Southern War Machine: The Augusta Powder Works Was an Unparalleled Accomplishment of Military Industry. " *Civil War Times*, June 2017.

Snyder, Dean. "Torpedoes for the Confederacy." Civil War Times, March 1985.

Sogoian, Tig. "CSA Montgomeries." *North South Trader's Civil War* 32, no. 4, 2007.

Suhr, Robert Collins. "Torpedoes, the Confederacy's Dreaded 'Infernal Machines.'" *America's Civil War*, November 1991.

Sylvia, Stephen W. "Publisher's Forum: Look out for Baseballs." *North South Trader's Civil War* 33, no. 2, 2008.

Zebrowski, Carl. "Frozen in Time: A Ghost Town and the Efforts of an Unflappable Organizer Have Kept Alabama's Fort Blakeley in Pristine Condition." *Civil War Times Illustrated*, December 1994.

Presentations

Thatcher, Joseph M. "Thomas Courtenay and the Coal Bomb," presentation at the American Civil War Museum, Richmond, VA, July 15, 2016.

Other Secondary Information Sources

Chaffin, Tom. "The H. L. Hunley: The Secret Hope of the Confederacy." Calhoun County Museum Archives. Port Lavaca, TX.

"Civil War - Aquia Landing." Stafford County Museum. Undated.

Dickinson, Clifford R. "Union and Confederate Engineering Operations at Chaffin's Bluff/Chaffin's Farm, June 1862–April 3, 1865," Advanced Research Grant, Eastern National Park & Monument Association, Department of the Interior, National Park Service, Richmond National Battlefield Park, Richmond, VA, September 29, 1989.

"E. C. Singer and the H. L. Hunley," Calhoun County Museum Archives. Port Lavaca, TX.

"Fort Donelson." National Battlefield Tennessee and Kentucky, National Park Service. 2018.

Guidry, Katie. "Indianola and the Civil War," *The Texas Public Employee*, April 1968. Calhoun County Museum Archives, Port Lavaca, TX.

"Illustrated Guide to Richmond, the Confederate Capital: A Facsimile Reprint of the City Intelligencer of 1862." Museum of the Confederacy, Richmond, VA, 1960.

Rhodes, George Fred. "The Hunley: The Confederate Secret Weapon." Calhoun County Museum Archives, Port Lavaca, TX.

Walraven, Bill. "Civil War Clashes in Area Recounted," *Corpus Christi Caller*, File. Calhoun County Museum Archives, Port Lavaca, TX.

Website References

American Battlefield Trust, "10 Facts: Cold Harbor," http://www.civilwar.org/learn/articles/10-facts-cold-harbor. Accessed May 12, 2017.

Barnhart, Don. "Masonic Saboteurs," Warriors of the Lone Star State, April 20, 2016. http://warriorsofthelonestar.blogspot.com/2016/04/masonic-saboteurs.html, Accessed January 27, 2019.

Bunn, Mike. Director, Historic Blakeley State Park, "Battle of Fort Blakeley." http://www.encyclopediaofalabama.org/article/h-3718, Accessed January 24, 2019.

Calhoun County Museum, Web Post, February 19, 2004. www.ancestry.com/boards/localities.northam.usa.states.texas.counties.calhoun/260.1/mb.ashx. Accessed January 19, 2019.

History.com Editors, "Sherman presents Lincoln with a Christmas gift." https://www.history.com/this-day-in-history/sherman-presents-lincoln-with-a-christmas-gift. Accessed January 27, 2019.

International Campaign to Ban Landmines. "History of Landmines." http://icbl.org/en-gb/problem/a-history-of-landmines.aspx

Son of the South, "The Richmond Campaign," http://www.sonofthesouth.net/leefoundation/richmond-campaign.htm. Accessed May 12, 2017.

South Carolina Historical Society, Gabriel J. Rains papers, 1840-65. https://beta.worldcat.org/archivegrid/collection/data/37521848. Accessed January 27, 2019.

Virginia Military Institute Archives, https://archivesspace.vmi.respositories/3/593. Accessed January 21, 2019.

Index